Apprecia

MW01295599

Truth on Tough Texts: Expositions of Challenging Scripture Passages

Dr. Watson has undertaken a project that would make most men tremble: he has studied and explained some of the most daunting passages of Scripture, and then has demonstrated the courage to publish his explanations for all of the theologians of Christendom to evaluate and contest! He has done so with remarkable care and thoroughness, and you will profit by reading the outcomes and learning from his methods.

—Dr. James Maxwell
President, Faith Baptist College and Seminary
Ankeny, Iowa

I had the privilege of teaching with Dr. Watson in Haiti in 2011 and providentially was able to read several issues of TOTT. These articles not only gave me an appreciation for his scholarship but an understanding and gratitude for a resource that is desperately needed by the serious student of the Word of God. The perspicuity of the Bible has been challenged throughout Church History, but *Truth on Tough Texts: Expositions of Challenging Scripture Passages* brings clarity to difficult texts using a sound biblical hermeneutic.

—Dr. Allen Monroe
Equipping Leaders International
Former Professor, Cedarville University

Challenging. Insightful. Biblical. Three words that accurately describe Doc Watson's writing in his new book, *Truth on Tough Texts: Expositions of Challenging Scripture Passages*. In this compilation of excellent articles, the author does something that is rare these days: he lets the Bible speak for itself. By applying a sound biblical hermeneutic and taking the Bible seriously, truth clearly emerges from the tough texts of Scripture. Pastors and laymen alike will benefit from the hours of study and careful scholarship that went into these pages.

—Dr. James Bearss
President, On Target Ministry
Teaching Faithful Men through International Education

If you have not been blessed to sit under the teaching ministry of Dr. Watson, in one of the most beautiful venues in God's creation, then do the next best thing and read his books. TOTT is a much needed antidote for a culture that overwhelmingly calls itself Christian but cannot enumerate its most basic and important truths. I heartily recommend you wrestle through the tough texts of Scripture with Doc's enlightened coaching.

—JD Wetterling
Author of *No one . . .* and
No Time to Waste

The vast majority of Scripture is clear and understandable to even the simplest of readers, but there are those "hard sayings," those confusing sections, those tough texts that take extra care and study to discern. Dr. Watson examines many of these "tough texts" through the lens of Scripture, making every effort to determine their true meaning and eliminate the layers of inadequate teaching that has covered many of them over the ages. I recommend this book to the serious student of the Word of God.

—Dr. Gary E. Gilley
Pastor, Southern View Chapel; Springfield, Illinois
Author, *This Little Church* series

Doc Watson's TOTT has served me and our church family with his willingness to tackle not only tough *texts* but also tough *topics*. I often post his recent article on my office bulletin board. As a pastor, I am all about helpful resources for myself and others, and that's what this publication offers. Where the commentaries give a brief statement, Doc gives you a concise and thorough explanation. Keep this book within reach on your shelf because you will use this as a reference source when discussions lead to a question about a biblical text or topic.

—Pastor Kevin Kottke, MDiv
Plainfield Bible Church
Plainfield, Indiana

Dr. Watson has taken from his extensive experience those biblical texts and issues that are most difficult and tackled them head-on. These are texts most commentaries skirt over or shy away from. Doc's manner is thorough and in-depth, using sound hermeneutic principles of exegesis. The results are profound studies and answers on important subjects. These rich studies have been very beneficial to me personally, and I recommend them to anyone who loves the truth of God's Word.

—Pastor Jim Bryant, MBS
Grace Bible Chapel; San Antonio, Texas

Upon This Rock

Studies in Church History and Their Application

The sequel to

Truth on Tough Texts: Expositions of Challenging Scripture Passages

Dr. J. D. Watson

Sola Scriptura
Publications

Upon This Rock: Studies in Church History and Their Application

Copyright © Dr. J. D. Watson

Published by Sola Scriptura Publications
P. O. Box 235
Meeker, CO 81641
sspmail1521@gmail.com

www.TheScriptureAlone.com

Unless otherwise noted, all Scripture quotations and word references are from *The Authorized King James Version*.

Cover picture: *Church on a Rock*; stock photo, www.Dreamstime.com

Library of Congress Cataloging-in-Publication Data

ISBN–13: 978-1481828437
ISBN–10: 1481828436

Dedication

This work is dedicated first to my dear Savior
and Lord, Jesus Christ,
and also to

Russell H. Spees

a "Christian Businessman" in every
sense of the term whose faithful adherence to
historical *truths* and *texts* is a blessing and encouragement.

Acknowledgements

As in the first volume, I want to thank each reader of the monthly articles that have appeared in *Truth On Tough Texts* since its premiere in August 2005. The response of readers to the monthly issues, as well as the first book, have been of tremendous encouragement.

Special thanks go out to my wife, Debbie, for her reading, editing, and critiquing of the monthly offerings. Special thanks also to Mark Phillippo, Jr. for his copy editing of the final book manuscript.

A warm thanks to several others who also greatly aided this endeavor: Joe Bruce, Rico Patterson, Russ Spees, Jim Spees, and Dr. James Bearss.

Soli Deo Gloria

Contents

Illustrations

Introduction

This book's predecessor, *Truth on Tough Texts: Expositions of Challenging Scripture Passages*, is a compilation of most of the articles that appeared in the first six years of the monthly publication, *Truth on Tough Texts*, launched by this author in August 2005. A few were omitted partly for space reasons but primarily because I felt a separate volume was in order to deal with the historical matters they address.

The Reformation, for example, is misunderstood by many, ignored by some, and even attacked by others. It is, therefore, a major emphasis here in chapters 3 through 8. Even Church History itself, as is history in general nowadays, is viewed by many as unimportant, if not wholly irrelevant. "Why look backward?" it is argued. "We should only look forward and be about our Father's business in the here and now."

Such an attitude, however, is not only foolish but downright dangerous. As we will note in chapter 1, Spanish-born American philosopher and writer George Santayana (1863–1952) made the now famous statement, "Those who cannot remember the past are condemned to repeat it." Well, the Church as a whole has, indeed, forgotten much of the past, and the lessons we should learn from it, and is repeating many of the same errors.

This book, therefore, begins in Part I with "Our Foundation," in which we examine the value of studying Church History and then study the deep significance of the words of our Lord in Matthew 16:16–19, "Upon this rock." Part II, "The Five Solas of the Reformation," is the heart of our study in which we examine the core issues of the Reformation and are challenged with their importance for our day. Part III, "Other History Lessons," addresses other historical figures and events that are critical for our understanding in a day of growing indifference to these matters. There are also 60 illustrations, most of which were not in the original articles.

As in the first volume, certain conventions have been used to aid in reading. *First*, each biblical text is noted at the beginning of the chapter and appears in **bold**. This is also true in the exposition itself. *Second*, noted figures from history are also in bold. *Third*, each chapter title is footnoted to indicate its original place in the history of the monthly publication and any other pertinent information. *Fourth*, all other notes appear at the end of each chapter. *Fifth*, Greek, Hebrew, and Latin words appear in a different font (e.g., *charis*, "grace") to contrast them from normal text.

I pray these studies will be to God's glory and the reader's good.

The Author
June 2012

The whole of history is incomprehensible without Jesus.

Ernest Renan
Introduction in *Life of Jesus*

Part I:

Our Foundation

1

Why Study Church History?*

Isaiah 51:1

Hearken to me, ye that follow after righteousness, ye that seek the LORD: look unto the rock whence ye are hewn, and to the hole of the pit whence ye are digged.

The story is told of little Johnny who said to his father, "I don't want to discuss the grade I got in history because that's all in the past." Clever, but not wise. Do you like history? I sure didn't until college, where I had a professor who just opened it up, and it is now an important consideration in any study of theological issues.

What often hangs people up about history is they think it is just about a bunch of dates, deeds, and dead guys. Who cares, right? But history is far less about dates and events than it is about *causes* and *consequences*. For example, what about the Reformation, which we will explore in later chapters? What is important is not so much that it started on April 18, 1521 when **Martin Luther** delivered his famous "Here I stand" speech.[1] What is important first is what *caused* that event, namely, the apostasy and abuses of Roman Catholicism that had been building for a thousand years. Second, what is also crucial are the *consequences* of that event (both good and bad) and what we can and should learn from it.

History is, therefore, critically important. A pastor friend of mine told me he once met another pastor who felt strongly that not only should pastors today have a degree in theology but another in history. His point is well taken. While we might not agree that a degree is necessary, we should recognize that pastors should be trained in history. Why? *Because we actually can understand little theology without history.* After all, think about it: are we not reading history every time we open our Bible?

Amazingly, many historians and philosophers see no real purpose to history. They say such things as: "There is no secret or plan to history"; history is made up of "irrationalities" of which no one can make any sense;

---

* This chapter was originally issue #64 of *Truth on Tough Texts* (hereafter abbreviated TOTT), November 2010. A few new historical illustrations have been added, however, because some of those in the original article appear elsewhere in this book with more detail.

there is no "harmony" in historical events; history is made up of "random events" in which we see "one emergency following another." Shakespeare reflected this attitude in the character Macbeth, who pessimistically declared that history is "a tale told by an idiot, full of sound and fury, signifying nothing."[2]

George
Santayana

How foolish! In contrast, as noted in the Introduction, no better words have been uttered on this than those of philosopher, essayist, poet, and novelist **George Santayana** (1863–1952); while sadly an "agnostic Catholic"(quite a combination!), he was certainly correct that, "Those who cannot remember the past are condemned to repeat it."[3] We today are, indeed, forgetting. I also read just recently what is perhaps the best explanation for studying history. It was uttered by the blind Czech historian **Milan Hubl** to the novelist Milan Kundera:

> The first step in liquidating a people is to erase its memory. Destroy its books, its culture, its history. Then have somebody write new books, manufacture a new culture, invent a new history. Before long the nation will begin to forget what it is and what it was. The world around it will forget even faster.[4]

If we may interject, that is exactly what is happening in America more every day. History (especially American history itself) is even being removed from the school curriculum.

Joseph Sittler

So, if all that is true for history in general, how much more important is it for the Christian to have at least some basic knowledge of Church History? As one of the greatest of church historians, **Phillip Schaff** (1819–1893), wrote:

> How shall we labor with any effect to build up the Church, if we have no thorough knowledge of her history, or fail to apprehend it from the proper point of observation? History is, and must ever continue to be, next to God's Word, the richest foundation of wisdom, and the surest guide to all successful practical activity.[5]

Likewise, while we would not agree with his Ecumenism, evangelical Lutheran theologian and professor **Joseph Sittler** (1904–1987) well said, and which has been quoted often:

> There is certainly nothing wrong with the Church looking ahead, but it is terribly important that it should be done in connection with the look inside, into the Church's own nature and mission,

and a look behind at her own history. If the Church does this, she is less likely to take her cues from the business community, the corporation, or the marketplace.

We note also the great 17th-century mathematician and Christian **Blaise Pascal** (1623–1662): "The history of the Church should more accurately be called the history of truth."[6] Returning to Phillip Schaff, he is worth quoting at some length:

Blaise Pascal

> The history of the Church has practical value for every Christian, as a storehouse of warning and encouragement, of consolation and counsel. It is the philosophy of facts, Christianity in living examples. If history in general be . . . as Diodorus calls it, "the handmaid of providence, the priestess of truth, and the mother of wisdom," the history of the kingdom of heaven is all these in the highest degree. Next to the Holy Scriptures, which are themselves a history and depository of divine revelation, there is no stronger proof of the continual presence of Christ with his people, no more thorough vindication of Christianity, no richer source of spiritual wisdom and experience, no deeper incentive to virtue and piety, than the history of Christ's kingdom. Every age has a message from God to man, which it is of the greatest importance for man to understand.
>
> The Epistle to the Hebrews [chap. 11] describes, in stirring eloquence, the cloud of witnesses from the old dispensation for the encouragement of the Christians. Why should not the greater cloud of apostles, evangelists, martyrs, confessors, fathers, reformers, and saints of every age and tongue, since the coming of Christ, be held up for the same purpose? They were the heroes of Christian Faith and love, the living epistles of Christ, the salt of the earth, the benefactors and glory of our race; and it is impossible rightly to study their thoughts and deeds, their lives and deaths, without being elevated, edified, comforted, and encouraged to follow their

Phillip Schaff

> holy example, that we at last, by the grace of God, be received into their fellowship, to spend with them a blessed eternity in the praise and enjoyment of the same God and Saviour.[7]

My Dear Christian Friend, the Christian Faith we know today was not just handed to us on a silver platter, but was planted, cultivated, and grown over the centuries. If I may repeat, *we can understand little theology without history*. I would, therefore, offer seven reasons why we should study church history. For most of them, I'll also submit an historical event that I hope will encourage you to desire to know more.

The Command of God

The Bible, particularly the Old Testament, repeatedly exhorts us to search out and remember the past. God instituted festivals and ceremonies, in fact, as a reminder. Passover, of course, reminded the Jews of their deliverance from Egyptian bondage. During the Feast of Tabernacles (or Booths) the people lived in huts made of boughs. It commemorated God's provision for them through the wilderness and celebrated the autumn harvest. It also foreshadowed the peace and prosperity of the millennial reign of Christ and will be celebrated during the Millennium (Zech. 14:16).

Our text is one of those truly beautiful verses of the Bible: **Hearken to me, ye that follow after righteousness, ye that seek the LORD: look unto the rock whence ye are hewn, and to the hole of the pit whence ye are digged.** In the next two verses God goes on to say, in effect, "Remember your past; remember where you came from; remember that your nation exists only because of My power that created that nation from an old man and an old woman who were beyond the age of child-bearing." We, too, should remember what we were—wretched, hell-bound sinners! But God loved us, had mercy on us, and sent His only begotten Son to die in our place. But we should also remember the countless events of church history that have helped mold our historical faith. As the "Five Solas of the Reformation" section of our study graphically illustrates, for example, we cannot understand or appreciate Christianity without an understanding of the Reformation. Sadly, however, many so-called evangelicals are actually trying to undo the Reformation.

To Comprehend Today

It has been wisely said, "History is not about the past but the present." Most people just do not realize that we cannot comprehend the present unless we understand the past. It shows us that we are really no different from our Christian brothers and sisters who have gone before us. It enables us to understand and sympathize with the difficulties they faced. It also helps us avoid the sins and errors they made.

During the first four centuries of the Church,[8] it grew progressively more secularized, and the same is occurring today. This caused (and is causing) serious doctrinal errors as well as a departure from biblical exposition. There were some, however, who saw what was occurring. Writing in the middle of the 2nd-century, the apologist **Justin Martyr** described a typical worship service of his day:

> And on the day called Sunday, all who live in cities or in the country gather together to one place, and the memoirs of the apostles or the writings of the prophets are read, as long as time permits; then, when the reader has ceased, the president verbally instructs, and exhorts to the imitation of these good things. Then we all rise together and pray, and, as we before said, when our prayer is ended, bread and wine and water are brought, and the president in like manner offers prayers and thanksgivings, according to his ability, and the people assent, saying Amen.[9]

Justin Martyr

That is of tremendous importance. Mark it down—*the reading and explanation of the Word of God was the absolute center of the worship service.* Not today. Central today is music, drama, comedy, discussion, or anything else we can think of *except* preaching. Today the pulpit ministry, that of expository preaching, is all but gone. This leads to a third reason.

To Consider Tomorrow

Such comprehension of the past and present, leads us right to considering the future. Where are current trends going to lead? Where are patterns of doctrine and conduct going to take us ultimately? Into what troubled waters will even a single teaching guide us?

Our historical illustration here is **Thomas Aquinas** (1224–74). While there is no arguing that Aquinas was one of the greatest thinkers and theologians in history (albeit thoroughly Roman Catholic), there is also no denying his fundamental error. As Francis Schaeffer submits, he began "to open the door to placing revelation and human reason on an equal footing."[10]

Thomas Aquinas

Frankly, it is troubling, indeed, that any Protestant Christian would laud Aquinas. His affinity for the philosopher Aristotle (and the typical high view of man among such pagans) is well known. It was the blending of such rationalistic philosophy with Christianity that led to a crippling of the foundational doctrines of the sovereignty of God and the depravity of man.

The real key to Aquinas, in fact, lies in his view of man. While he be-lieved man rebelled against God and was fallen, he did not think that fall was total. In contrast to the semi-Pelagian (also Arminian and Catholic) error that the *will* remained unfallen, Aquinas' error was that it was actual-ly the *intellect* that was unaffected. As a result, man is able to rely on his own human thinking. Therefore, Aquinas maintained, since his intellect is unfallen, man can be convinced of God's existence through reason (alt-hough deeper truth, such as the Trinity, for example, must come from reve-lation). As one historian well puts it, "Accepting Aristotle's principle—every effect has a cause, every cause has a prior cause, and so on back to the First Cause—Thomas declared that creation traces back to a divine First Cause, the Creator."[11] This is the old Cosmological Argument for God's existence.

So, where did Aquinas' blending of philosophy and Christianity ulti-mately lead? It led us to what are called Classical Apologetics, which de-fends the faith through rational arguments for the existence of God, using evidence to substantiate biblical claims and miracles. It also led us to Evi-dential Apologetics, which defends the faith through the evidence of the miracles of the Bible, especially the evidences for Christ's resurrection, as well as fulfilled prophecies and scientific evidence for creation. All this is clear simply because it is man's intellect and reason that is appealed to. "Give a man enough evidence," it is argued, "and he will recognize the truth."

As we have noted elsewhere,[12] is it not odd that we think our well rea-soned arguments, however compelling or convincing they might be, can actually persuade someone to believe apart from the power of God? And if it is the power of God that saves, why do we need compelling arguments in the first place? Or is it that we need both?

No, it is not arguments that win anybody to Christ, rather it is "the Gospel of Christ" *itself* (the Gospel *in and of itself* without anything added) that is "the power of God unto salvation to every one that believeth; to the Jew first, and also to the Greek" (Rom. 1:16). Paul, in fact, prefaced that statement with the assertion that he wasn't ashamed of that Gospel, rather he preached *that alone* as God's power. So, we do not use *reason*; we use *revelation*. We don't *debate* the issues in arrogance; we *deliver* the Truth[13] in humility. That is evangelism.

As noted earlier, it is extremely troubling that Aquinas is painted in brilliant colors by many Protestants. Just as his philosophy was thoroughly pagan, his theology was blasphemously Roman Catholic. He taught such doctrines as: Christ *won* grace while the Church *imparts* it; Christians need the constant infusion of "cooperating grace" by which they can gain merit in God's sight; saving grace comes through the sacraments; submission to the Pope is necessary for salvation; transubstantiation (the bread and wine of the Lord's Supper being the literal body and blood of Christ) is a true and continuing sacrifice of Christ on the Cross; and the list goes on.[14]

A common attitude of our day is, "Well, we can glean truth from anyone." I have heard this said about even the worst false teachers of our day, often cleverly expressed with phrases such as: "Even a stopped clock is right twice a day," or, "Even a blind squirrel finds a nut once in awhile." We would submit, however, that such an idea is like looking for a few kernels of edible corn in a pig pen or rummaging through a dumpster in the hope of finding a sandwich.

It is interesting, indeed, that the great Reformer **Martin Luther** did not buy into any of this. He was well versed in medieval philosophy, including Aquinas, and its heavy emphasis on Aristotle and pulled no punches in his condemnation:

> The Universities also require a good, sound Reformation. I must say this, let it vex whom it may. . . . the blind heathen teacher, Aristotle, rules even further than Christ. Now, my advice would be that the books of Aristotle be altogether abolished . . . My heart is grieved to see how many of the best Christians this accursed, proud, knavish heathen has fooled and led astray with his false words. God sent him as a plague for our sins.[15]

We would, therefore, submit that it is absolutely essential that we study history to remind us to always examine a new doctrine, a new trend, a new method, a new ministry, or anything else to consider where it will ultimately lead and what the consequences of it will be.

To Contemplate Providence

There are three aspects of the Sovereignty of God: His *decrees*, His *preservation*, and His *providence*. Space permits only brief mention of the last one. God's *providence* means that He continuously fulfills His original plan and design through the events that occur in the universe. What a staggering thought! I constantly ponder the providence of God in history and repeatedly marvel at how He has worked to bring certain things to pass through amazing events that most people just call "coincidence." Mark it down: *Our sovereign God is always at work through providence.*

Mary Tudor

To illustrate, when **Mary Tudor** (Bloody Mary) became Queen of England in 1553, she was determined to put an end to the Protestant

Reformation once-and-for-all and reestablish Roman Catholicism as the national religion. While she was challenged by the English Protestants, she was not deterred. Almost 300 Protestants were burned at the stake and hundreds more escaped to Europe. Many of those godly exiles, among whom were some of the finest theologians and Bible scholars in history, found refuge in Geneva, Switzerland and were determined to translate the Bible into English, and with that the *Geneva Bible* was born. Coming more than 50 years before the 1611 KJV, the Geneva was translated from 1557 to 1560 and was the first English translation to be translated solely from the original Hebrew and Greek. It was even the first Bible that could be classed as a "Study Bible" because of its abundant notes, annotations, cross references, and commentary.

The First page of the Gospel of John in the 1599 Geneva Bible

King James I, however, was infuriated by the strong emphasis of the Doctrines of Grace in the *Geneva Bible* (as are many people today), not to mention its sanctioning of civil disobedience when rulers violate God's law (e.g. Ex. 1:19). This prompted him to authorize a group of Puritan scholars to produce a translation without such notes. It has been speculated, in fact, that if it had not been for James' outrage, the also excellent King James Version might never have been born.

It's significant, indeed, that when the Pilgrims set foot in the New World in 1620, it was the *Geneva Bible* they held in their hands, and it continued to be the Bible of the home for 40 years after the publication of the KJV and went through 144 editions. It was the *Geneva Bible* from which the Scottish Reformer John Knox preached at St. Giles Cathedral in Edinburgh, and it was the Bible of William Shakespeare, John Milton, John Bunyon, and, of course, the Puritans.

Sadly, it lost this prominence only after the KJV was widely promoted by the King and after he outlawed the printing of the Geneva in the English realm. While it has often been called "The Forgotten Bible," the *Geneva Bible* has also been rightly dubbed "The Heartbeat of the Reformation." Outspokenly anti-Roman Catholic (especially in Revelation), it was hated by Rome, just as Rome hated (and still hates) the historic doctrines of the Reformation. It's ironic, indeed, that while many Protestants today, myself included, lovingly embrace the KJV (which reads 90% the same as the Geneva), it is really the *Geneva Bible* that is our true heritage. While in the end the KJV makes for a better and richer translation (see chapter 12), the Geneva laid the solid foundation. In fact, even the preface to the KJV, titled "The Translators to the Reader," took its own Scripture quotations from the *Geneva Bible*.

Here, then, is an amazing example of God's providence. Despite the attacks of man, God's purpose was thwarted in not the slightest degree in bringing us the Bible in English. We will see this in even more detail in chapter 12.

To Conquer Error

One of the most important aspects of Church History is how Theology has developed through the centuries. One of the main reasons for that has been the reaction of godly men against error and apostasy. One doesn't have to study very long to discover *repeated* examples of error. Error is recorded in Scripture (such as the Judaizers of Acts 15 and the entire book of Galatians). Knowing Church History is a priceless tool in fighting error today.

For example, countless cults and false religions deny the Deity of Christ. To the Jehovah's Witnesses, Jesus was not equal to Jehovah and was not God in human flesh but was rather a created being and was actually Michael the Archangel in his preexistent state, having a brother named Lucifer who rebelled against God.[16] Likewise, to the Mormon, Jesus—like all men, in fact—was a preexistent spirit who took his body at birth in this world; He is set apart from the rest of us only by the fact that He was the first-born of God's spirit-children.[17] Other cults, such as Christian Science, the Unity School of Christianity, The Way International, and others illustrate why they are all called "a cult," namely, because they deny the deity of Christ or in some way pervert that doctrine.

But all this is nothing new in Church History; it is simply a revival of the ancient heresy called Arianism. Arius, a 4th-century parish priest in Alexandria, taught that Jesus was not coequal with God and was, in fact, a created being (see chapter 10 for a deeper study of Arianism and the man who stood virtually alone against it).

The popular book, *The Da Vinci Code*, by Dan Brown (Doubleday, 2003) is another graphic illustration. While seemingly just another thriller novel set in the present-day, it has a hidden agenda that makes it far more. Starting with the murdered curator of a Paris museum, the hero and heroin of the story must decipher the clues left behind by the murdered man and thereby uncover an ancient and sinister plot. *And what is that ancient secret?* The supposed "true" story that Christianity has been trying to hide for 1,600 years, namely, that Jesus was just another man who actually ended up marrying Mary Magdalene.

Error is everywhere, but knowing history makes it much easier to spot.

To Compare People

Have you ever been reading an incident in history where a person did something remarkable and then thought, "I could never have done that?" Indeed, comparing ourselves to some of the great people of history will humble us like nothing else will. Not only will studying people of the past teach us about *them*, but it will also teach us about *ourselves*.

For example, one of the fundamental traits missing in society today is personal *integrity*. The essence of integrity is allegiance, standing firm for what is right without duplicity, double-mindedness, or divided allegiance.

Whenever I think of the word *integrity*, I am immediately reminded of the Huguenots of 16th-century France. They held strong morals and possessed high integrity. To be "honest as a Huguenot" was said to have been the highest praise of one's integrity. Put simply, what the Puritan was in England, the Huguenot was in France. A conservative estimate says that by 1561 one-sixth of France was strong in the historic doctrines of Christianity, which were reasserted in the Reformation, and blameless moral character; other estimates say one-fourth.

But history then reveals that the Huguenots were forced to leave France in 1685 and hence settled in England, Prussia, Holland, South Africa, and the Carolinas here in America. (I had the joy of once visiting a Huguenot Church in Charleston, South Carolina.) What's especially significant about that exodus is that it was a terrible economic blow to France, since most Huguenots were skilled artisans and professional men of the middle class (paralleled by the tax-paying middle class in America). Does that not explain the intellectual emptiness and moral debauchery that permeates France to this very day? Does that not explain the virtually incomprehensible ramblings of French philosophers such as Voltaire (1694–1778), André Maurois (1885–1967), and especially Jean Paul Sartre (1905–1980)?

French Huguenot Church in Charleston, South Carolina

In a day when there is little integrity among politicians, businessmen, and sadly even some religious (and so-called Christian) leaders, the need for integrity cannot be overemphasized. While society today places virtually no value at all on personal integrity, it is a trait that is at the very core of a true believer.

To Cultivate Endurance

Our Lord declared, "Ye shall be hated of all men for my name's sake: but he that shall endure unto the end, the same shall be saved" (Mk 13:13). The true believer is the one who endures to the very end. We also read in Hebrews 6:11, "And we desire that every one of you do show the same diligence to the full assurance of hope unto the end." James likewise declares, "Blessed is the man that endureth temptation: for when he is tried, he shall receive the crown of life, which the Lord hath promised to them that love him" (Jas. 1:12).

When we look at faithful people of the past, it is a tremendous encouragement. There are scores of those who have endured hardship and even death for the faith. They were each committed to the Truth and anticipated Christ's return. They did, indeed, endure to the end.

Of countless illustrations, one that strikes us profoundly, and one that we would do well to remember in our day, is that of the Pilgrims. Who were those 102 Pilgrims who left England in search of religious freedom and landed at Plymouth, Massachusetts in December of 1620? The story is a fascinating one.[18]

About 1602 **William Brewster** (c.1563–1644), a Cambridge educated man and Puritan, began meeting in his home with a group of Puritans of

William Brewster

Scrooby, England who wanted religious freedom. Also involved was another Cambridge educated man and Puritan, **John Robinson** (c.1575–1625), who soon became the pastor of the group, while Brewster was the ruling elder. The movement grew, and when persecution forced them to leave the Church, they founded the Separatist Church of Scrooby in 1606. At this time part of the group moved to Amsterdam, Holland seeking greater freedom of worship. Two years later the rest followed. Another year later they moved to Leyden, where the congregation grew to 300.

By 1620, Brewster and Robinson both promoted immigration to America to seek religious freedom. While Robinson stayed behind to pastor those who decided to remain in Holland, Brewster led about one-third of the group to America. Sailing first to England on the *Speedwell*, they then boarded the *Mayflower* and sailed from Southampton on September 16. They sighted land (Cape Cod) on November 19, and landed at Plymouth on December 26. It is also interesting that because of storms at sea, they landed in Plymouth instead of Virginia. But this was the sovereignty of God at work, for they would have been persecuted as much in Virginia as they had been in England.

In the opening lines of his famous poem, "Sea Fever," John Masefield (1878–1967) wrote of the romance of sailing: "I must go down to the seas again, / to the lonely sea and sky, / And all I ask is a tall ship, / and a star to steer her by." He wrote something quite different, however, about the pilgrims who made that voyage, a voyage that can be accurately described as horrific:

The ship was very small, and crowded with people. Counting the crew, she must have held nearly a hundred and fifty people, in a space too narrow for the comfort of half that number. The passengers were stowed in the between decks, a sort of low, narrow room, under the spar deck, lit in fine weather by the openings of hatchways and gun-ports, and in bad weather, when these were closed, by lanterns. They lived, ate, slept, and were seasick in that narrow space. A woman bore a child, a man died there. They were packed so tightly, among all their belongings and stores, that they could have had no privacy. The ventilation was bad, even in fine weather. In bad weather, when the hatches were battened down, there was none. In bad weather the pilgrims lived in a fog, through which they could see the water on the deck washing from side to side, as the ship rolled, carrying their pans and clothes with it. They could only lie, and groan, and pray, in stink and misery, while the water from ill-caulked seams dripped on them from above.[19]

All that, however, was just a warm up for what they faced on the shores of this new continent. The "want of fresh food," Masefield goes on to recount, "the harshness of the change of climate, the exposure and labour in the building of the town, and the intense cold of even a mild New England winter, were more than they could endure. Nearly half of them were dead within six months." But they endured, and within the next twenty years were joined by some 20,000 more Puritans.

Who were those Puritans? They were godly, Scripture-saturated people who clung to the precious doctrines of the Reformation—the Doctrines of Grace. Their desire was to govern themselves biblically for the glory of God. No matter how the revisionists try to rewrite American history, there is no denying that the principle of "the laws of nature and nature's God" was the heart of early America. While not all the Founding Fathers were Christians, the majority were. Unlike today, an acknowledgment of Christian belief was required for holding public office during the years of the Founding Fathers.

Consider also the foundation of American education. Harvard University, for example, is the oldest American college. Founded (1636) with a grant from the Massachusetts Bay Colony and named (1638) for its first benefactor, John Harvard, it was intended as a training ground for Puritan ministers but evolved a more generalized program of education. The first president of Harvard, in fact, was the Puritan leader Thomas Shepard, and several of our Founding Fathers attended there, including: John Adams, John Hancock, and Samuel Adams. Further, the requirements of a student to attend Harvard were quite specific:

Let every student be plainly instructed and consider well the main end of his life and studies is to know God and Jesus Christ and therefore to lay Christ in the bottom as the only foundation of all sound knowledge and learning . . . Everyone shall so exercise himself in reading the Scriptures twice a day that he shall be ready to give an account of his proficiency therein.

The landing of our Pilgrim Fathers in New England

History also reveals that other colleges, such as Yale, and especially Princeton, had similar requirements. Princeton's founding statement was, "Cursed be all learning that is contrary to the cross of Christ," and it did, indeed, produce some of the greatest theological minds in American history. Ah, how times have changed!

One historian well summarizes: "It's only a slight exaggeration to say that most of the good in America began with the Puritans and most of the bad has come from rejecting their worldview."[20] While some would argue, "But the Puritans are gone now; they haven't endured at all, so why cite them as cultivating endurance?" we would submit the very opposite. Besides the persecution they endured, as well as the sea voyage and early years in America, their legacy still endures today. A monument to them, for example, endures in the pieces of the *Mayflower* that have been restored and are on display in Skagit County Museum in La Conner, Washington.

But far more enduring is what the Puritans left behind via the printed page. Several publishers continue to reprint the works of the Puritans, and we do well to read them. Their passion for preaching, the authority of Scripture, theological exactness, moral purity, and more provide us invaluable lessons that we ignore at our peril. Indeed, the Puritans challenge us today to cultivate endurance.

Recommended Reading

If you would like to go further in a basic study of Church History, an easy starting place is S. M. Houghton's wonderful, *Sketches from Church History* (Banner of Truth Trust). Another that provides simple, daily readings, is Rick Cornish's *5 Minute Church Historian* (NavPress). To go a step deeper, read Bruce Shelley's excellent *Church History in Plain Language*, 3rd Edition (Thomas Nelson).

NOTES

[1] It can, of course, be argued that it all started on October 31, 1517 when Luther nailed his 95 Theses to the church door in Wittenberg.

[2] *Macbeth*, 5.5.19.

[3] Santayana, *The Life of Reason*, Vol. 1., 1905.

[4] Quoted by Milan Kundera in his novel, *The Book of Laughter and Forgetting*.

[5] Philip Schaff, *What is Church History: A Vindication of the Idea of Historical Development* (J. B. Lippincott and Co., 1846), 5.

[6] *Pensées* (Section XIV, polemic 858.

[7] Philip Schaff, *History of the Christians Church*, Vol. 1, "General Introduction," § 5. Uses of Church History.

[8] The publisher has chosen to capitalize "Church" as a proper name throughout this book when it refers to the Church as a whole, that is, the Body of Christ. We view it as a "transcendent idea," such as "the Truth" (see note 13 below). Lowercase ("church" or "churches") is used when referring to a local church.

[9] *The Ante-Nicene Fathers*, Vol. 1; Ages Digital Library, "The First Apology Of Justin," Chapter 67.

[10] Francis Schaeffer, *How Should We Then Live?* (Feming H. Revell, 1976), 43.

[11] Bruce Shelley, *Church History in Plain Language*, 3rd Edition (Thomas Nelson, 2008), 201.

[12] See chapter 21, "Apologetics and the Gospel," in the author's *Truth on Tough Texts: Expositions in Challenging Scripture Passages* (Sola Scriptura Publications, 2012), 210.

[13] The publisher has chosen to capitalize "Truth" as a proper name throughout this book when referring to "the Truth." As the *Chicago Manual of Style* offers: "Words for transcendent ideas in the Platonic sense, especially when used in a religious context, are often capitalized [such as]: Good; Beauty; Truth; One" (7.82). Lowercase ("truth") is used when the word has a modifier, such as "a biblical truth," for example.

[14] Shelley, 201–202.

[15] *Letter to the German Nobility* (III.25).

[16] *The Kingdom is at Hand*, p. 49. Cited in *Handbook of Today's Religions*, p. 46.

[17] *Handbook of Today's Religions*, 70–71.

[18] A more detailed account appears in the author's *Salvation is of the Lord: The Doctrines of Grace Expounded by a Former Arminian*, which is scheduled for release in 2013 by Sola Scriptura Publications.

[19] *Chronicles of the Pilgrim Fathers*, with an Introduction by John Masefield (New York: E. P. Button & Co., nd.), xi–xii.

[20] Rick Cornish, *5 Minute Church Historian* (NavPress, 2005), 194. For a study of worldviews, see chapter 49, "What in the World is a Biblical Worldview?" in the author's *Truth on Tough Texts: Expositions of Challenging Scripture Passages* (Sola Scriptura Publications, 2012), 478–86.

2

𝕌𝔭𝔬𝔫 𝕋𝔥𝔦𝔰 ℜ𝔬𝔠𝔨*

Matthew 16:16–19

And Simon Peter answered and said, Thou art the Christ, the Son of the living God. And Jesus answered and said unto him, Blessed art thou, Simon Barjona: for flesh and blood hath not revealed it unto thee, but my Father which is in heaven. And I say also unto thee, That thou art Peter, and upon this rock I will build my church; and the gates of hell shall not prevail against it.

hat is "the Church"? A simple definition, offered by evangelical theologian William Evans in his classic work, *The Great Doctrines of the Bible*, is: "The Church is composed of the body of believers who have been called out from the world, and who are under the dominion and authority of Jesus Christ."[1] One will find similar definitions and descriptions (with more detail, of course) among many other evangelical theologians and expositors.

What is the Church?

The above evangelical view of the Church is based upon an understanding of three Greek words.

First, there is the unique word *ekklēsia*. It is comprised of *ek*, "out," and *kaleō*, "to call," and therefore means "a called-out assembly." It is found in Classical Greek from the 5th-century BC onward and was used for the assembling of citizens of the city (*polis*) for legislation and other public business.

Second, while *ekklēsia* occurs about 100 times in the Septuagint for the gathering of Israel for some definite purpose, the usual word is *sunagōgē* ("synagogue"), which appears about 225 times to translate various Hebrew words. It is amazing that Jesus' followers didn't describe their meetings using *sunagōgē*, since this would have been the natural word for Jews to use. When it *is* used, it refers to the meeting place of the local Jewish community or assembly.

---

* This chapter was originally issue 79 of TOTT, September/October 2012. It was the last to be added to this collection and inspired the book's title.

So again, *ekklēsia* is unique indeed, appearing some 116 times. As our Lord declared in our text, **Upon this rock I will build my church.** Our Lord truly transformed this word, using it to refer to *His* assembly, making it distinct from Judaism.

Third, our English word **church** actually comes from *kuriakos*, which is derived from *kurios* (Lord), and literally means "belonging to the Lord" (translated "Lord's" in 1 Cor. 11:20 and Rev. 1:10).

So, combining all that, the Church can be defined simply as: *the called-out assembly of New Testament believers that belongs to the Lord.* The Universal Church (the church as an *organism*) is comprised of all believers everywhere. Our Lord's words in our main text, for example, emphasize His **church**, not *churches* (cf. 1 Cor. 15:9; Col. 1:18, 24; Eph. 5: 23–27). The Local Church (the Church as an *organization*) is a local assembly of believers organized according to Scriptural guidelines (e.g., Jerusalem, Acts. 8:1; Antioch, 13:1; Ephesus, 20:17; Galatia, Gal. 1:2; Judea, 1 Thess. 2:14; and Asia Minor, Rev. 2–3).

When one turns, however, to "other branches of Christianity," as some erroneously term it, he finds something quite different. In Mormonism, for example, the structures of authority and authorization outlined in the *Doctrine and Covenants* comprise the "Church." Without that authority, it is insisted, you have no "Church" in the capital "C" sense, but merely a lower-case "church." God might love a Baptist or a Lutheran, for example, and be pleased with his work, but if he doesn't accept the one authorized baptism of Mormonism, he is not of the "Church."

Turning in still another direction, Roman Catholicism, the Church is again defined far differently than it is in true biblical Christianity. As stated in one of the most authoritative works of Catholicism, *Fundamentals of Catholic Dogma*, by Ludwig Ott:

> In the wider sense the designation "Mystical body of Christ" means the communion of all those made holy by the grace of Christ. These include: the faithful on earth; those in the place of purification [i.e., Purgatory] who are not yet completely justified; and the perfectly justified in Heaven. . . . In the narrower sense the Mystical body of Christ means the visible Church of Christ on earth.[2]

Robert Bellarmine

Even such a basic definition clearly states some of the false doctrines of Catholicism, such as Purgatory and the idea that people can become "completely justified" at some point *after* death.

Another definition, this one the classic by "Saint" **Robert Bellarmine** (1542–1621), Italian Jesuit and Cardinal, stated: "The Church is a union of men who are united in the profession of the same Christian Faith, and by the participation in the same Sacraments, under the direction of their lawful pastors [i.e., priests], especially of the one representative of Christ on earth, the Pope of Rome."[3] The errors here are even more dramatic: the sacramental system is at the core of "church membership"; priests are pictured as mediators; and, mostly notably, *the Pope is lifted up as being the actual representative of Christ on earth.*

What is the Rock?

It is that latter theory that commands our attention. For more than fifteen hundred years, the Roman Catholic Church has dogmatically asserted that the Pope is the supreme and authoritative representative of Christ on the earth, and it is our text that is appealed to as the chief "proof" that Peter was the first Pope and from whom all others have descended. So presumptuous and arrogant is this assertion, in fact, that the first Vatican Council (1870) pronounced a curse upon anyone who would dare challenge it:

> If anyone says that the blessed Apostle Peter was not established by the Lord Christ as the chief of all the apostles, and the visible head of the whole militant Church, or, that the same received great honour but did not receive from the same our Lord Jesus Christ directly and immediately the primacy in true and proper jurisdiction: let him be anathema.[4]

Now, is this really all that important? What difference does it make? Well, it is not an overstatement to say that this is actually central to the entire Roman Catholic system. In his classic exposé, titled simply *Roman Catholicism,* **Loraine Boettner** (pronounced Bet-ner, 1901–1990) wrote:

> The whole structure of the Roman Church is built on the assumption that in Matthew 16:13–19 Christ appointed Peter the first pope and so established the papacy. Disprove the primacy of Peter, and the foundation of the papacy is destroyed. Destroy the papacy, and the whole Roman hierarchy topples with it. Their system of priesthood depends absolutely upon their claim that Peter was the first pope at Rome, and that they are his successors.[5]

Loraine Boettner

Again, that is not even the slightest exaggeration. It is absolutely essential for true Bible believing Christians to recognize that *everything* in the Roman system hinges on this single dogma. Therefore, if the Papacy can be shown to be without a shred of biblical support, what does that say about the entire system? What does that say also of the Reformation? Does it not dramatically demonstrate that the Reformers were, indeed, returning to biblical salvation? Does it not then say that those today who call themselves evangelicals but who are actually in sympathy with Rome and trying to undo the Reformation, and thereby return to Rome, are as apostate as the system they are defending?

Well, it is our purpose here to show with crystal clarity that the evidence against the Roman Papacy, and therefore the entire system, is utterly overwhelming. We also hope to demonstrate that any compromise with it is a betrayal of our Lord and His Word.

First, the words **Peter** and **rock** are, of course, central to the issue. **Peter** is the Greek *petros*, which refers to a stone that is small enough to throw. The word **rock**, however, is the Greek *petra*, which refers to a large rock, such as a boulder, cliff, bedrock, or even a mountain chain. So, it is a well known fact that this is a simple play on words. There are, however, a couple of ways this play on words has been understood.

One view maintains that our Lord is simply saying He will build His church, not on Peter (*Petros*, a throwable stone), as Catholicism teaches, but on Himself (*Petra*), who is the large rock, the bedrock. More specifically, it is to the Divine revelation and profession of faith in Christ in verses 16–17.

Another view also notes the two different words but with a different contrast, namely, that *petros* is masculine while *petra* is feminine. Based upon that, it is submitted, *petros* refers to Peter himself while *petra* refers to the larger group of apostles with Peter as the chief representative. This view, as well as the first one, matches Ephesians 2:20, which clearly proclaims the Church is built upon "the foundation of the apostles and prophets, Jesus Christ himself being the chief corner stone," not Peter alone.

We can conclude from this that whichever of these views is the true meaning of **Peter** and **rock**, one thing is certain: the Roman view is wrong at its core. If that is not yet obvious, however, let us go on.

Second, if **Peter** was intended, why did our Lord change to the feminine *petra* (**rock**) in the middle of the sentence? Boettner puts this in a clever way, as if Jesus were saying, "And I say unto thee, that thou art Mr. Rock, and upon this, the Miss Rock, I will build my church." The simple fact is that the Roman view simply cannot answer the change in gender. Like all false teaching, it is based upon faulty exegesis.

Third, even more basic than that, if Peter was actually the **Rock**, is it not probable that Jesus would have simply said, "Thou art Peter, and upon *you* I will build my church"? Would not this have cleared up any ambiguity?

Fourth, what seems to be ignored is our Lord adds that it is because of that foundation that **the gates of hell shall not prevail against** (*katischuō*, "overcome, overpower, vanquish") His Church. Was this true of Peter? Indeed not, for we read just a few verses later that Peter (the supposed **Rock** of the Church) actually rebuked the Lord Jesus for His talk about going to Jerusalem to be killed. What was Jesus' response? "Get thee behind me, Satan: thou art an offence unto me: for thou savourest not the things that be of God, but those that be of men" (vv. 21–23). Does that sound like Pope material?

Fifth, if Peter was, in fact, the first Pope, why do the disciples ask Jesus in Matthew 18:1, "Who is the greatest in the kingdom of heaven?" Since they heard Peter's confession and our Lord's response, would they not already know that Peter was obviously the greatest? On the other hand, if they had just forgotten that little fact, would not Jesus have here reminded them of Peter's superiority and again cleared up any confusion? A similar situation arose, in fact, two chapters later (20:20–21), the details of which are in Mark 10:35–37. This time it is James and John asking for chief honors. But again, why would they ask if Peter's superiority had already been made clear to them?

Sixth, would not Peter himself have first *recognized* his superiority and then *reminded* others of it? Yes, he identified himself as an Apostle (1 Pet. 1:1; 2 Pet. 1:1), but not once did he claim a superior rank or position over the others. In fact, he referred to himself merely as a fellow "elder" with others (1 Pet. 5:1) and a "servant [*doulos*, bond slave] of Jesus Christ" (2 Pet. 1:1). Is all that not a far cry from the Pope today who quite readily accepts genuflecting at his presence and kisses on his foot?

Seventh, is it reasonable to think that an infallible Pope comes from the fallible Peter? Not only do we see Peter's miserable failure in Matthew 16:21–23, as noted above, but we see another recorded in Galatians 2:11–21. Paul "withstood [Peter] to the face" because of his compromise of doctrine, namely, complicity with the Judaizers in compelling Gentile believers to live as Jews.

Eighth and finally, there is no definitive proof whatsoever that Peter was ever actually in Rome. Now, Roman Catholics will take me to task on this, but the evidence is ambiguous at best. Their chief "proof," of course, is 1 Peter 5:12–13: "I have written briefly, exhorting, and testifying that this is the true grace of God wherein ye stand. The church that is at Babylon, elected together with you, saluteth you; and so doth Marcus my son." Based upon this, it is dogmatically asserted that this proves "Peter's stay in Rome" because "Babylon is a symbolic designation for Rome."[6] The fact of the matter is, however, that there are several possibilities as to the meaning of "Babylon" here. Besides the *symbolic* Roman view, there was also a *literal* Roman outpost in northern Egypt named Babylon, which was a political, military, and Judean center. There was also, of course, the Babylon of Mesopotamia. As John Gill submits, in fact, "It is best therefore to understand it literally, of Babylon in Assyria, the metropolis of the dispersion of the Jews, and the center of it, to whom the apostle wrote; and where, as the minister of the circumcision, he may be thought to reside, here being a number of persons converted and formed into a Gospel church state." Another obscure view was that "Babylon" was symbolic of Jerusalem because of its wickedness and resemblance to Babylon. (Still another is that it is symbolic of America!)

If I may also interject, any symbolic meaning here simply does not fit. Peter's writing was consistently literal and practical. He was not the type to use symbolism. He consistently said what he meant and meant what he said. We would, therefore, submit that if he had *meant* Rome, he would have *written* Rome.

I also found it interesting during my research that, like Gill, older commentators (e.g., Albert Barnes, Calvin, Adam Clark, the Puritans [see Matthew Henry and *Geneva Bible* note], etc.), take Babylon in one or the other literal sense, while many contemporary ones actually defend the Rome view. Some, for example, make it sound more compelling by saying that Peter, writing from Rome, used "Babylon" as a code word so as not to endanger persecuted Christians in Rome in case his letter were found after his death. They cite John's use of "Babylon" for Rome in the Book of Revelation as another example of this practice. But this again *assumes* a figurative meaning of Babylon there as well. A view that is growing in credibility today is that Babylon in Revelation does not refer to the revived Roman (European) Empire at all, as has been commonly taught for decades, rather *literal* Babylon in the form of Islam.[7] In any case, is it not troubling that some evangelicals today seem to go out of their way to side with (or at least be tolerant of) Rome in subtle (and sometimes not so subtle) ways? If I may also lovingly add, *a typical trend in our day is to see things in the text that are not actually there.*

It is also asserted that certain Early Church authorities confirm that Peter was in Rome. Irenaeus (c.115–c.202), for example, maintained this, but on the other hand, he maintained that Peter also ministered with Paul while in Rome, an idea that is even more unprovable. Eusebius (c.263–339) also insisted that Peter was in Rome, but then again he also wrote that Peter founded the church at Antioch, which is clearly incorrect.

In the same vein, while those authorities say Peter was in Rome, does it not seem odd that there is not a single word from the greatest New Testament authority, *the Apostle Paul*, that Peter was in Rome? After all, Paul wrote four of his epistles during his first imprisonment there and two more during the second. But in all that correspondence, we read not even a hint of Peter's presence, even though Paul mentions many other Christians, including fellow laborers, by name in his letters. One would think that the great Peter would get at least a mention if he were actually laboring in Rome.

Further, what about the letter to the Romans? In chapter 15 Paul mentions 27 members of that church, but no Peter. Why is this significant? Simply because Paul wrote that letter about AD 58 and Catholicism says Peter was there from 42 to 67 and was the head of the Church. Do you see the problem? Are we to believe that Peter had already been the head of that church for 16 years when Paul wrote but Paul didn't bother to mention it?

Here's another little tidbit to ponder in Romans. Note Paul's statement in 1:11: "For I long to see you, that I may impart unto you some spiritual gift, to the end ye may be established." "Established" is *sterizō*, from *histēmi*, "to make to stand up, raise, awaken, or rouse (of persons lying down or sleeping)." As M. R. Vincent puts it, "The word implies fixedness." But wait! Are we to think that Peter had already been in Rome for 16 years but the believers there were not properly established? In fact, with Peter there, why did they even need this greatest of doctrinal treatises in the first place?

So, we say again, there is no definitive proof that Peter was ever in Rome. Is it possible? Of course it is, though highly improbable. But for the Roman Church to say this dogmatically is indefensible and clearly prejudicial simply because it conveniently fits their theory of the Papacy. It says Peter was the **Rock** in Rome, and anyone who disagrees, regardless of any biblical or historical data, is cursed.

What is the Only Possible Conclusion?

Besides what we have already seen, the errors of Roman Catholicism are almost incomprehensible. The Mass alone, the recrucifying of Jesus and partaking of his literal body and blood is so blasphemous that it should literally nauseate us. Through the ages, Catholicism has steadily added this doctrine, that ritual, this other custom, and that other tradition to ultimately build such a monstrosity that it is unthinkable that any true evangelical Christian would speak even a single positive word for it.

Here are but a few developments with their approximate dates: prayers for the dead and making the sign of the cross (300); veneration of angels and dead saints, and the use of images (375); The Mass as a daily celebration (394); exaltation of Mary, the "Mother of God" (431); doctrine of Purgatory, (593); prayers directed to Mary, dead saints, and angels (600); kissing the pope's foot (709); worship of the cross, images, and relics (authorized in 786); worship of St. Joseph (890); fasting on Fridays and during Lent (998); celibacy of priests (1079); The Rosary (1090); sale of indulgences (1190); Transubstantiation (1215); doctrine of Seven Sacraments affirmed (1439); Tradition declared of equal authority with the Bible (Council of Trent, 1545); infallibility of the pope in matters of faith and morals (Vatican I, 1870); and more. Added to that abbreviated list, consider also: saints, monks, nuns, monasteries, convents, forty days of Lent, holy week, Palm Sunday, Ash Wednesday, All Saints day, Candlemas day, fish day, meat days, Christmas Day, Maundy Thursday, Easter Sunday, incense, holy oil, holy palms, Christopher medals, charms, novenas, and still more, all invented by Roman Catholicism, not only with no biblical support whatsoever but also with the influence and overtones of paganism.

If we may ask here: Should it not appall us when we hear these terms used in our evangelical churches? Should not the origins of such doctrines grieve us who profess to believe in the authority and sufficiency of Scripture alone—the Reformation doctrine of *sola Scriptura*? Should this not trouble us all the more as we see a growing number of Christians being influenced by ancient Roman Catholic mysticism? This is dramatically demonstrated, for example, by how many evangelicals embraced the movie *The Passion of Christ*, as well as how many are falling for the so-called Spiritual Formation Movement.

So what is the conclusion? The unvarnished answer to that question offends many today, but the irrefutable fact is: *Roman Catholicism is not true Christianity*. To defend it as such, or try to find "common ground" as is often vocalized today, is utter folly and a betrayal of the true Christian Faith. I think Harry Ironside, in his commentary on Revelation, put it better than anyone I have ever read: "Romanism is Christianity, Judaism, and Heathenism joined together; and the Lord abhors the vile combination."

Inexplicably, in spite of all that (*and much more*), there are still those in Evangelicalism who downplay and even ignore that Christianity and Catholicism are, in plain fact, polar opposites. I would submit here a truly fascinating illustration of this that I pray you will carefully and prayerfully consider. In 1917, William C. Irvine published his book, *Timely Warnings*, the first of the modern counter-cult books. Renamed to *Heresies Exposed* in 1921, it went through 39 printings by 1985. In it he warned Christians of false religions and cults that denied the essential doctrines of biblical Christianity. Irvine's book stood alone for some 20 years as the single polemic against cults and false religions, and it is extremely significant that included in that book was a chapter exposing the cult that Roman Catholicism truly is. Inexplicably, however, that view vanished from virtually every book that followed. While *The Chaos of the Cults* (J. K. Van Baalen) came in 1938, followed by *The Kingdom of the Cults* (Walter Martin) in

1965, and others soon after, what is conspicuously absent from those two, and practically every other work that has followed since, is an exposé of Roman Catholicism. Why? Writing in 1938, Van Baalen himself gives us a clue in *The Chaos of the Cults*:

> The writer has been asked repeatedly why Roman Catholicism has not been included as one of the major cults. The answer is that the Roman Catholic Church is a stone with many faces. It is a corrupt and exceedingly dangerous political machine, and it is a religious body full of doctrinal error and superstition. But it is also a church that stands upon the solid foundation of the Apostles Creed. It holds and defends such cardinal Christian doctrines as that of the Trinity, the Deity of our Lord, His resurrection, His second coming to judge the world, and the atonement by His substitutionary blood. Some of the outstanding apologetic work in our day is done by Roman Catholic scholars. Such a body does not come under the heading of unchristian cults as described in the present volume.[8]

Such misunderstanding of Roman Catholic dogma and its agenda is hard to fathom. It violently opposes true biblical Christianity as set forth in the five solas of the Reformation and is nothing short of blasphemous in its doctrines and practices. I know this is strong language, but there is no hiding the fact that it is *apostate* in its theology, *arrogant* in its attitudes, and even *amoral* in some of its practices. Inexplicable also is that while cult books point out the apostasy and wickedness of Mormonism, Jehovah's Witness, and others, they ignore the demonstrable fact that Catholicism is essentially no different; it is just another works based religion. Frankly, in light of growing tolerance, we cannot help but wonder if even Mormonism will one day be removed from such cult exposés.

A noted exception to such cult books is Fritz Ridenour's, *So What's the Difference?* Updated and expanded in 2001, it is one of today's more honest polemic works, examining twenty worldviews, faiths, and religions in comparison to Christianity. Even it, however, has an ever so slight weakness in dealing with Roman Catholicism. While it does a good job pointing out Catholicism's departures from biblical Christianity, it does so in a section titled "Other Trunks of the Christian Tree," a section that also includes Eastern Orthodoxy. A better choice, we submit, would have been something such as, "Imitators of Christianity," because these are *not* part of the "True Vine" of Christianity at all. Another tiny weakness appears in the statement, "While Roman Catholics place high value on their liturgy and sacramental system, it is incorrect to say that they believe they are 'saved by works.' Roman Catholicism teaches that Christ's blood 'has become the instrument of atonement for the sins of all men.'"[9] That is poor wording, for faith *plus* works is no longer faith at all. Thankfully, Ridenour goes on to write in the very next sentence, "At the same time, they insist that faith in what Christ did on the cross in and of itself is not enough." That is correct and again underscores that Catholicism is not the true Christian Faith.

In dramatic contrast to such anemic books noted earlier, prior to our modern era, in fact, the recognition that Catholicism is not Christianity was *never* called into question by Christian leaders (please read that again). A graphic example appears just a few years before William C. Irvine's book was published. In 1909 the first of twelve marvelous volumes, entitled *The Fundamentals*, appeared and was devoted to the exposition and defense of Evangelicalism. Completed in 1915, the set contained 90 articles defending the crucial, non-negotiable doctrines of the Christian Faith. Contributors included: James Gray, G. Campbell Morgan, A. T. Pierson, J. C. Ryle, Thomas Spurgeon (Charles Spurgeon's son), Charles Feinberg, and dozens more. Another was **T. W. Medhurst**, a Scottish pastor who was the first student at Charles Spurgeon's Pastor's College; Spurgeon even officiated at Medhurst's marriage in 1859. In an article titled "Is Romanism Christianity?" Medhurst began by writing (see the Appendix for a complete reprint of this article):

> I am aware that, if I undertake, to prove that Romanism is not Christianity, I must expect to be called "bigoted, harsh, uncharitable." Nevertheless I am not daunted; for I believe that on a right understanding of this subject depends the salvation of millions.
>
>
>
> One reason why Popery has of late gained so much power in Great Britain and Ireland, and is gaining, power still, is that many Protestants look on it now as a form of true Christianity; and think that, on that account, notwithstanding great errors, it ought to be treated very tenderly. Many suppose that at the time of the Reformation, it was reformed, and that it is now much nearer the truth than it was before that time. It is still, however, the same; and, if examined, will be found to be so different from, and so hostile to, real Christianity, that it is not, in fact, Christianity at all.

T. W. Medhurst

Dear Christian Friend, does that not well explain exactly what is happening today? Please recall that the purpose of that set of articles was to defend the crucial, *non-negotiable* doctrines of the Christian Faith, so where does that put us today? Are we not, in fact, renegotiating? Does not any compromise or complicity with Catholicism betray biblical Christianity? "To aid such a system," Medhurst wrote, "is to fight against God."

Before we close, I do not want to overlook a very important question: Does all this mean we hate Catholics? Certainly not! *Roman Catholics are a mission field*, a point we shall make again as we continue. While the common attitude among much of Evangelicalism today is that we should embrace our "Catholic brethren," nothing could be further from the truth. While there are certainly some Roman Catholics who are true believers, *those who hold to that system* are blind and need the true Gospel of Jesus Christ. Why? Because *He* is the **Rock**!

NOTES

[1] William Evans, *The Great Doctrines of the Bible*, Revised Edition by S. Maxwell Coder (Moody, 1912, 1974), 182.

[2] Ludwig Ott, *Fundamentals of Catholic Dogma* (Tan Books and Publishers, 1955, 1960, 1974), 271.

[3] Ibid.

[4] Cited in Ott, 279, from Vatican I: Dogmatic Constitution "Pastor Aeternus" §1 (July 18, 1870).

[5] Loraine Boettner, *Roman Catholicism* (Presbyterian and Reformed, 1962), 105.

[6] Ott, 283.

[7] See Joel Richardson, *Mideast Beast* (WND Books, 2012).

[8] *The Chaos of the Cults* (Grand Rapids: Eerdmans, 1972), 5.

[9] Fritz Ridenour, *So What's the Difference?* (Regal Books, 1967, 1979, 2001), 42–43. He quotes from the *Catechism of the Catholic Church* (Doubleday, 1995), paragraph 1992.

God speaks by the Church (the true Church we mean); but He speaks nothing by her but what He speaks in the Scriptures, which she does only ministerially to us; and therefore the authority of God and His law is above hers, who, though she publish, yet did not make it, but is herself subject to it.

John Owen
Puritan Golden Treasury

Part II:

The Five Solas of the Reformation

3

𝔗𝔥𝔢 ℜ𝔬𝔬𝔱𝔰 𝔬𝔣 𝔱𝔥𝔢 ℜ𝔢𝔣𝔬𝔯𝔪𝔞𝔱𝔦𝔬𝔫*

Jeremiah 3:6–15, 20—4:2

hat was the Reformation? Was it just a time of religious confusion? Was it merely a bunch of Christians who were fighting amongst themselves? Was it simply two factions in the Church that were making mountains out of molehills? Further, was the Reformation a mistake, a black mark on the Church's history caused by a bunch of intolerant, narrow-minded trouble-makers who divided an otherwise unified church? Should we today try to reverse what occurred then and return to the days prior to that tragic event?

This section seeks to answer such questions. For the last several decades, there has been an enormous amount of misunderstanding about what the Reformation was about. Worse, there have been a series of attacks against the Reformation, most of which have insisted that it was, indeed, a mistake that needs to be undone.

Whatever view one takes of the Reformation, at the heart of it was a five-fold foundation, five key truths that defined the movement. Each beginning with the Latin word *sola*, meaning "alone," they formed the rebuilt "pillars" of biblical Christianity that had been demolished by the Roman Catholic Church over the preceding 1,000 years. These five pillars were: *sola scriptura* (Scripture alone), *sola gratia* (grace alone), *sola fide* (faith alone), *solus Christus* (Christ alone), and *soli Deo gloria* (to God alone be glory).

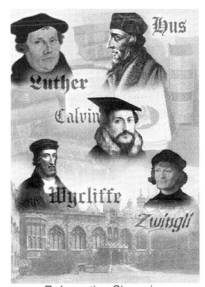

Reformation Champions

---

* A much abbreviated version of chapters 3–8 originally appeared in TOTT issues #60 and 61, July and August 2010. These chapters reproduce the full original lectures, with a few additions as well.

The purpose of this section of our little book is to revisit those days. We will first look at the roots of those Reformation days by examining some of the unscriptural (and often blasphemous) doctrines that were (and still are) taught in the Roman system. We will then examine each "*sola*" by defining it and demonstrating how it is an essential principle of biblical Christianity. We will discover, in fact, that the five "*solas*" are at the very core of the Christian Faith and that without them Christianity does not (and cannot) exist.

Why is this necessary? Because the pillars are once again in jeopardy. They are once again being demolished by contemporary thought. Based on a series of messages preached to various congregations, I pray that these studies will serve to warn true Christian believers of what is happening in the Church today and that it will encourage them to "earnestly contend for the faith once delivered to the saints" (Jude 3).

Since this is a series of studies on the Reformation, I thought it would be appropriate to take our main text for each study from that "Heartbeat of the Reformation," *The Geneva Bible*, which we noted in an earlier study. If you are using the KJV, you will see only slight differences. This brings us to our introductory text, Jeremiah. 3:6–15, 20—4:2:

The Lord said also unto me, in the days of Josiah the King, Hast thou seen what this rebel Israel hath done? for she hath gone up upon every high mountain, and under every green tree, and there played the harlot.

And I said, when she had done all this, Turn thou into me: but she returned not, as her rebellious sister Judah saw.

When I saw, how that by all occasions rebellious Israel had played the harlot, I cast her away, and gave her a bill of divorcement: yet her rebellious sister Judah was not afraid, but she went also, and played the harlot.

So that for the lightness of her wholesome she hath even defiled the land: for she hath committed fornication with stones and stocks.

Nevertheless for all this, her rebellious sister Judah hath not returned onto me with her whole heart, but feignedly, saith the Lord.

And the Lord said unto me, The rebellious Israel hath justified her self more then the rebellious Judah.

Go and cry these words toward the North and say, Thou disobedient Israel, return, saith the Lord, and I will not let my wrath fall upon you: for I am merciful, saith the Lord, and I will not always keep mine anger.

But know thine iniquities: for thou hast rebelled against the Lord thy God, and hast scattered thy ways to the strange gods under every green tree, but ye would not obey my voice, saith the Lord.

O ye disobedient children, turn again, saith the Lord, for I am your Lord, and I will take you one of a city, and two of a tribe and will bring you to Zion,

And I will give you pastors according to mine heart, which shall feed you with knowledge and understanding. . . .

But as a woman rebelleth against her husband: so have ye rebelled against me, O house of Israel, saith the Lord.

A voice was heard upon the high places, weeping and supplications of the children of Israel: for they have perverted their way, and forgotten the Lord their God.

O ye disobedient children, return and I will heal your rebellions. Behold, we come unto thee, for thou art the Lord our God.

Truly the hope of the hills is but vain, nor the multitude of mountains: but in the Lord our God is the health of Israel.

For confusion hath devoured our fathers labor, from our youth their sheep and their bullocks, their sons and their daughters.

We lie down in our confusion, and our shame covereth us: for we have sinned against the Lord our God, we and our fathers from our youth, even onto this day, and have not obeyed the voice of the Lord our God. . . .

O Israel, if thou return, return unto me, saith the Lord: and if thou put away thine abominations out of my sight, then shalt thou not remove.

And thou shalt swear, The Lord liveth in truth, in judgment, and in righteousness, and the nations shall be blessed in him, and shall glory in him. (*Geneva Bible*, emphasis added)

This passage recounts Jeremiah's second message of his book (the first is 2:1—3:5). He tells the story of two sisters, Israel (the Northern Kingdom) and Judah (the Southern Kingdom) Israel had committed spiritual adultery against God, that is, the worship of idols, specifically, the fertility cult of the ancient world. God waited for her to return, but she refused to do so, so He gave **her a bill of divorce** and sent her away (v. 8), a clear reference to the destruction of the Northern Kingdom and the Assyrian captivity in 722 BC. In spite of the object lesson this provided Judah as she watched that scene, she did not learn from it, would not turn away from idolatry, and also was taken into captivity, this time by the Babylonians in 605–602 BC.

Two words stand out in this passage. One is "backsliding," as it is translated in the KJV seven times (vs. 6, 8, 11, 12, 14, 22 [twice]). The Geneva uses **rebel** (v. 6), **rebellious** (vs. 8, 11), and **disobedient** (vs. 12, 14, 22). The Hebrew words used in these verses (*shôbāb* and *meshûbâ*) are very strong. While most modern translations render these as "faithless," that is not strong enough. The Hebrew indicates apostasy, backsliding, and deliberately turning away from Truth, not occasionally but rather as a way of life. While some use the term "backslidden Christian," that is inappropriate. This is an exclusively Old Testament term that spoke of willful, perpetual apostasy.

The other word that stands out is **return** (or **returned**), which appears five times (vs. 7, 12, 22, 4:1 [twice]). In its simplest sense, the Hebrew (*shûb*) means to return, to restore, to go back, as when, for example, Abraham's descendants in their fourth generation would return to Canaan (Gen. 15:16).[1]

While this passage is Old Testament and, of course, Jewish, it nonetheless provides a picture for the Church to consider. As we will see in a moment, before the Protestant Reformation, the Church had drifted far from God and His revelation in Scripture. Back in chapter 2, we noted the first sentence of Harry Ironside's graphic summary of Roman Catholicism from his commentary on Revelation. Here is the rest:

> Romanism is Christianity, Judaism, and Heathenism joined together; and the Lord abhors the vile combination. God gave Rome space to repent, and she repented not. Go back to the days of Savonarola (Italy), Wickliffe and Cranmer (England), John Knox (Scotland), Martin Luther (Germany), Zwingle (Switzerland), Calvin (France)—all those mighty reformers whom God raised up throughout the world to call Rome to repent of her iniquity, but she repented not. *If she had any desire to get right with Him, she would have repented in the sixteenth century* [emphasis added].

Harry Ironside

That last statement is extremely important, as we will see. As also noted in chapter 2, contrary to popular thought, and as shocking as it is to most ears, *Roman Catholicism is not Christian* and has never repented from her idolatry. As the passage before us illustrates, then, the Church, like Israel, was apostate in the extreme and was in need of a **return** to God. As we will see, there is also today a critical need to **return**.

So, at the root of the Reformation were five key truths, all of which began with the Latin word *sola*, meaning "alone." They were:

- *Sola Scriptura*, the Scripture alone
- *Sola Gratia*, grace alone
- *Sola Fide*, faith alone
- *Solus Christus*, Christ alone
- *Soli Deo Gloria*, to God alone be glory

We could put these together in one statement that summarizes the true, biblical Christian Faith:

It is *Scripture* alone that declares that salvation comes by *grace* alone, through *faith* alone, in *Christ* alone, by which *God* alone is glorified.

So pivotal, so essential, so axiomatic are these truths that neither the Reformation nor Christianity itself can in any way be understood apart from them.

That is what this section of our study is about—*it is about the very core of the Christian faith*. Without these truths, in fact, Christianity does not exist. To *distort* even *one* of them, is to *destroy all* of them, for they are, indeed, one indivisible truth. These truths also enable us to evaluate the Church as a whole and individual churches in particular. The existence of these truths reveals the orthodoxy of *the* Church (or *a* church), while their absence reveals, to use a biblical image, *Ichabod*, "the glory is departed" (1 Sam. 4:21). As we will see, much of the glory of God has departed from the Church (and churches) simply because these truths have all but vanished. Today's church is a blur of activity, but without the compass of Truth she has lost her way and is in need of a **return** to truth.

📖   📖   📖

Before dealing with these five principles, however, it is absolutely essential to examine briefly the state of the Church prior to the Protestant Reformation. Sadly, few Christians even know what the Reformation was, much less the issues at stake. If you asked the average Christian, "What was the Reformation?" appallingly few would be able to define it. If you asked them, "Well, are you a Catholic or a Protestant?" they would no doubt say "Protestant," but they would not be able to tell you why. If you investigated further by asking, "What exactly are you protesting?" they might say, "The Catholic Church," but they would not be able to elaborate on what is wrong with Catholicism, especially because many evangelicals are saying that Protestants and Catholics are essentially the same, that we are all "brothers and sisters in Christ."

What, then, was the Reformation about?

To say that the Church at that time was in sad condition is the height of understatement. Just as it is darkest before the dawn in our physical world, there was a thick veil of spiritual darkness over the Church and even society itself. Gone were such things as the simplicity of faith, the fervency of love, and the assurance of hope, all of which were true of the Apostolic Age. There was no joy, no peace, no certainty, and certainly no truth. Outwardly, there was pomp and regal display, but inwardly there was emptiness. Worship was hollow and "preaching" was devoid of content. Sermons were not in the language of the people but were in Latin, which amounted to little more than "profane and vain babblings" (1 Tim. 6:20; 2 Tim. 2:16) because only scholars understood it, leaving the people in ignorance and superstition.

Beautiful cathedrals were built in the Middle Ages (more accurately the Dark Ages from the 5th to the 15th centuries), but within their walls lived no truth whatsoever. The gravest of errors were taught (and are *still* taught) by the Roman Church. Added to the two simple ordinances establish by the Lord Jesus (which were never meant for a means of salvation but were only memorial and testimonial in nature), the Roman Church founded a seven-fold sacramental system that it says is the way God's grace and merit are earned by the sinner. Those sacraments are: holy order of the priesthood, infant baptism, confirmation as a youth, marriage as an adult, receiving mass (eating Christ's literal body and drinking His literal blood) regularly throughout life, penance for confessed sin throughout life, and extreme unction on one's deathbed (also called anointing the sick and Last Rites). As is made clear in its own *Baltimore Catechism*, Catholicism teaches "that among the chief means provided by Christ for our sanctification are the sacraments. They are outward signs instituted by Christ to give grace. . . . When the sign is applied to the one who receives the sacrament, it signifies inward grace and has the power of producing it in the soul."[2]

If that is not clear enough, one of the most authoritative works of Catholicism, *Fundamentals of Catholic Dogma*, by Ludwig Ott, states:

> Scholastic Theology coined the formula: *Sacramenta operantur ex opere operato*, that is, the Sacraments operate by the power of the completed sacramental rite. The Council of Trent sanctioned this expression which was vigorously combated by the Reformers. . . . . All Catholic theologians teach that the Sacraments are not merely conditions or occasions of communication of grace, but true causes (*causae instrumentales*) of grace. . . . The Council of Trent declared against the Reformers, who, following the precedent of Wycliffe, denied the sacramental character. . . . As there are various Sacraments having various signs, and as the differences in the sacramen-

tal signs also point to a difference in the effecting of grace, it must be assumed that each individual Sacrament, corresponding to its special purpose, conveys a special or specific sacramental grace.[3]

Salvation in Catholicism, therefore, is not by faith *alone* but by faith *plus works*, by the infusing of grace into man by means of his practicing the sacraments. While the Reformers staunchly combated this as the apostasy it is, today many are trying to say that such theology is Christian.

Added to the sacramental system was (and is) the teaching concerning purgatory, adopted into the Church about 593 AD. Here is a place, somewhere between heaven and hell, in which the soul passes through the fire of purification before it enters heaven. All believers, it is taught, even the highest clergy but excluding the martyrs, are still encumbered with some degree of sin and must go to purgatory for a certain amount of time, usually several thousand or even millions of years, until all sin is purged, after which they are translated into heaven.

This led to another teaching, *limbus patrum*, that is, "limbo of fathers." The literal idea of *limbus* is "fringe or border," and the basic idea in the word "limbo" is "a state or place of confinement." So the teaching in the term *limbus patrum*, which was chosen in the Middle Ages, refers to a place on the border of Hell that, as the *Catholic Encyclopedia* puts it, was the place where "the just who had lived under the Old Dispensation, and who, either at death or after a course of purgatorial discipline, had attained the perfect holiness required for entrance into glory, were obliged to await the coming of the Incarnate Son of God and the full accomplishment of His visible earthly mission. Meanwhile they were 'in prison' [awaiting] the higher bliss to which they looked forward."[4]

If that doesn't shock you, how about this? A similar teaching is *limbus infantium* ("children's limbo"), which is the place where unbaptized infants go, according to Rome; since they weren't baptized, they can't go to heaven, but because they have done no wickedness, they go a place of happiness and no "positive pain." This is why infant baptism is so strongly emphasized to parents, so that they will be able to see their children again in Heaven. If I may go "from preaching to meddling" for a moment, we have adopted practically the same thing in the Protestant ceremony called "baby dedication."

One's time in purgatory can be reduced, Rome taught (and still teaches), by doing penance to make up for sins committed and to try to gain "indulgences," that is, remissions of sin. Just prior to the Reformation, the *selling* of indulgences had reached epidemic proportions (and is actually returning to Catholic practice after being removed from practice by Vatican II in the 1960s). By paying a fee to the Church, one could buy forgiveness of sins not only *already* committed but also even for sins not *yet* committed. Most of Luther's famous "95 Theses" that he nailed to the church door in Wittenberg dealt with the unconscionable abuse of indulgences by the infamous John Tetzel.

Particularly troubling was (and is) Catholicism's teachings concerning Mary. Shockingly, she is considered to be the "Co-Redemptrix" with Christ, that is, she cooperates with Christ in the work of saving sinners. While the Vatican II council (1963–65) brought certain reforms, it changed nothing of Catholicism's underlying theology. In that council it was stated that Mary was "used by God not merely in a passive way, but as cooperating in the work of human salvation through faith and obedience. . . . She conceived, brought forth, and nourished Christ. She presented Him to the Father in the temple, and was united with Him in suffering as He died on the cross."[5] In other words, while Catholicism does not teach that Mary literally died for our sins, it does teach that by giving birth to Christ, nurturing Him through life, and even suffering with Him on the cross, she indirectly contributed to the work of salvation. Putting it bluntly, Mary was elevated to goddess status, just as Semiramis was in Babylon, Ishtar in Assyria, Astarte in Phoenicia, Isis in the Egypt, Aphrodite in Greece, and Venus in ancient Rome.

Luther and his 95 Theses

Further still, Mary is also considered to be "Mediatrix," that is, she now dispenses God's grace and blessings to the spiritually needy. Once again, Vatican II reaffirmed:

> This maternity of Mary in the order of grace began with the consent which she gave in faith at the Annunciation and which she sustained without wavering beneath the cross. This maternity will last without interruption until the eternal fulfillment of all the elect. For, taken up to heaven, she did not lay aside this saving role, but by her manifold acts of intercession continues to win for us gifts of eternal salvation.
>
> By her maternal charity, Mary cares for the brethren of her Son who still journey on earth surrounded by dangers and difficulties, until they are led to their happy fatherland. Therefore the Blessed Virgin is invoked by the Church under the titles of Advocate, Auxiliatrix, Adjutrix, and Mediatrix.[6]

Not only was (and is) Mary central to the Roman system, but also of great value is the veneration of and prayers to the saints, something that again comes from paganism. There are almost as many saints and saints' days as there are days in the year. There was a saint for virtually every business, age, calling, and vocation. Even nations had their patron saints. These saints, it is taught, have a surplus of good works that can benefit people on earth and can be prayed to and asked for aid in sickness and misfortune.

As if all that were not appalling enough, however, nothing was (and is) more characteristic of the Roman system, however, and more typical of *paganism*, in fact, than the veneration of relics and statues of the martyrs. Blatantly shaking its fist in the face of God, who commanded, "Thou shalt not make unto thee any graven image [or] bow down thyself to them" (Ex. 20:5–6), a command reiterated several times in the New Testament (Acts 17:29–31; 1 Cor. 8:4–6, 10:14; Col. 3:5; 1 Jn. 5:21), Catholicism does just that. Relics include supposed pieces of the cross, bones of martyrs, pieces of the silver coins Judas took for betraying Christ, pieces of cloth woven by the Virgin Mary, and even vials of milk from her breasts. By visiting and venerating such relics, worshipers are promised less time in purgatory. There is also the veneration of statues of Mary and the saints by kissing them, bowing down to them, and burning candles and incense before them. And if I may meddle a little further, what do we do in churches today? We have "candlelight services." What is the matter with us? Are we ignorant or just rebellious? All this is *without argument* totally pagan in origin. Among the Egyptians, for example, the god Osiris was venerated by relics. There were sepulchers of that martyred god all over Egypt, all containing an arm, a leg, or even a skull, all of which were claimed to be genuine. Idols! And if I may meddle one more time, and I do so in love, what do we do at Christmas time? We pull out our "nativity scenes" and place them on the church lawn.[7]

Doctrine always works out in practice, so it is not surprising that the lifestyle of the clergy at the time of the Reformation was as perverted as its theology. Elated upon seeing the city of Rome in the distance on his journey there in 1510, **Martin Luther** fell to his knees and cried, "*Salve! Sancta Roma* [Hail to thee, Holy Rome!] thrice holy for the blood of martyrs shed here." But upon touring the city the next day, his estimation soon diminished. While he had pictured streets filled with Christians and holy sites teeming with godly pilgrims, what he found was the very opposite, a city permeated by wickedness, a place overflowing with vice and corruption. The clergy was the worst of all. He saw no poverty or self-denial among them, just money and luxury. Cardinals lived in sin with their mistresses, while some considered themselves virtuous simply because they confined themselves to women. Pope Julius II lived in splendor, was at the time waging war with France, and had just returned from laying siege to another town.

The light, however, was about to dawn. In *southern* Europe, the 15th-century Renaissance, which means the rebirth of culture or learning, finished setting the stage for the Reformation. While it brought about intellectual development, the movement turned to Humanism to try to find meaning to life. The cry of the Renaissance was *man is the center of all things*; he can do whatever he wills and can accomplish anything to which he sets his mind. As noted in chapter 1, the seed of this was actually planted in the Middle Ages by **Thomas Aquinas** (1227–74), the Roman Catholic Schoolman who mixed Christian thought with pagan thought, especially his hero Aristotle. By teaching that while man fell in his *will*, his *intellect* did not, the inevitable result was the idea that man could think his way out of his problems. This tainted the Church as well. No longer was the Bible the authority; rather the Church became the authority. We should also in-

Michelangelo's *David*

terject that that idea is still with us today, even among evangelicals. While we give the Bible lip service, it is far from being the *sole* authority in all that we believe and do in the Church; we look to our intellect, our understanding, and our ideas. I would submit, we have never wholly escaped Thomas Aquinas, who is still studied today as one of the greatest thinkers of Church History. Additionally, right in line with Humanism, Renaissance thought further tainted the Church by adding human works to the work of Christ for salvation.

At first, Humanism seemed true and workable. The art and architecture of the Renaissance, for example, especially in Florence, Italy, is breathtaking to this day. **Michelangelo's** (1475–1564) statue *David* still stands as the ultimate statement of the Renaissance. It pictures man as supreme in his own strength and breathtaking beauty. It is significant, however, as Francis Schaeffer observes, "there are signs that by the end of his life Michelangelo saw that humanism was not enough."[8] Likewise, the incredibly brilliant **Leonardo da Vinci** (1452–1519) truly epitomized Renaissance man; he was not only an artist, but also a chemist, musician, architect, anatomist, botanist, and mechanical engineer. His accomplishments still stagger the mind 500 years later. But it is again noteworthy that he, too, "anticipated where humanism would end" and even "saw . . . its coming defeat."[9]

There is a staggering paradox here that truly sets the stage for the Reformation, namely, *thinking does not lead to the Truth*. While René

Descartes (1596–1650) said, "I think, therefore I am," that ultimately means nothing. While a man might "be," he is still lost in his "being." Truth is not *discovered*; Truth is *revealed*. Man can never discover Truth; only God reveals Truth, and He reveals it in one place only. He reveals it not in rationalism, visions, dreams, or "meditative states," rather He reveals truth in Scripture alone.

While all that was happening in the *south* of Europe, however, another movement was arising in the *north*. Men there struggled with the same questions of morals and life, but they came to a *conclusion*, and therefore *results*, that were the polar opposite of Renaissance man. As had the forerunners of the Reformation—**John Wycliffe** (c. 1320–1384) and **John Huss** (1369–1415)—the Reformers started with *God*, not man. As Solomon tells us, "The fear of the LORD is the beginning of knowledge" (Prov. 1:7), so unless we begin with that presupposition, we can know nothing. By starting with God, not man, the Reformers first realized that man is not the center of all things but rather is a depraved creature who fell in his entire being. *It is, here, in fact, that we find the key to all our Theology.* We must start with *God* and work *down*, not start with man and work up.

That principle, in fact, is at the very foundation of biblical salvation doctrine, and we will return to this theme as we continue our study. If one does not believe that, he simply does not believe what Scripture declares about by sin, salvation, and the Savior. Every false teaching—whether it be Arianism, Pelagianism, Arminianism, or any other—has at its core an unbiblical view of man. Every one of those, in fact, views man as having either not fallen at all and basically good, or that his fall was only partial, that there is a little good (or at least a little ability) left in there somewhere. In stark contrast, the Reformers recognized the biblical teaching of man's totally fallen and perverse nature, that his entire being—his intellect, emotions, and will—is hopelessly fallen. One writer puts it well, "To speak of a sinner as totally depraved does not mean that he is as bad as he could possibly be, but rather that sin contaminates the totality of his being."[10]

No passage sums this up better than Ephesians 2:1–3. When it says that man is "dead in trespasses and sins," it means that he is in a hopeless state. Can he respond to God in his own strength? No, for he is dead. Can he in and of himself believe the Gospel without God's intervention? No, for he is dead. Man must be regenerated before God then gives him the faith to believe (Eph. 2:8–9; cf. Jn. 6:65; Acts 18:27; Phil. 1:29). Unless we start here, we do not have the true, biblical, historical Christian Faith.

The Reformers also considered the Bible as the Word of God and the only authority over men's lives. By removing Humanism from their thought, the Reformers rediscovered the Truth of the Gospel. The leaders of the Reformation were men such as Martin Luther (1483–1546) in Germany, who nailed his Ninety-five Theses on the church door in Wittenberg (Oct. 31, 1517), John Calvin (1509–64) in Switzerland, who wonderfully outlined biblical truth in his monumental *Institutes of the Christian Religion* in 1536, and John Knox (c.1513–72) in Scotland, who said the Catholic mass was idolatry and whose preaching turned that country upside down. Indeed, these men called Catholicism what is was (and still is)—a non-Christian, pagan religion.

When one reads the Reformers, the Puritans, and their descendants, he gets the impression that when those great leaders used the word "papacy," they spit it out of their mouths because they understood its true nature. I am convinced beyond a shadow of a doubt, if I may be so bold, that anyone who does not truly and deeply loath Roman Catholicism is not a true, biblical evangelical. Now, I did not say he is not a *Christian*, but he is certainly not an evangelical. A true evangelical proclaims the Evangel, the Good News of grace alone by faith alone in Christ alone, and Catholicism does none of that. It is the worst perversion of Christianity ever conjured up by Satan and fostered upon man. It is unthinkable, as we will document in other studies, how many evangelicals still want to embrace that satanic system.

If I may interject, was the Reformation perfect? No, far from it. It had some profound shortcomings, and we could spend a study or two detailing them and their consequences. Lehman Strauss well summarizes: "The Reformation raised up a group of men who came out from Romanism and who rescued much from the mortuary of Rome. But they did not go far enough"[11] (see the "Conclusion" for a little deeper look).

That, however, is not our purpose here. What the Reformation accomplished, and gloriously so, was bringing the Church out of the darkness that had ruled for 1,000 years and was the first major attempt to return to biblical Christianity. Its primary accomplishments were the bringing back of *salvation truth* and a return to the authority and sufficiency of Scripture. Neither are these studies meant to glorify the Reformers themselves, for they clearly erred in certain areas. Rather we note their attempt to a return to Scripture and its pure doctrines of salvation.

Before closing this Introduction, commentator Philip E. Hughes writes something today's church really needs to hear. Calling Catholicism "ecclesiastical despotism," he submits:

> As we look back over nineteen centuries of the history of the Christian Church, we cannot help being struck by the manner in which for most of the time so many of its adherents seem to have been content lamely to tolerate the impositions and extortions of ecclesiastical despots whose lives are a contradiction of the meekness and gentleness of Christ and whose concern has been less for the

souls of the perishing than for the buttressing of their own reputation in the eyes of the world. The Reformation of the sixteenth century was a breaking away from this dark spirit of tyranny and the recovery, through returning to the pure doctrine of the New Testament, of that liberty in the gospel which is the birthright of every Christian.[12]

Disastrously, however, few are standing up in the face of the salvation truth that is again being challenged in our day, even from within the ranks of Evangelicalism. Some so-called evangelicals maintain that the Reformation was the most tragic mistake of Church History, that it split the Church and destroyed unity. If I may be so blunt, such teaching from so-called evangelicals is beyond comprehension. It demonstrates either ignorance of Catholicism's true nature or simply tolerance in spite of it. When we advocate embracing a system that is pagan in its origin and blasphemous in its practice, we have abandoned true Christianity.

Now, perhaps you are thinking, "Pastor, do you hate Catholics?" Most certainly not! On the contrary, as noted back in chapter 2, they are lost and in need of salvation. They are a true mission field. "Pastor, do you think there are Catholics that are true Christians?" Perhaps, but if so, they are in spite of that system. No, it is not Catholics we hate, rather the Catholic *system* we loathe, for it is among Satan's greatest tools of blinding men of the truth of the Gospel. As we will see, the five solas, the very foundation stones of Christianity, are foreign to that system.

So, what drove the Reformation? What were the key truths that powered it? It was the "five *solas*." It was the **return** of the core truths that

> *Scripture* alone declares that salvation comes by *grace* alone, through *faith* alone, in *Christ* alone, by which *God* alone is glorified

that fueled the Reformation and returned light to a world that had been in darkness for a thousand years. In a day when even so-called evangelicals are saying that the Reformation was a mistake, these truths need to be reemphasized and loudly proclaimed like never before since the 16th-century. *To abandon these truths is to return to darkness and even to deny the finished work of the Lord Jesus Christ.*

In the next five chapters, therefore, we will examine these five *solas* to see what they provide for us:

- *Sola Scriptura*, the Scripture alone — our Only *Model*
- *Sola Gratia*, grace alone — our Only *Method*
- *Sola Fide*, faith alone — our Only *Means*
- *Solus Christus*, Christ alone — our Only *Mediator*
- *Soli Deo Gloria*, to God alone be glory — our Only *Motive*

If I may also interject as we conclude this introduction, we will mention a few modern trends as we continue, but what has really caused them? Movements such as Relativism, Secularism, Pragmatism, Mysticism, Psychology, Open Theism, and the Emerging Church, have not only infiltrated our churches, but in many cases have totally taken them over. Why? *Because we have abandoned doctrine.* "Doctrine divides, love unites," is the mantra of our day. But without doctrine, without *absolute Truth*, we have *absolutely nothing*. And at the very foundation of it all are these doctrines of salvation.

If we may repeat one more time those famous words of George Santayana, "Those who cannot remember the past are condemned to repeat it." We have not only forgotten, but we also are doing all we can to prevent our memory from improving. We, therefore, close with this statement: *as these biblical truths fueled the Reformation, they are desperately needed again today to revive a dying Evangelicalism.*

NOTES

[1] For a deeper study of the preceding Hebrew words, see the author's *A Hebrew Word for the Day* (AMG Publishers, 2010), 90–91.

[2] John A. O'brien (prepared by), *Understanding the Catholic Faith: An Official Edition of the revised Baltimore Catechism No. 3* (Ave Maria Press, 1941, 1955), 189.

[3] Ludwig Ott, *Fundamentals of Catholic Dogma* (Tan Books and Publishers, 1955, 1960, 1974), 329–330, 332–333.

[4] "Limbo" in *Catholic Encyclopedia*, Classic 1914 Edition (http://www.newavent.org/cathen).

[5] Walter M. Abott, S.J., General Editor, *The Documents of Vatican II* (Guild Press, 1966), 88, 91.

[6] Ibid, 91.

[7] For a deeper study, see chapter 43, "The Pestilence of Idolatry," in the author's *Truth on Tough Texts: Expositions of Challenging Scripture Passages* (Sola Scriptura Publications, 2012), 421–432.

[8] Francis Schaeffer, *How Should We Then Live?* (Fleming H. Revell, 1976), 72.

[9] Schaeffer, 74, 78.

[10] Robert Spinney and Justin Dillehay, *Not the Way I used to Be: Practical Implications of the Bible's Large Doctrine of Regeneration* (Tulip Book, 2007), 2.

[11] Lehman Strauss, *Book of Revelation* (Loizeaux Brothers, Inc., 1964), 73.

[12] Philip E. Hughes, *The Second Epistle to the Corinthians, The New International Commentary on the New Testament* (Eerdmans, 1992), 401.

We hold that neither man or angel is any wise to add or detract any thing, to change or to alter any thing from which the Lord hath set down in His Word.

John Penry
Puritan Golden Treasury

4

Sola Scriptura: Our Only Model

2 Tim. 3:14–17; 1 Pet. 4:11

But continue thou in the things which thou hast learned, and which are committed unto thee, knowing of who thou hast learned them: And that thou hast known the holy Scriptures of a child, which are able to make thee wise unto salvation, through the faith which is in Christ Jesus. For the whole Scripture is given by inspiration of God, and is profitable to teach, to convince, to correct, and to instruct in righteousness, That the man of God may be absolute, being made perfect unto all good works. (Geneva Bible)

If any man speak, let him speak as the oracles of God; if any man minister, let him do it as of the ability which God giveth: that God in all things may be glorified through Jesus Christ, to whom be praise and dominion for ever and ever. Amen. (KJV)

Among the last words that Paul wrote before his martyrdom, he challenged Timothy concerning the singular place Scripture must have in his life and ministry. He made it clear that "wisdom," and **salvation** itself, come from Scripture alone. He went on to say that Scripture alone is **profitable** (ōphelimos, useful, beneficial, advantageous) first **to teach** ("doctrine" in the KJV). It is the only way to teach spiritual truth, although this has all but vanished in our day.

Scripture is also profitable **to convince** ("reproof" in the KJV). What a word this is! It is the Greek *elegchō*, which, as Greek authority Richard Trench writes, "means to rebuke another with the Truth so that the person confesses, or at least is convinced, of his sin."[1] In his commentary on Ephesians, John Calvin adds, "It literally signifies to drag forth to the light what was formerly unknown."[2] What a vivid picture! We must drag error kicking and screaming into the light to expose it, but that too is unfashionable in today's church.

Scripture is also designed **to correct**. Here is another fascinating word, *epanorthōsis*, which actually consists of three words. The root *orthos* means "upright, straight, correct" and is where we derive such English words as *orthodontist* (who corrects and straightens teeth), *orthopedics* (the correcting of bone injuries, deformities, and diseases), and *orthodox* (conforming to correct doctrine or belief). Add to this the prefix *epi*, "to" or "upon," and the prefix *ana*, denoting repetition (as in the word *again*), and the result is "to set upright again, to straighten again." Scripture, then is the only thing that can set things right, bring them back to where they are supposed to be.

Finally, Scripture is meant **to instruct in righteousness**; **instruct** is *paideia*, training and discipline, so in this case, in the things that are right. The result of all that, Paul concludes, is so that Timothy will be **absolute** ("perfect" in the KJV; *artios*, suitable, complete, capable, and sound) and also **made perfect** (or "thoroughly furnished"; *exartizō*, "fitted out, altogether fitted, fully equipped) **unto all good works** (that is, for worship, holy living, and Christian service).

Those verses vividly demonstrate that in the early church *Scripture was elevated to its rightful position as sole, sufficient authority*. It was absolute and ruled unilaterally in all matters. It was the sole and sufficient authority *in* everything and *for* everything. Sadly, however, it did not take long for that began to change.

One fascinating example, which is quite probably the first major departure from Scripture after the apostolic days, was the decision to regard the terms "bishop" and "elder" (or "pastor") as *different* positions in the church hierarchy. Now, the incontrovertible fact is that the Early Church viewed all three of these terms as referring to one and the same person: *elder* refers to the man's *character*, *bishop* refers to his *position* as ruler and guardian, and *pastor* refers to his *function* as a teacher and feeder of the sheep. This fact is beyond any doubt, as is found in the writings of the Church Fathers, such as early 4th-century scholar Hilary and late 4th-century Roman scholar Jerome, as well as contemporary theologians of Jerome, such as Chrysostom, and in-turn his successors: Pelagius, Theodore of Mopsuestia, and Theodoret.[3]

This was deliberately changed, however, supposedly to fight heresy. As early as the 2nd-century, "bishops" were elevated over "elders." Bishops soon became rulers over groups of churches, and some bishops were even elevated over other bishops, and were eventually called cardinals. Ultimately, in the western church (Roman Catholicism), one bishop emerged as supreme over all. Between 313 and 590, the bishop at Rome was considered "first among equals," but in 590 the Roman bishop was given supremacy over all other bishops (see chapter 2 for more about the Papacy). In the strict sense of the term, this bishop (who in 590 was Gregory I) became the first "Pope." The Papacy then, to prop up its teaching of "apostolic succession," had to go back through history and arbitrarily choose certain men (several of very questionable character) through whom they could trace the pope back to Peter.

Now, let's stop and think a moment. It was, therefore, one early, deliberate, calculated departure from clear Scripture precedent that created the hierarchy of Rome that exists to this day (and sadly even in some Protestant denominations). Worse, the result was that this "supreme bishop," the Pope, became the absolute authority over the Church and every member of it. When the Pope speaks *ex cathedra* ("from the chair"), his declarations are not only *equal* to Scripture, but are *superior* to Scripture and *supercede* Scripture. Prior to the Reformation, the laity was forbidden even to read Scripture. All interpretation was in the hands of the Pope and other officers of the Church. The official Catholic interpretation of Scripture was dubbed with the name *Magesterium*, and it was the Church that gave birth to the Scriptures, not Scripture who bore the Church.

What is absolutely crucial to understand here is that Roman Catholicism actually does accept the authority of Scripture. It readily admits to its authority and infallibility, but that is what is misleading and is why many do not recognize Catholicism as being a cult. While it recognizes the Scripture's *authority*, it rejects its *sufficiency*, that it *alone* is the authority. It maintains that the Church's traditions and teachings as well as the Pope's *ex cathedra* declarations are equal to Scripture authority. In practical application, these are actually superior to the Scriptures, for if the Pope declares something that is unscriptural, it is that declaration, not Scripture, that is followed. As we will note in another study, this makes Catholicism not one bit different than a cult such as Mormonism, which also recognizes the Bible but elevates the Book of Mormon over it.

It was the Reformation, however, that met this apostasy head-on and *rejected it in its entirety*. In July 1519, at the Leipzig Debate with John Eck, when Eck accused Luther of appealing to Scripture alone and not papal authority, Luther responded:

> A simple layman armed with Scripture is to be believed above a pope or a council without it. . . . [N]either the Church nor the pope can establish articles of faith. These must come from Scripture. For the sake of Scripture we should reject pope and councils.

In October 1520 came a papal bull (Latin, for "seal," as in a seal on an official document) condemning Luther and his writings and demanding that he recant. Luther defiantly refused; instead of burning his own writings, he publicly burned the papal bull, saying the bull condemned Christ Himself. What a scene!

It was then in April 1521 that Luther was summoned to the final showdown at the Diet (assembly) in the city Worms. The Roman Church requested that Emperor Charles V, himself a Roman Catholic, deal with the case of Luther, which he agreed to do. On that fateful day, the crowd that gathered was enormous, so huge, in fact, that it was difficult for Luther and his supporters to even reach the conference hall. Besides the Emperor, there were 206 high ranking officials, including dukes, archbishops, bishops, ambassadors, and papal nuncios. The diet began on April 17 with the brilliant Johann von Eck serving as the presiding officer. He asked Luther pointedly if he was the author of the numerous writings that had been placed on a table in the conference hall and asked if he was willing to retract the doctrines in them that contradicted the accepted doctrines of the Church. Luther admitted he was the author but asked for some time for reflection before answering the other charge. After all, Luther knew that his answer might very well cost him his life, and we can only imagine the pressure he felt. After a night of much prayer, Luther was asked again in the crowded hall if he was willing to retract his teachings. To this he replied the now famous words:

Martin Luther

> Unless I am convinced by Scripture and plain reason—I do not accept the authority of popes and councils, for they have contradicted each other—my conscience is captive to the Word of God. I cannot and I will not recant anything, for to go against conscience is neither right nor safe. Here I stand; I cannot do otherwise. God help me. Amen.[4]

The hall exploded in uproar, with everyone speaking at once. The Emperor was enraged and left the hall, later saying "he could not see how a single monk could be right and the testimony of a thousand years of Christendom wrong." What a scene indeed!

Do we not hear similar words today? We hear, "That's the way we've always done it," or, "That's what I was taught," or, "That's the tradition of our denomination." As in Luther's day, there is much in the Church today that not only is not *based* on Scripture, but much of which even *contradicts* Scripture. In my humble view, in fact, the key to Luther's statement is that to go against a conscience that is "captive to the Word of God . . . is *neither right nor safe*," for that is precisely what is happening today. The Church is simply not captive to Scripture, not driven by God's Word alone. In his wonderful book, *Whatever Happened to the Gospel of Grace*, his final book, in fact, before his promotion into glory, **James Montgomery Boice**, wrote:

The most serious issue [facing the Church today], I believe, is the Bible's *sufficiency*. Do we believe that God has given us what we need in this book? Or do we suppose that we have to supplement the Bible with human things? Do we need sociological techniques to do evangelism, pop psychology and pop psychiatry for Christian growth, extra-biblical signs or miracles for guidance, or political tools for achieving social progress and reform?[5]

Ponder this a moment. By what is today's church really guided? In the final analysis, virtually every aspect of the Church today is driven by *popular culture*. Instead of pointing people to God's Word alone for answers to life problems, they are given "therapeutic counseling" to make them feel better about themselves in their world. Instead of giving people the biblical Gospel of sin, salvation, and service, we appeal to their felt needs so they will feel comfortable. Instead of preaching the pure truth of Scripture, we entertain the MTV generation so it will enjoy coming to church. Everything today, from Bibles, to church programs, to tee shirts, is marketed using a pretty wrapper that appeals to what people want, that is, to their flesh. We submit again, it is *culture* that rules the Church not *Scripture*. Thankfully, some church leaders are seeing the problem. Michael Horton, for example, writes:

> . . . *sola Scriptura* meant that the Word of God was sufficient. Although Rome believed it was infallible, the official theology was shaped more by the insights of Plato and Aristotle than by Scripture. Similarly today, psychology threatens to reshape the understanding of the self, as even in the evangelical pulpit sin becomes "addiction"; the Fall as an event is replaced with one's "victim" status; salvation is increasingly communicated as mental health, peace of mind, and self-esteem, and my personal happiness and self-fulfillment are center-stage rather than God's holiness and mercy, justice and love, glory and compassion. Does the Bible define the human problem and its solution? Or when we really want facts, do we turn somewhere else, to a modern secular authority who will really carry weight in my sermon? Of course, the Bible will be cited to bolster the argument. Political ideology, sociology, marketing, and other secular "authorities" must never be allowed priority in answering questions the Bible addresses. That is, in part, what this affirmation means, and evangelicals today seem as confused on this point as was the medieval church.[6]

Indeed, we are as confused today as in the days of the Reformation. Writing in 1991, another discerning Christian leader, John MacArthur, agrees:

A widespread lack of confidence in Christ's sufficiency is threatening the contemporary church. Too many Christians have tacitly acquiesced to the idea that our riches in Christ, including the Bible, prayer, indwelling spirit, and all the other spiritual resources we have in Him are not adequate to meet peoples' real needs. Entire churches are committed to programs built on the presupposition that the apostle's teaching, fellowship, the breaking of bread, and prayer (Acts 2:42) aren't a full enough agenda for the Church as it prepares to enter the complex and sophisticated world of the twenty-first century.[7]

Sadly, however, such comments are in the shrinking minority nowadays. Gone is the Reformation principle of *sola Scriptura*—Scripture alone. So central was this, that it has been called the "formal principle" of the Reformation. By "formal" is meant that this principle is the authority that *forms and shapes* the entire movement from beginning to end. Scripture alone, then, gave form to everything involved in the Reformation. Without that, there could be no form, no content, and no Truth because all those demand an authority. Without authority, there can be nothing else.

The purpose of sola Scriptura, then, was to reposition the Bible as the final authority over the Church. It was, indeed, the only *model*. That is why we deal with it first. Without it, the other "*solas*" are meaningless because they have no foundation or authority; they are no more than the theological opinion of a bunch of dead guys. While Roman Catholicism had elevated the Church and the Pope over Scripture and therefore made the Scripture inferior to the Church, the Reformers (Luther, Zwingli, Calvin, and others) reaffirmed the authority of Scripture *alone*. To them Scripture was not a *norma normata* (determined norm), rather it was the *norma normans* (determining norm). Scripture is not determined by anyone; rather it is the "The Determiner."

Many Scriptures proclaim the centrality and sufficiency of Scripture. In addition to our text (2 Tim. 3:14–17), we read:

> Deuteronomy 4:2: Ye shall not add unto the word which I command you, neither shall ye diminish ought from it, that ye may keep the commandments of the LORD your God which I command you.
> Psalm 19:7: The law of the LORD is perfect, converting the soul: the testimony of the LORD is sure, making wise the simple.
> Hebrews 1:2: [God] in these last days spoken unto us by his Son.
> Revelation 22:18–19: For I testify unto every man that heareth the words of the prophecy of this book, If any man shall add unto these things, God shall add unto him the plagues that are written in

this book: And if any man shall take away from the words of the book of this prophecy, God shall take away his part out of the book of life, and out of the holy city, and from the things which are written in this book.

One term used in the Bible, however, is especially fascinating and pivotal. It is the term **oracles of God**, which appears three times in the KJV: Romans 3:1–2, Hebrews 5:12, and 1 Peter 4:11, the latter of which is of the greatest significance and is our second text:

> **If any man speak, let him speak as the oracles of God; if any man minister, let him do it as of the ability which God giveth: that God in all things may be glorified through Jesus Christ, to whom be praise and dominion for ever and ever. Amen.** (KJV)

Throughout the ages, men have tried to divine the future. Examining the entails of animals, interpreting dreams, gazing at crystals, observing the movements of fish in a tank, snakes in a pit, and the stars and planets in the sky have all been used to try to divine the future. During the Shang dynasty in China, shoulder blades of oxen and bottom shells of tortoises were inscribed and heated. A message was then derived from the cracks formed by the heating.

One of the more interesting methods of divination was that of listening to and watching the movement of birds. In Rome, public officials called "augurs" (Latin for "bird") would listen to birds to decide whether or not an official ceremony should proceed. Others would watch the flight of birds, deducing meaning from what direction the birds flew. Our English word "auspices" in fact, comes from the Latin *auspicium*, which in turn comes from *auspex*, "bird seer." So when we speak of an "auspicious" occasion, we are actually speaking of an occasion that is favorable because the birds say it is.

If such things sound foolish, what can we say of modern oracles, such as reading palms and tea leaves, consulting horoscopes, interpreting dreams, practicing religious rituals, following man's rationale, and accepting the pronouncements of a Pope or councils? Why do men do such things? *Because they have abandoned the Word of God.*

Like the Romans, the Greeks had their pagan oracles, which they referred to using the Greek words *manteion* and *creoterion*. This is not the word Peter uses, however. He uses the common Greek word *logion*, which comes from *logos*, "word" (Lk. 5:1; Jn. 17:6; Acts 4:29, 31; 8:14; Col. 1:25; 1 Thes. 2:13; Tit. 1:3; Heb. 13:7; etc.). Used in this way, *logos* speaks of *the utterance of God*. Think of it! It is His very utterances that God has committed to men. Think of it! Through our Bibles, we hold in our hands the very words of the same God who spoke other words to call the universe into existence. Are we truly captivated by that thought?

Sadly, some translators criticize the translation of *logion* as "oracles," submitting that even though this is a legitimate translation, it seems unsuitable here. They argue that since "oracles" refers to pagan religions and rites, then this was the furthest thing from Paul's mind. We would submit, however, that oracles is actually the best rendering in this context. Why? *Because this translation much more powerfully demonstrates to the English reader the contrast between* men's *oracles and* God's *oracles.* Roman Catholicism, for example, makes no apology for following the oracles of the pope. Paul's point, in stark contrast, is that God entrusted His oracles to men and that these oracles are infinitely superior to man's.

First Peter 4:11, therefore, is a tremendously powerful and significant statement: **If any man speak, let him speak as the oracles of God.** In other words, *if a man has something to say, it had better be the Word of God.* Notice that the verse does *not* say that whatever a Bible teacher or preacher (or Pope, for that matter) says *is* the oracles of God. On the contrary, the verse declares that whatever a man says must *conform* to the oracles of God. We have just the opposite today, however. A preacher can get on TV or radio and utter anything about God and most Christians think it is great. "After all," they say, "he's talking about Jesus so it must be good." But the question this verse demands we ask is: *do his words really conform to the oracles of God? Is this man really speaking the utterances of God?*

Not only does this verse clearly condemn Roman Catholic dogma, but it also speaks directly to Evangelicalism today, which is driven more and more by pop culture, each person's individual feelings and "felt needs," as well as those who claim new revelation through visions and inner urges. Likewise, many preachers, teachers, and leaders today are saying many things, but many of them simply do not conform to **the oracles of God**. Their words do not come from Scripture.

If I may be bold and blunt for a moment, if a man is not going to minister and preach according to **the oracles or God**, then he should just hold his tongue, and most certainly get out of the pulpit. Our sole authority is **the oracles of God**, nothing *less*, nothing *more*. In other words, as Paul told Timothy, the only thing we should be doing is preaching the Word, as declared in 2 Timothy 4:1–4:

> I charge thee therefore before God, and the Lord Jesus Christ, who shall judge the quick and the dead at his appearing and his kingdom; Preach the word; be instant in season, out of season; reprove, rebuke, exhort with all longsuffering and doctrine. For the time will come when they will not endure sound doctrine; but after their own lusts shall they heap to themselves teachers, having itch-

ing ears; And they shall turn away their ears from the truth, and shall be turned unto fables.

It there was, in fact, one key thing that the Reformers returned to, it was biblical, expository preaching. Prior to the Reformation, this had vanished from the Church, and it has all but vanished in our day, having been replaced by topical, issue-oriented, political, and psychological sermons that accomplish nothing spiritual, much less anything eternal. The popular notion of our day, as one mega-church guru has clearly stated it, "The ground we have in common with unbelievers is not the Bible, but our common needs, hurts, and interests as human beings. *You cannot start with a text.*"[8] Such a statement is almost beyond belief!

The Reformers, in contrast, were wholly committed to the text and its exposition. Luther, for example, often preached four times on Sundays and left behind some 2,300 sermons. In direct contrast to the devaluation of preaching in the Roman Church, Luther's preaching, as well as all Reformation preaching, was instructive, expository, and built on the text alone. "My best craft," Luther said, "is to give the Scripture with its plain meaning; for the plain meaning is learning and life."

The pulpit was the absolute heart of **John Calvin's** ministry. During his four years in Strasbourg, he preached almost everyday and twice on the Lord's Day. In Geneva, from 1541 until his death in 1564, it was also twice on Sunday, and every other week he preached each weeknight. His Sunday sermons covered the New Testament, his weeknight sermons the Old Testament. Those sermons were recorded by a stenographer and became, along with his other lectures, the basis of his many commentaries. The pulpit truly was the heart of his ministry, as he moved through the Scriptures verse-by-verse, book-by-book,

John Calvin

always seeking the natural meaning of the text followed by its application. He also correctly believed that preaching was the primary task of the pastor and was how God educates His people. Commenting in 1 Peter 4:11, in fact, he wrote in his *Institutes*:

> What else is this than to banish all the inventions of the human mind (whatever be the head which may have devised them), that the pure word of God may be taught and learned in the Church of the faithful,—than to discard the decrees, or rather fictions of men (whatever be their rank), that the decrees of God alone may remain steadfast?[9]

If I may quote again, even more powerfully did Calvin write in his commentary of 1 Peter, which in-turn was based upon his *preaching*:

In the meantime, we learn from these words of Peter, that it is not lawful for those who are engaged in teaching to do anything else, but faithfully to deliver to others, as from hand to hand, the doctrine received from God; for he forbids any one to go forth, except he who is instructed in God's word, and who proclaims infallible oracles as it were from his mouth. He, therefore, leaves no room for human inventions; for he briefly defines the doctrine which ought to be taught in the Church. . . . This was, indeed, commonly the case formerly with false prophets; and we see at this day how arrogantly the Pope and his followers cover with this pretense all their impious traditions. But Peter did not intend to teach pastors such hypocrisy as this, to pretend that they had from God whatever doctrine it pleased them to announce, but, he took an argument from the subject itself, that he might exhort them to sobriety and meekness, to a reverence for God, and to an earnest attention to their work.

Oh, how we need that challenge in our day! If I may quote Calvin one more time, he added this powerful statement in his *Institutes*, "The ministry of the Word . . . and how far our reverence for it should go, that it may be to us a perpetual token by which to distinguish the Church."[10] In other words, it is our love *for* and preaching *of* the Word that demonstrates our true love for God and distinguishes us from Rome. And sadly, most modern ministry is not distinguished by the word of God and its proclamation.

We would go so far as to submit that Calvin would agree with the statement that a "church" that does not have preaching at the core is not a biblical church. We need to carefully consider that point. There are countless evangelical "churches" today, but if Calvin was right—and according to what the Bible says, he was—then many of those "churches" are not truly churches at all. They are entertaining, they are appealing, they are great social centers, but they are not New Testament churches. *Where the Word of God is not exposited as the central ministry, there is no true church.*

We should also interject here the effect Calvin's preaching had on Geneva. Biblical, expository preaching today is considered by most as irrelevant, impractical, and even counter-productive, but it transformed the city of Geneva. Here was a city notorious for riots, gambling, drunkenness, adultery, and literally every vice known to man. People would actually run through the streets naked singing indecent songs and blaspheming God. Calvin's preaching, and the social reforms that flowed from it, transformed that city, bringing to it unheard of things such as personal cleanliness, education for all ages, love of work, industry, and religious and political liberty. We would do well today to recognize that people will not be changed by "seeker-sensitivity" or by having their "felt-needs" addressed. *They will be transformed only by the proclamation of Truth.* This was true in the days of the prophets, in the days of Jesus and Paul, in the days of Luther and Calvin, and it is still true today.

Huldrych Zwingli (1484–1531) while not of the notoriety of Luther and Calvin, valued preaching even more than they and was inexhaustible in the pulpit. He maintained that "preaching is the sign of the true pastor."[11] He said this was so because, as he put it, he submitted to "the tyranny of the book." He was committed to the Bible as the direct Word of God and practiced the plain, simple exposition of it. It wasn't popes or councils that should rule the Church in Zwingli's view, rather the Scripture alone. Many preachers in the years to come followed his example. Likewise, **John Knox** (c.1513–72) was not only a doc-trinal preacher but also an incredibly stirring one. He preached daily during his pastorate at Saint Giles, Edinburgh.

Huldrych Zwingli

We would close, therefore, with this statement on *sola Scriptura*, as stated in The Cambridge Declaration of the Alliance of Confessing Evangelicals on April 20, 1996:

> We reaffirm the inerrant Scripture to be the sole source of written divine revelation, which alone can bind the conscience. The Bible alone teaches all that is necessary for our salvation from sin and is the standard by which all Christian behavior must be measured.
>
> We deny that any creed, council or individual may bind a Christian's conscience, that the Holy Spirit speaks independently of or contrary to what is set forth in the Bible, or that personal spiritual experience can ever be a vehicle of revelation.

Dear Christian Friend, Scripture alone, then, is the only *model*, the only form and shape of the Christian Faith. It is Scripture alone, which is the Word who became flesh, empowered by the Holy Spirit, that is the sculptor, the artist, the architect of our faith. Scripture alone is the blueprint and owner's manual that dictates everything about building and maintaining the Church and each of its bricks. To depart from this foundation is to abandon the Christian Faith and return to the darkness of Rome. Let us, therefore, say with Luther, "Here I stand; I cannot do otherwise. So help me God."

NOTES

[1] Richard Trench, *Synonyms of the New Testament* (Hendrickson, 2000), 29, 30.

[2] *Calvin's Commentaries: Ephesians* (electronic edition; *Online Bible*), comment on Ephesians 5:11.

[3] For a more in-depth study of these three terms and their history, see the author's *Truth on Tough Texts: Expositions of Challenging Scripture Passages* (Sola Scriptura Publications, 2012), 157–172

[4] As report by Roland H. Bainton, *Here I Stand* (Abingdon Press, 1978), 144.

[5] James Mongomery Boice, *Whatever Happened to the Gospel of Grace* (Crossway Books, 2001), 72 (emphasis in the original).

[6] Michael Horton, from an address, "Reformation Essentials," delivered at a conference jointly sponsored by the National Association of Evangelicals and Trinity Evangelical Divinity School held at the Trinity campus in Illinois; May, 1989: (http://www.monergism.com/ updates/reformation_essentials_by_mich.php)

[7] John MacArthur, *Our Sufficiency in Christ* (Word Publishing, 1991), 19.

[8] Rick Warren, *The Purpose Driven Church* (Zondervan, 2002), 295 (emphasis added).

[9] *Institutes*, IV.8.9 (Beveridge translation).

[10] *Institutes*, IV.2.1.

[11] Cited in *The Company of the Preachers* (p. 174) from G. R. Potter, *Zwingli* (Cambridge University Press, 1976), 135, 378.

5

𝕾𝖔𝖑𝖆 𝕱𝖎𝖉𝖊: 𝕺𝖚𝖗 𝕺𝖓𝖑𝖞 𝕸𝖊𝖆𝖓𝖘

Hab. 2:4; Rom. 1:17; Gal. 3:11; Heb. 10:38

Behold, he that lifteth up himself, his mind is not upright in him, but the just shall live by his faith. (Geneva Bible)

For by it the righteousness of God is revealed from faith to faith: as it is written, The just shall live by faith. (Geneva)

And that no man is justified by the Law in the sight of God, it is evident: for the just shall live by faith. (Geneva)

Now the just shall live by faith: but if any withdraw himself, my soul shall have no pleasure in him. (Geneva)

The background of our first text, Habakkuk 2:4, is the conceit and arrogance of the Babylonians. The Hebrew behind **lifteth up** (*'āpal*), which appears only here in the Old Testament, literally means "to swell." They were, indeed, swollen, puffed up in their pride and self-confidence. In stark contrast, God declares that the righteous person will live by **faith**. So pivotal is this principle that it is quoted three times in the New Testament. By quoting this text in Romans 1:17, Paul says that *salvation* is by faith, in Galatians 3:11 he emphasizes that that salvation is *not by works*, and in Hebrews 10:38 he adds that we now *live* by faith in all things.

From an early age, **Martin Luther** received religious training. In 1502 he received his B.A. and in 1505 he received his M.A. It appeared he was on his way to a career in law, but turned instead toward the Church and became an Augustinian monk in the monastery in Erfurt in 1505. Some historians explain this sudden change as possibly due to the deep impression made on him by the death of his close friend Alexis and his own narrow escape from lightning. While that might certainly be true *externally*, another historian, Henry Sheldon, has a better explanation of what was happening *internally*:

But those who believe in the Reformation will claim a deeper explanation, and will say that Divine Providence sent Luther through the legal, monastic regime of the [monastery], that he might be more perfectly prepared to serve as the evangelical reformer; that *he needed the Pauline experience of enslavement to law, in order to become the herald of the Pauline doctrine of grace.*[1]

That last statement is especially striking. God allowed Luther to go through the bondage and despair of enslavement to law that he found in Roman Catholic monasticism (and the entire Roman system) to prepare him for the earth shattering doctrine of grace alone through faith alone. Luther's story is indeed an amazing one.

Luther was constantly aware of his need for salvation, and even as early as 1506 he was becoming more and more dissatisfied with the teaching of the Catholic Church and more and more conscious of personal sin. He just could not rid himself of feelings of guilt over his sin and was besieged by the thought, *How can a sinner ever become a saint?*

He then spent hours in study and prayer. He observed the minutest details of discipline. No one equaled Martin in prayer, fasting, night vigils, or self-mortification. He would later write, "If ever a monk could get to heaven by monkery, I would have gotten there." In all his efforts, his only concern was to become a saint and earn a place in heaven. But no matter what

Johann von
Staupitz

he did, nothing lifted him from his despair and feelings of abject unworthiness. He never felt that he was getting closer to his goal. So deep set was Luther's guilt that instead of weakly confession, the normal practice of the other monks, he confessed every day. On one occasion, he spent six hours confessing only his sins from the previous day.

So deep was Luther's despair, that **Johann von Staupitz** (1460–1524), Doctor of Divinity and Vicar-General over all the Augustinian monasteries in Germany and Luther's mentor in those days, tried to help him. After explaining his struggles to Staupitz, the vicar asked Luther if in all his reading he had not read of God's love, mercy, and goodness? Luther responded with these staggering words:

Oh, Father, is it not against all natural reason that God out of his mere whim deserts men, hardens them, damns them, as if He delighted in sins and in such torments of the wretched for eternity, He Who is said to be of such mercy and goodness? This appears iniquitous, cruel, and intolerable in God, by which very many have been offended in all ages. And who would not be? I have been so driven to the very abyss of despair that I have wished I had never been created. Love God? I hate Him!

What utter, hopeless despair! Sitting on his bed one specific night, Luther contemplated his state and decided on a course of action. "I must mortify the flesh even more," he thought. "It is the body that keeps me from knowing holiness." Looking at the whip that lay beside him, he picked it up, stood, and swung his arm in an arc in front of him and then over his shoulder as hard as he could. The whip dug into his flesh, raising welts immediately. He stifled a cry from the pain, and then repeated the action again and then again. Sometimes he would change his swing so he could strike the back of his thighs. The pain was so intense there that he had to bite a piece of leather to suppress a scream. He continued in this manner until his back bled, but still he did not feel right with God. He inflicted thirty more lashes to no avail, and then thirty more. By this time he was on his knees and was beyond agony, but he would not stop until he could feel his guilt lift. After still another thirty lashes, he passed out and lay on the floor all night.

Wittenburg in Luther's Day

Luther was ordained a priest in 1507, called to teach for a semester at the newly founded University of Wittenburg in 1508, and back to Erfurt to teach there in 1509. As we noted in an earlier study, he was thrilled in 1510 when he was sent to Rome on business. He hoped he would find peace for his troubled heart. On approaching the city, he fell on his knees and cried, "Hail, holy Rome!" But what he found was far from holy. He saw a worldly, warlike pope (Julius II) who lived in luxury, and terribly corrupt priests who even mocked the ritual of the Church and rushed through the mass. He returned to Wittenberg in 1511 more disillusioned than ever. The corruption he had witnessed left a sour taste in his mouth and a dark cloud over his soul that he could not escape. He simply could not comprehend how supposed "men of God" could live as they did in Rome. In a letter home, Luther wrote, "It is incredible what sins and atrocities are committed in Rome. They must be seen and heard to be believed; so that it is usual to say, 'If there be a hell, Rome is built above it; it is an abyss from whence all sins proceed.'"

Inevitably, this began to cast doubt in Luther's mind of the Church itself, and it was that doubt that deepened his fear for his own soul. If salvation is not in relics, he thought, not in self-denial, not in shrines, not in good works, not even in Rome, where is it? For the second time he found himself thinking, sometimes I hate God. There was no way Luther could have known, of course, but what he had seen in Rome and his increasing self-doubt were preparing him for the turning point of his life that was just ahead.

Despite his doubts, Luther was not dissuaded from his duties. By October of 1512, he had completed all the requirements for his Doctor of Theology degree. It was Johann von Staupitz himself who placed the Doctor's cap on Luther's head during the colorful ceremony, and it was Staupitz whom Luther would now succeed as Professor of Theology at the University of Wittenberg, the position he would hold for the remaining thirty-four years of his life.

In spite of his struggles, Luther launched into the study of the Scriptures like never before because of his new responsibilities of teaching. Having always been strong on the mastery of the Biblical languages, he once insisted:

> And let us be sure of this: we will not long preserve the gospel without the languages. The languages are the sheath in which this sword of the Spirit is contained; they are the casket in which this jewel is enshrined; they are the vessel in which this wine is held; they are the larder in which this food is stored; and, as the gospel itself points out, they are the baskets in which are kept these loaves and fishes and fragments. . . . Hence, it is inevitable that unless the languages remain, the gospel must finally perish. . . . The preacher or teacher can expound the Bible from beginning to end as he pleases, accurately or inaccurately, if there is no one there to judge whether he is doing it right or wrong. But in order to judge, one must have a knowledge of the languages; it cannot be done in any other way. Therefore, although faith and the gospel may indeed be proclaimed by simple preachers without a knowledge of languages, such preaching is flat and tame; people finally become weary and bored with it, and it falls to the ground. But where the preacher is versed in the languages, there is a freshness and vigor in his preach-

ing, Scripture is treated in its entirety, and faith finds itself constantly renewed.[2]

This attitude now drove all Luther's study, as he prepared lectures that he then delivered twice a week. From 1513–1515, he lectured on the Psalms and from 1515–1517 on Romans and Galatians. It was somewhere during this time—no one knows exactly when, for even Luther recorded no specific date—that this man, who had struggled for so long, who had lived in despair for so many years, who had hidden his uncertainties from his students, finally found the answer he had sought for so long. While seated at his desk on the second floor of a tower in the Black Monastery, he meditated on the words of the Apostle Paul in Romans 1:16–17: "For I am not ashamed of the gospel of Christ: for it is the power of God unto salvation to every one that believeth; to the Jew first, and also to the Greek. For therein is the righteousness of God revealed from faith to faith: as it is written, The just shall live by faith."

Luther lecturing at Wittenburg

At first, those verses terrified him all over again. "If God is righteous and just," he thought, "then I must be damned. How can I expect God to forgive me?" As he compared this with other Scriptures that deal with "penance," however, the light began to dawn. He saw that the Latin in 2 Peter 3:9 and many others verses read *poenitentia*, which means "penance"—and unknown to Luther would be so translated in every future Roman Catholic Bible in English even to this day. He then discovered, however, that the original Greek in such verses is *metanoia*, which means "repentance, a change of mind from evil to good." This showed him that salvation came not by *penance*, that is, by fasting, pilgrimages, prayers to the saints, and so forth, but by *repentance*, a change of mind about sin, a turning from sin. The curtain opened in his mind and he saw for the first time that salvation is not by *outward effort* but by *inward attitude*. He saw that through the merits of the finished and sufficient work of Christ, a righteous and just God declared men righteous through faith. Luther would later write in his work, *Justification By Faith*:

> I greatly longed to understand Paul's Epistle to the Romans and nothing stood in the way but one expression, "the justice of God," because I took it to mean that justice whereby God is just and deals justly in punishing the unjust. My situation was that, although an

impeccable monk, I stood before God as a sinner troubled in conscience, and I had no confidence that my merit would assuage him. Therefore I did not love a just and angry God, but rather hated and murmured against him. Yet I clung to the dear Paul and had a great yearning to know what he meant.

Night and day I pondered until I saw the connection between the justice of God and the statement that "the just shall live by faith." Then I grasped that the justice of God is that righteousness by which through grace and sheer mercy God justifies us through faith. Thereupon I felt myself to be reborn and to have gone through open doors into paradise. The whole of Scripture took on a new meaning, and whereas before the 'justice of God' had filled me with hate, now it became to me inexpressibly sweet in great love. This passage of Paul became to me a gate to heaven.

If you have a true faith that Christ is your Saviour, then at once you have a gracious God, for faith leads you in and opens up God's heart and will, that you should see pure grace and overflowing love. This it is to behold God in faith that you should look upon his fatherly, friendly heart, in which there is no anger nor ungraciousness. He who sees God as angry does not see him rightly but looks only on a curtain as if a dark cloud had been drawn across his face.

Martin Luther's true conversion to Christianity would not only have long-range affects on history—influences that Luther could never have fathomed—its immediate result was the transformation of his preaching and teaching. While he did not break with Rome immediately—he would, in fact, remain in sympathy with its teachings and only criticize its excesses—what he now believed and taught would transform his preaching in such a way that it would quickly cross the lines of Church teaching and force him to forsake the Roman Church. He would now begin preaching the Truth, which always tends to bring controversy and even hatred.

During the next four years, Luther's understanding of *sola fide*, the biblical doctrine of justification "by faith alone," molded his thought into a solid theology, a theology which powered all his teaching and preaching. He was appointed preacher of the monastery, and by 1516 a great number came to hear him and desired that he preach every day. Students came from all over Germany to hear him lecture.

It was, therefore, *sola fide* that became what has been called the "material principle" of the Reformation. While a "formal principle"—which was *sola Scriptura*—speaks of the authority that forms and shapes an entire movement or system, a "material principle" is the *central teaching* of a movement or system. When properly defined and understood, a material principle provides indispensable help in understanding all other teachings of the system. In other words, an entire doctrinal system can be explained in relationship to its material principle. As we saw in our previous study, *sola Scriptura* is the *model* (form and pattern) of salvation; we now see that *sola fide* is the only *means* (way, channel, agency) of salvation.

No other principle of Christianity, therefore, more encapsulates its entire system of doctrine than does *sola fide*. Salvation does not come by *works*, which is the material principle of *Catholicism* and *all* religion; rather salvation comes through *faith*. Luther, in fact, stated, "The article with and by which the Church stands, without which it falls."[3] He went on to state about its pivotal place:

> This doctrine is the head and the cornerstone. It alone begets, nourishes, builds, preserves, and defends the Church of God; and without it the church of God cannot exist for an hour.[4]

So what was the Reformation about? *The Reformation was about a repudiation of the whole idea of human effort through his own works as a way to commend the sinner toward God and the recovery of the Gospel of faith in Christ alone.* As a note in the *Geneva Bible* so well declared it 400 years ago:

> We are justified by faith without works, taken from the end of Justification. The end of Justification is the glory of God alone: therefore we are justified by faith without works: for if we were justified either by our own works only, or partly by faith, and partly by works, the glory of this justification should not be wholly given to God. (Comment on Rom. 3:27)

That alone, in fact, *is* the Gospel, the good news, as declared in Galatians 2:16; 1:8–9; Romans 3:21–22 and 30, and many other verses. Salvation comes not by *ceremony*, but by the *cross*. It is not by the *ritual* of the *Church*, but the *righteousness* of *Christ*. It is not by the *bondage* of the *Law* but by *blood* of our *Lamb*. It is not by our *continuous works* but by His *completed work*. In short, the righteousness of God is not *granted* by *works*, but is a *gift* of *faith*.

This doctrine is hated and repudiated by Catholicism because, as one great writer puts it, half of its errors stem from the rejection of *sola fide*. That wonderful champion of Evangelicalism, **J. C. Ryle** (1816–1900), wrote this scathing summary:

J. C. Ryle

> . . . the absence [in Catholicism] of the doctrine of justification by faith alone in Christ's work alone accounts for half the errors of the Roman Catholic Church. The beginning of half the unscriptural

doctrines of Popery may be traced up to rejection of justification by faith. No Romish teacher, if he is faithful to his church, can say to the anxious sinner, "Believe on the Lord Jesus Christ, and thou shalt be saved." He cannot do it without additions and explanations, which completely destroy the good news. He dare not give the Gospel medicine without adding something which destroys its efficacy and neutralizes its power. Purgatory, penance, priestly absolution, the intercession of saints, the worship of the Virgin, and many other man-made services of Popery, all spring from this source. They are all rotten props to support weary consciences. But they are rendered necessary by [Rome's] denial of justification by faith.

Romanism in perfection is a gigantic system of church-worship, sacrament-worship, Mary-worship, saint-worship, image-worship, relic-worship, and priest-worship. . . . it is, in one word, a *huge organized idolatry*.[5]

Should we not ask here: Where are the men today who will stand up and tell the truth, as did Ryle?

Rome, therefore, fought the Reformation tooth and nail, its biggest guns coming out at the Council of Trent, which began in 1545 and continuing for almost twenty years. High on Trent's hit list was *sola fide*. One of its "canons" (principle tenets), for example, which has remained unchanged through Vatican I and II, was: "If anyone says that *by faith alone* the sinner is justified, so as to mean that nothing else is required to cooperate in order to obtain the grace of justification . . . let him be anathema" (session 6, canon 9). Trent went on to declare that the *instrumental* cause of justification (i.e., the means by which it is obtained) is not faith, but "the sacrament of baptism" (session 6, chapter 7) and that justification is forfeited whenever the believer commits a mortal sin (session 6, chapter 15). This without question makes justification dependent on human works in the Roman system. But such religion is *precisely* what Paul referred to in Galatians 1:8–9, where he declares that any other Gospel than that of faith alone (and as we will examine in our next study, grace alone) is itself cursed of God.

Is this issue really all that important? Is it worth fighting for? Most certainly! To deny *sola fide* is to deny the finished work of Christ. To deny *sola fide* is to align ourselves with a pagan system that repudiates the true Gospel of Jesus Christ. As we have noted, this is why Catholicism is not Christianity.

Finally, if we are going to understand *sola fide*, we must also understood the doctrine of *justification*, which is the legal transaction whereby God declares us just (i.e., righteous). Luther thundered that justification is "the chief article from which all other doctrines have flowed," and that it is "the master and prince, the lord, the ruler, and the judge over all kinds of doctrines."[6] Calvin likewise called justification "the main hinge on which religion turns."[7] That great Puritan **Thomas Watson** echoed Calvin when he wrote:

> Justification is the very hinge and pillar of Christianity. An error about justification is dangerous, like a defect in a foundation. Justification by Christ is a spring of the water of life. To have the poison of corrupt doctrine cast into this spring is damnable . . . In these latter times, the Arminians and Socinians[8] have cast a dead fly into this box of precious ointment.[9]

Thomas Watson

Those words make clear that what we believe about *justification* will dictate what we believe about *salvation*. The Reformation, then, focused on *how* a person is justified. On what grounds does God declare us just? Must we first become just by works before He declares us so, or does He declare us just before we are just? It is for this very reason that we repeat once again: Roman Catholicism and Biblical Christianity are polar opposites. We must be absolutely clear on this point. There is no unity or agreement between these two warring systems. Catholicism teaches a totally different gospel, namely, a gospel by which we are justified by faith *plus* works, not by grace through faith *alone*.

What, then, is *justification*? In its bare essence, justification is a legal (or forensic) term. It means "to declare or pronounce righteous and just, not symbolically but actually." Justification does not imply that there is no guilt. On the contrary, we are worthy of death. We who were once under condemnation are now declared to be righteous because of Christ. Justification is the declarative act of God, as the Judge, whereby He declares that the demands of justice have been satisfied so that the sinner is no longer condemned. Think of a criminal before the judge; he has been convicted beyond a reasonable doubt and is justly condemned to die, but the judge says, "You *are* guilty and deserve to die, but I by my mercy and grace declare you righteous. You are no less guilty, but you are no longer condemned."

In the strict sense of the word, however, justification does not *make* us righteous, nor does it change our behavior, for these are accomplished by *regeneration*[10] and *sanctification*.[11] While all three of these work together, they are still distinct. Further, justification is more than just pardoning the sinner, as we just described in the analogy above. Again, justification is a declaration, not of *innocence*, but of *satisfaction*. In our analogy, then, true justification would demand the judge say, "While I am declaring *you* right-eous, *someone* else will have to die for your crime." *That* is justification.

To understand justification fully, we need only contrast it with for-giveness. While justification includes forgiveness, it goes beyond it. Justi-fication means that the righteousness of Christ has been "imputed" to use, that is, charged to our account (Rom. 4:3–25; 5:17–19; Eph. 1:6–7; 2 Cor. 5:21). He is the satisfaction; He went to the gallows for us. We stand justi-fied, that is, no longer condemned, not because of our own righteousness, but because of Christ's righteousness. This demonstrates that there is a change in our relationship to God and there is now no guilt. In contrast, however, if our sins were merely "forgiven," there is no change in our rela-tionship to God and no guilt is removed. Why? Because the next time we sinned, we would have to be forgiven again, and this process would have to be repeated over and over again, which is what occurred in the old Mo-saic sacrificial system. Glory to God! Forgiven *and* justified!

The important thing to notice here is that it is God who has justified us in the past. It is not our *faith* that justifies, rather it is *God* who justifies (Rom. 8:33), totally apart from works, merit, or action. Put another way, *faith* is not the ground of justification, rather the *righteousness of Christ* is the ground of justification.

What part, then, does faith play? After all, Romans 4:5—"But to him who does not work but believes on Him who justifies the ungodly, his faith is accounted for righteousness"—makes it plain that faith is involved, so how does it relate? We can state the relationship this way: while the right-eousness of Christ is the *cause* of justification, faith is the *channel* by which it is applied. To put it another way: while God *instigates* justifica-tion by the righteousness of Christ in the *past*, He *implements* it in us through faith in the *present*.

One other question demands our attention. Is such faith some kind of nebulous belief, just a mental assent to a few facts concerning Christ? That is, indeed, the view of many today. "Easy Believeism" is another American invention that has captured today's church. Appallingly, the necessity for repentance is denied and salvation is divorced from discipleship. James Montgomery Boice again writes in *Whatever Happened to the Gospel of Grace?*

> For many evangelicals faith is only mental assent to certain doc-trines. It is something we exercise once at the start of our Christian lives, after which we can live more or less in any way we please. It does not matter in terms of our salvation whether or not this "faith" makes a difference. Some evangelicals even teach that a person could be saved and secure if he or she possessed a dead or dying faith or, incredible as this seems, if he or she apostatizes, denying

Christ. In contrast to such an eviscerated faith, throughout church history most Bible teachers have insisted that saving, biblical faith has three elements: "knowledge, belief, and trust," as Spurgeon put it; "awareness, assent, and commitment," as D. Martyn Lloyd-Jones said.[12]

Those men are right. In fact, the Greek verb behind "faith" and "believe" (*pisteuō*) implicitly and indisputably carries the idea "to obey." As one Greek authority puts it:

> The fact that "to believe" is "to obey," as in the OT, is particularly emphasized in Heb. 11. Here the *pisteuein* [faith] of OT characters has in some instances the more or less explicit sense of obedience. . . . Paul in particular stresses the element of obedience in faith. For him *pistis* [faith] is indeed *hupakoun* [obey] as comparison of Rom. 1:5, 8; 1 Thes. 1:8 with Rom. 15:18; 16:19, or 2 Cor. 10:5 with 10:15 shows. Faith is for Paul to *hupakouein tō euangeilō* [literally, "obedient to the good news"], Rom. 10:16. To refuse to believe is not to obey the righteousness which the Gospel offers by faith, Rom. 10:3. . . . He coins the combination *hupakon pisteuō* [literally, "obedience of faith"], Rom. 1:5.[13]

It is distressing, indeed, that many today are teaching that salvation does not really alter anything, that it does not result in a "new creature" at all, in which "old things are passed away" and "all things are become new" (2 Cor. 5:17). Is it faith plus good works and obedience that saves? Certainly not! But, as James makes crystal clear, it is a faith *that* works and obeys. Salvation is not *caused* by obedience, but it most certainly *results* in obedience. To deny this, quite frankly, is to deny the Gospel. It is a sad travesty that the so-called "Lordship debate" continues to rage, because it is a debate that should not even exist among true evangelicals.

We close again with a statement from The Cambridge Declaration of the Alliance of Confessing Evangelicals on April 20, 1996:

> We reaffirm that justification is by grace alone through faith alone because of Christ alone. In justification Christ's righteousness is imputed to us as the only possible satisfaction of God's perfect justice.

> We deny that justification rests on any merit to be found in us, or upon the grounds of an infusion of Christ's righteousness in us, or that an institution claiming to be a church that denies or condemns *sola fide* can be recognized as a legitimate church.

What is the object of our faith? *The righteousness of Christ.* We are clothed not in our own garments of works because "all our righteousnesses are as filthy rags," that is, a menstrual cloth (Isa. 64:6). We *have* no righteousness. No matter how many works we might perform, no matter how many sacraments we might practice, it will not be enough. If anyone could ever have gotten to heaven by works, it would have been good old Martin Luther, but that is not enough. We are clothed rather in the spotless garments of the Lamb, the true "coat of many colors" that is our Savior Himself. It is faith and trust in the righteousness of Christ alone that saves us. Indeed, *sola fide* is the only *means* of salvation.

NOTES

[1] Henry Sheldon, *History of the Christian Church*, Vol. III, 47 (emphasis added).

[2] Written in a 1524 circular titled "To the Councilmen of All Cities in Germany That They Establish and Maintain Christian Schools."

[3] Martin Luther, *What Luther Says: An Anthology*, ed. Ewald M. Plass, 3 vols. (Concordia, 1959), 2:704 n.5.

[4] Ibid, 2:704.

[5] J. C. Ryle, *Warnings to the Churches*, Banner of Truth, 1992, 158 (emphasis in the original).

[6] Martin Luther, *What Luther Says: An Anthology*, Edwald M. Plass, Editor (Concordia, 1959), Vol. 2, 702, 715.

[7] *Institutes*, III.11.1.

[8] Adherents of a 16th-century Italian sect holding Unitarian views, including the denial of the divinity of Christ and the Trinity.

[9] Thomas Watson, *A Body of Divinity* (Banner of Truth Trust, 1992 reprint), 226.

[10] Regeneration is the "new birth" (Jn. 3:3–7; Jas. 1:13; I Pet. 1:23), the act of the Holy Spirit whereby He imparts new life (Jn. 5:21, 25; Eph. 2:1) and a new nature (2 Pet. 1:4).

[11] While regeneration is birth, sanctification is growth, the continuous work of the Holy Spirit whereby He makes us holy and more Christ-like (Rom. 8:29) in attitude, action, and affection (Rom. 12:1–2; 1 Cor. 6:9–11, 19, 20; Eph. 4:22–32; 1 Thes. 5:23; 2 Thes. 2:13).

[12] James Mongomery Boice, *Whatever Happened to the Gospel of Grace* (Crossway Books, 2001), 137–138.

[13] Gerhard Kittel (Editor). *Theological Dictionary of the New Testament* (Eerdmans, 1964; reprinted 2006), Vol. VI, 205.

6

Sola Gratia: Our Only Method

Ephesians 2:8–9

For by grace are ye saved through faith, and that not of your selves: it is the gift of God, Not of works, least any man should boast himself. (Geneva Bible)

We have so far examined two tenets of the true Christian Faith, and likewise two pillars of the Reformation: *sola Scriptura*, Scripture alone, our only *model*, and *sola fide*, faith alone, our only *means*.

We turn now to a third: *sola gratia*, grace alone, which is our only *method* of salvation. This brings us, in fact, to the very core of the Doctrines of Grace, a term that simply means that *saving* grace is *sovereign* grace, that salvation, from beginning to end, and everything in between, is by God's sovereign grace, apart from any contribution from man whatsoever. Salvation is either *all* of grace or *none* of it is of grace. Adding anything to grace, negates grace.

In a sense, it is this point that is the crux of the whole Reformation debate, perhaps, in fact, the key to the whole debate. This is seen by recounting one of the most pivotal moments in theological history, namely, the debate between **Martin Luther** and **Desiderius Erasmus**. Erasmus (1466–1536) was a Dutch humanist and theologian. While ordained a priest in 1492, it appears he never actively worked as a priest and, like Luther, criticized some of the Church's excesses. He and Luther greatly respected one another, but they had a fundamental disagreement over the human will. In 1524, Erasmus published his book *The Freedom of the Will*, which dealt with the issue of grace, but from a subtle, roundabout way. He chose to make the biggest issue of all the question of "free will," that is, how much impact sin had (or did *not* have) on man's will. In it he wrote, "By free choice in this place we mean a power of the human will by which a man can apply himself to the things which lead to eternal salvation, or turn away from them."[1] In other words, man has voluntary or free power in and of himself to choose the way which leads to salvation apart from the grace of God grace (the same basic heresy Pelagius taught 1,000 years earlier, which we will examine later). In short, in Erasmus' mind, God and man work together to bring man's salvation. It is not a work accomplished totally by God.

Desiderius
Erasmus

Luther responded to Erasmus by publishing his most famous work, *The Bondage of the Will*, in 1525. Amazingly, while disagreeing with virtually everything Erasmus wrote, Luther actually *commended* Erasmus for recognizing the real core issue separating Rome and Bible believers. He wrote, in fact, one of the most important statements in theological history:

> . . . unlike all the rest, you alone have attacked the real thing, the essential issue. You have not wearied me with those extraneous issues about the Papacy, purgatory, indulgences and such like . . . you and you alone have seen the hinge upon which it all turns, and aimed for the vital spot. For that I heartily thank you.[2]

In short, Erasmus was not so foolish as to defend any of the major points, for they are indefensible. Rather, he pointed out "the hinge upon which it all turns." The issue of "free will" to Luther was the crux of the whole matter, namely, whether Christianity is a religion of *pure* grace or *partial* grace, that is, either *all* of God or *partly* of God with man. Would God simply supply the grace and man in his own power (his unfallen "free will") would supply the faith, or would God supply it all?

Sola gratia, then, declares that God supplies not only *forgiveness* and *justification* by grace, but also even *faith* by grace. That is why Christ is called "the author and finisher of our faith" (Heb. 12:2), for He is the beginning and the ending of it. He has done all of it. In fact, the doctrine of *sola fide* cannot be understood in its fullest apart from *sola gratia*. What is the source of faith? Is it the God-given means to salvation or is it a condition to salvation that man is left to himself to fulfill? Is grace God's contribution while faith is man's contribution? Is salvation wholly of God or does it ultimately depend upon something that we do for our salvation, namely, exercise our faith?

It was this issue that drove the Reformers. Did they believe in the hated doctrines of the sovereignty of God and election, doctrines that are mocked, maligned, and mutilated in our day? *They most certainly did!* Why? Because they believed in *sola Scriptura*, which clearly declares that man fell so far that even his will was effected. As Paul wrote to the Romans:

> As it is written, There is none righteous, no, not one: There is none that understandeth, there is none that seeketh after God. They

are all gone out of the way, they are together become unprofitable; there is none that doeth good, no, not one. (Rom. 3:10–12)

"Gone out of the way" translates a single word in the Greek, *ekklinō*. The root *klinō* is a verb that literally means "to bend something from a straight position," and so metaphorically "to swerve or turn away." The prefix *ek* basically means "out of or from, so we could translate this as "to swerve from the path." Man has swerved, turned away, from the path of God's righteousness so radically that he not only cannot get back on that path, but also has no desire to seek to do so even if he knew where it was.

It is precisely because of that condition that Scripture goes on to say that God has given man the faith to believe, as our text declares: **For by grace are ye saved through faith, and that not of your selves: it is the gift of God**. The clear and obvious antecedent for the pronoun "it" is faith. Faith *had* to be God's gift, for without that gift, fallen man would *never* believe. Several other Scriptures strongly substantiate this principle:

> And [Jesus] said, Therefore said I unto you, that no man can come unto me, *except it were given unto him of my Father*. (Jn. 6:65, emphasis added)
>
> For unto you it is *given* [granted] in the behalf of Christ, not only to *believe* on him, but also to suffer for his sake. (Phil. 1:29, emphasis added)
>
> And when [Apollos] was disposed to pass into Achaia, the brethren wrote, exhorting the disciples to receive him: who, when he was come, helped them much which had *believed through grace*. (Acts 18:27, emphasis added)

The words "through grace" are especially important. The Greek actually reads *dia tēs charitos*, "through the grace." "Through" is *dia*, which in this construction indicates agency, means, or instrumentality. Added to this is the presence of the definite article "the" (*tēs*). How does one believe? Not by his own power, rather by the agency, means, and instrumentality of the grace of God.

Another often quoted verse is John 1:12: "But as many as received him, to them gave he power [i.e., right] to become the sons of God, even to them that believe on his name." Many Gospel preachers quote that verse, as they rightly should, but sadly they stop without quoting the very next one: "Which were born, not of blood, nor of the will of the flesh, *nor of the will of man*, but of God." Where did we get the will to believe? In ourselves? No, because we were dead (Eph. 2:1–3), and a dead man can't do anything. Rather it was God's grace that gave us the will to believe. Man's will has nothing to do with salvation, not even with believing. It is all of

God. Were we born again *because* of our will? No, glory be to God, we were born again *in spite* of our will.

Matthew Henry

That beloved Puritan commentator **Matthew Henry** (1662–1714), who could read the Bible when he was only three years old, and of whose commentary Spurgeon said, "Every minister ought to read it entirely and carefully through once at least," said it well when he wrote:

> We do not become the children of God as we become the children of our natural parents. Grace does not run in the blood, as corruption does. It is not *produced* by the natural power of our own will. As it is not of *blood*, nor of *the will of the flesh*, so neither is it of the *will of man*. It is the grace of God that makes us willing to be *His* (emphasis in the original).

To illustrate, did any of us have anything to do with our physical birth? We obviously had nothing to do with the conception. And every mother would be quick to say that we most certainly did not have anything to do with the birth. That was all her with us as the whole problem. Likewise, none of us had anything to do with being born again. It was not *our* will but *God's* will.

Some 100 years before Matthew Henry, John Calvin likewise wrote:

> Ought we not then to be silent about free-will, and good intentions, and fancied preparations, and merits, and satisfactions? There is none of these which does not claim a share of praise in the salvation of men; so that the praise of grace would not, as Paul shews, remain undiminished.[3]

In other words, let us stop prattling on about free-will and other human merit. It is all of grace. Still another writer, this time a Greek authority, writes:

> God does not merely give to both Jews and Gentiles the possibility of faith; He effects faith in them. Ephesians 2:8 makes it especially plain that all is of grace and that human merit is completely ruled out. To understand the Pauline and then the Lutheran doctrine of justification it is essential to make it clear that faith is not a new human merit which replaces the merit of works, that it is not a second achievement which takes the place of the first, that it is not something which man has to show, but that justification by faith is an act of divine grace. Faith is not the presupposition of the grace of

God. As a divine gift, it is the epitome and demonstration of the grace of God.[4]

Spurgeon also dealt with this truth in his sermon "All of Grace." It continues to amaze me how many evangelicals argue that Spurgeon did not believe in the Doctrines of Grace, or like some choose to spit out of their mouths "*Calvinism.*" Well, bless their hearts, they obviously have not read very much Spurgeon, for he was a strong, staunch, and very vocal defender of the doctrines of sovereign grace. Of our present subject he wrote:

> Even the very will thus to be saved by grace is not of ourselves, but is the gift of God. . . . I ask any saved man to look back upon his own conversion, and explain how it came about. You turned to Christ, and believed on his name: these were your own acts and deeds. But what caused you thus to turn? What sacred force was that which turned you from sin to righteousness? Do you attribute this singular renewal to the existence of a something better in you than has been yet discovered in your unconverted neighbor? No, you confess that you might have been what he now is if it had not been that there was a potent something which touched the spring of your will, enlightened your understanding, and guided you to the foot of the cross.[5]

Dear Christian Friend, what touched your dead, depraved heart and drew you to the foot of the cross, regenerated your soul, and gave you the faith to believe? *Sovereign grace.*

It is truly interesting when we articulate that word **grace**. Why? Because there is absolutely no doubt whatsoever that few words are more misunderstood, misused, or misapplied than **grace**. It is bandied about by just about everyone today. Two people can be discussing grace, in fact, but mean two entirely different things. Other words in this category are "election," "predestination," "foreknowledge," and others, but grace is at the heart of every one of those, as well as other concepts, so to misunderstand grace is to be totally clueless as to what biblical Christianity and its doctrines are about. If we do not understand grace, we understand nothing of the Christian Faith.

A case in point again is again Roman Catholicism. Yes, it most certainly speaks of grace, but it means something *vastly different* from what Scripture says and what the Reformers defended. Again, in response to the Reformers, here's what the Council of Trent declared:

> If anyone says that by the said sacraments of the New Law [a term that refers to the Trent's canons and decrees on the seven sacraments] grace is not conferred through the act performed [*ex opere*

operato, lit., "the work worked"] but [says] that faith alone in the divine promises is sufficient for the obtaining of grace, let him be anathema.[6]

In other words, grace is not *received* from God by *faith*, but is rather *infused* by man's *works*, specifically, through his performing of the sacraments. The Catholic Church, therefore, maintains that it is the dispensary of grace. It is through Roman Church that grace emanates from Christ and is dispensed to the individual through the sacraments. Such apostasy and blasphemy is beyond imagination, but what is far worse is how many "evangelicals" are jettisoning the Reformation and embracing the Roman Church.

The word **grace** translates the Greek *charis*. In Classical Greek it meant "that which affords joy, pleasure, delight,"[7] and from there several meanings developed: grace, favor, thankfulness, gratitude, delight, kindness, etc.[8] Originally, then, the word didn't carry the idea of something "unmerited" because Greek philosophy (which is at the root of our western culture) believed in human merit and self-sufficiency. Even then, however, the Greeks thought they needed "a little help," so they prayed to their gods for favors and gifts.

It was, therefore, in the New Testament that *charis* was transformed. While some of the meanings from the Classical Greek *are* found, the New Testament usage is unique because *New Testament grace is coupled with the person and work of Jesus Christ*. If you remove Christ, and therefore **grace**, all you have left is another religion that is based on human merit. You have ten practical commandments, many ethical principles for living, but all you have is mere religion.

One example of this appears in John 1:17: "Grace and truth came by Jesus Christ." Does that say grace and truth came by religion, works, or human merit? No, for the ultimate manifestation of God's grace is Jesus Christ. Throughout the New Testament, in fact, grace is coupled with Christ, for He is the ultimate manifestation of the grace of God. Further, Christ is the focus of all Scripture, in fact. The Old Testament *pointed* to Him, the Gospels *presented* Him, and the Epistles *propagated* Him. *Grace is about Christ*. This transformation of *charis* is summed up by Greek scholar Kenneth Wuest:

> In pagan Greece, the word referred, among other things, to a favor done by one Greek to another, out of the spontaneous generosity of his heart, without hope of reward. Of course, this favor was always done to a friend, not an enemy. When the word is used in the [NT], it takes an infinite leap forward, and acquires an additional meaning which it never had in pagan Greece, for this favor was

done by God at the Cross, not to one who loved Him, but to one who hated Him.[9]

Grace, therefore, can be clearly defined as *the unmerited favor of God toward man manifested primarily through the person and work of Jesus Christ, apart from any merit, work, or action of man.*

If we may be so bold, if anyone defines grace differently than that (or similar to that), let them be accursed (Gal. 1:8–9). Anyone who does not preach that doctrine of grace—and Roman Catholicism most certainly does not—is a false teacher. Many verses of Scripture substantiate that definition. Especially pointed is Romans 11:5–6:

> Even so, then, at this present time also there is a remnant according to the election of grace. And if by grace, then is it no more of works, *otherwise grace is no more grace.* But if it be of works, then is it no more grace . . . (emphasis added).

To speak of grace plus works—*and "free will" is simply another aspect of human merit*—is in essence to redefine grace as something other than grace. Consider just two other passages:

> While by the proving of this ministration they glorify God for your professed subjection unto the *gospel of Christ*, and for your liberal distribution unto them, and unto all men, and by their prayer for you, who long after you for the exceeding *grace of God* in you. Thanks be unto God for His unspeakable *gift* (2 Cor. 9:13–15, emphasis added).

> That the name of our Lord Jesus Christ may be glorified in you, and ye in Him, according to the grace of our God and the Lord Jesus Christ (2 Thes. 1:12).

Before we close this chapter, one more historical note is essential, which again involves the human will, as noted earlier. The depth of Erasmus' error, as well as Catholicism's error, is Arminianism, which is serious error because of its view of the human will. While such a statement causes a firestorm when uttered in some groups, the roots of Arminianism go back to a man named **Pelagius** (c. 360–420), a British monk and theologian. About 400 he postulated his ideas of how man is saved. He believed each person has the same "free will" that Adam had and, therefore, is able to choose good or evil for himself. He said that this is possible because each person is created separately and uncontaminated by the sin of Adam. Sin, therefore, is a matter of *will*, not *nature*. It is just as easy for a man to choose good as it is to choose evil. Why, then, is there so much sin we must ask? Pelagius maintained that the reason is not a corruption of the will by original sin, but rather by the simple weakness of human flesh. The obvious problem with that, however, is where does the weakness of human flesh come from?

After the resounding defeat of Pelagius' views (Pelagianism) at the Council of Ephesus in 431, **John Cassianus** (c.360–435) tried to find a compromise. While he taught that all men are sinful because of the fall, and that the fall *weakened* the will, he still, like Pelagius, rejected that the fall totally corrupted the will. He taught that the will is partially free and can, therefore, cooperate with divine grace in salvation, which is exactly what Erasmus would argue 1,000 years later. The Semi-Pelagian maxim, therefore, was, "It is mine to be willing to believe, and it is the part of God's grace to assist." While these views were condemned at the Synod[10] of Orange in 529, it is very enlightening to note one historian's comment: "[Cassianus'] doctrine lay somewhere between that of Augustine and that of Pelagius (hence called Semi-Pelagian) *and was not essentially different from the accepted Catholic doctrine*."[11] What is Roman Catholicism? It is Semi-Pelagianism, plain and simple. What does this say about evangelicals who maintain the same view?

Which brings us to **James Arminius** (1560–1609), who became the

James Arminius

spokesman for several ministers in Holland who did not agree with the Doctrines of Grace. Reluctant to make his views public, Arminius finally agreed to do so at a national synod. He died, however, nine years before it was called in 1618. His followers, therefore, presented his views in a five-point statement, called the "Remonstrance" (protest, opposition). While many today enjoy blasting away at the so-called "five points of Calvinism," it was actually the "five points of Arminius" that came *first* and *attacked the orthodox doctrines of sovereign grace that had stood for centuries*. (Please read that last sentence again.) In essence, the Remonstrance stated:

- While man did inherit Adam's sin and is under God's wrath, he is still able to initiate his salvation after God grants him grace to cooperate.
- God's election had "its foundation in the foreknowledge of God." Therefore, election is conditional on man's acceptance.
- Christ's death did not actually save but made salvation *possible* to those who believe.
- While God's grace is needed, God doesn't draw man effectually, rather man believes only in his power and can resist the Holy Spirit's call.

- Finally, God gives believers the ability to win out over all sin and not fall from grace, but Scripture also seems to indicate that it is possible for a believer to fall away from salvation.

That is the Arminian system, a system that rejects true sovereign grace to such an extent that grace can even be lost and regained. How unthinkable it is!

Once again, however—and for the third time—these views were totally rejected, this time at the Synod of Dort in 1618. Of the 130 present, only thirteen defended these views. Is it not instructive that on three separate occasions false doctrine on the exact same subject was rejected? Three times men tried to water down the Gospel of Sovereign Grace, and three times those who wanted a pure Gospel did "earnestly contend for the faith which was once [for all] delivered to the saints" (Jude 3). "No," those champions of faith cried, "it is all of God!"

Another great theologian, one of the most brilliant men in American history, **Jonathan Edwards** (1703–1758) greatly contributed to this debate in his book *The Freedom of the Will*, in which he actually proved it is *not* free. While most people think the will is its own entity and therefore free to make a choice, Edwards rightly viewed the *will* as part of the *mind*, which means that we choose what the mind thinks is most desirable. Additionally, Edwards discussed not only the *mind* but also *motives*, which drive the mind to choose the things that are best. The crux again, however, is that man's mind does not want God

Jonathan Edwards

or His sovereign rule because he doesn't think that is better. He wants his sin and invariably chooses it because he thinks that is better.

In spite of all the biblical and historical evidence, however, it is happening once again! Sadly, proving that something is wrong doesn't make it go away, and the same was true of Arminianism. On the contrary, Arminianism deeply imbedded itself into theological thought. In his Introduction to Luther's classic, *The Bondage of the Will*, J. I. Packer wrote that "the present-day Evangelical Christian has semi-Pelagianism in his blood."[12] How true that is! Countless evangelicals hold the Arminian view because they fail to stop and just think what the words **for by grace are you saved** really mean. Arminianism (historically and today) is nothing but warmed-over Roman Catholicism, with which we can have absolutely no compromise, regardless of what many "evangelicals" today are saying to the contrary. While there are a few who are standing and condemning this fourth attack, their voices are being overpowered by the masses of preachers and teachers who are Arminian. They market Jesus like they are selling shoes, tell people to "walk the aisle" and "say this prayer," and have turned the Gospel into just another religion.

A case in point was the 19th-century so-called revivalist **Charles Finney** (1792–1875), who we will detail in a later study. No less than a full-blown Pelagian, he rejected the Doctrines of Grace in their entirety, along with any semblance of orthodoxy.

We close with this statement on *sola gratia*, as stated in The Cambridge Declaration of the Alliance of Confessing Evangelicals on April 20, 1996:

> We reaffirm that in salvation we are rescued from God's wrath by his grace alone. It is the supernatural work of the Holy Spirit that brings us to Christ by releasing us from our bondage to sin and raising us from spiritual death to spiritual life.
>
> We deny that salvation is in any sense a human work. Human methods, techniques or strategies by themselves cannot accomplish this transformation. Faith is not produced by our unregenerated human nature.

What is *sola gratia*? It is that salvation is solely by grace from beginning to end, that grace is the only *method*. If we do not embrace this core tenet of the Reformation and Christianity itself, we have returned to the errors of Pelagius and the darkness of Rome. Let us rejoice in *sola gratia*, our only *method*.

NOTES

[1] E. Gordon Rupp, P. Watson, *Luther And Erasmus: Free Will And Salvation* (Westminster Press, 1969), 47.

[2] Martin Luther, *The Bondage of the Will* (Fleming H. Revell, 1992), 319.

[3] Calvin's *Commentaries* (Ephesians).

[4] H. Hanse in *Theological Dictionary of the New Testament*, ed. Gerhard Kittel, trans. and ed. by Geoffrey W. Bromiley (Eerdmans, 1967), Vol. IV, 2.

[5] *Metropolitan Tabernacle Pulpit*, Vol. 61 (published 1915). One very outspoken preacher makes the unbelievable blunder, "Charles Haddon Spurgeon never preached one sermon a year on 'the five points of Calvinism.'" A quick review of Spurgeon's preaching proves this to be incredibly ridiculous. Spurgeon's *The New Park Street Pulpit* is a six-volume work covering Spurgeon's first six years at that church. After the completion of the new tabernacle, the series name was then changed to *The Metropolitan Tabernacle Pulpit*. The fact is that in his first year (Volume 1, 1855) Spurgeon preached three sermons dedicated to sovereign grace subjects: "Election" (two parts) and "Free-will—a Slave." In his second year, he preached four: "Sovereignty in Salvation"; "Effectual Calling"; "Final

Perseverance"; and "Divine Sovereignty." In his third year, he preached two: "Particular Election" and "Salvation is of the Lord." In his fourth year, he preached five: "The Death of Christ"; "Particular Redemption"; "Human Inability"; "Providence"; and "Sovereign Grace and Man's Responsibility." In his fifth year, he preached three: "Free Grace"; "Predestination and Calling"; and "Man's Ruin and God's Remedy." Finally, in his sixth year, Spurgeon preached three: "The Treasure of Grace"; "Election and Holiness"; and "High Doctrine." It was then in the very next year (April 11, 1861), when Spurgeon opened the Metropolitan Tabernacle, he sponsored a Bible Conference on the theme "Exposition of the Doctrines of Grace." He and five other speakers expounded on "Election," "Human Depravity," "Particular Redemption," "Effectual Calling," and "Final Perseverance of Believers in Christ Jesus." We should also add that all these sermons are merely the obvious ones. The message of sovereign grace permeates all Spurgeon's preaching

[6] Session 7, canon 8.

[7] Thayer, 675.

[8] Colin Brown, *The New International Dictionary of New Testament Theology* (Zondervan, 1975, 1986), Vol. 2, 115.

[9] *Wuest's Word Studies (1 Timothy 1:1)*

[10] A "synod" or "council" was a meeting of various church leaders who gathered to establish church policy, determine doctrine, combat heresy, or settle other issues. The first Church Council was held in Jerusalem to combat the heresy of the Judaizers (Acts 15). Because of the dominance and corruption of Roman Catholicism, each council must be analyzed to determine its real good.

[11] Elgin Moyer, *Who Was Who in Church History* (Moody Press, 1951), 78 (emphasis added).

[12] "Historical and Theological Introduction," *The Bondage of the Will*, 58.

God does not justify us because we are worthy, but by justifying us makes us worthy.

Thomas Watson
Puritan Golden Treasury

7

Solus Christus: Our Only Mediator

Heb. 10:10–12, 14; 9:23–28

By the which will we are sanctified, even by the offering of the body of Jesus Christ once made. And every Priest standeth daily ministering, and oft times offereth one manner of offering, which can never take away sins: But this man after he had offered one sacrifice for sins, sitteth for ever at the right hand of God . . . For with one offering hath he consecrated for ever them that are sanctified. (Geneva Bible)

It was then necessary, that the similitudes of heavenly things should be purified with such things: but the heavenly things them selves are purified with better sacrifices then are these. For Christ is not entered into ye holy places that are made with hands, which are similitudes of ye true Sanctuary: but is entered into very heaven, to appear now in ye sight of God for us, Not that he should offer himself often, as the high Priest entered into the Holy place every year with other blood, (For then must he have often suffered since the foundation of the world) but now in the end of the world hath he been made manifest, once to put away sin by the sacrifice of him self. And as it is appointed unto men that they shall once die, and after that commeth the judgment: So Christ was once offered to take away the sins of many, and onto them that look for him, shall he appear the second time without sin unto salvation. (Geneva)

We approach these verses with reverent hesitation. They address our Lord and Savior directly, and there is a feeling of inadequacy when speaking of such things. Jesus Christ is the center of Scripture, the Gospel itself, so how we address Him will dictate our entire theology. Jesus is everything. If we do not preach Him, we have nothing to say, and if we do not preach Christ *alone*, we preach a false Gospel. We, therefore, look now at *solus Christus*, Christ alone, our only *Mediator*.

Solus Christus

We begin again with a little history. The Roman Catholic Mass was a dramatic, even gripping, scene in the days prior to the Reformation. The holy altar stood at the front of the church. Thin, round wafers, enough for all worshippers present, lay in a golden dish. Beside it stood a golden chalice filled with wine. The priest entered the scene in brightly colored vestments and with bowed head. There was no singing; there were no spontaneous prayers. There was just the priest, who would in a moment—with the power that had been bestowed upon him by the bishop at his ordination—turn the plain bread and wine into the literal body and blood of Jesus Christ.

The people had been taught to revere this moment more than any other, because the Mass, the Roman Church taught, is the *same sacrifice* as the sacrifice of the Cross. In a moment, through the act of *transubstantiation*—meaning "a change of substance"—the priest would perform a miracle just as real as those of Jesus. So central was this to Romanism, that in response to the upheaval the Reformers would make in a few years, the Council of Trent would declare of the Mass in 1562:

> If any one denieth, that, in the sacrament of the most holy Eucharist, are contained truly, really, and substantially, the body and blood together with the soul and divinity of our Lord Jesus Christ, and consequently the whole Christ; but saith that He is only therein as in a sign, or in figure, or virtue; let him be anathema.
>
> If any one . . . denieth that wonderful and singular conversion of the whole substance of the bread into the Body, and of the whole substance of the wine into the Blood . . . let him be anathema.
>
> If any one saith, either that the principal fruit of the most holy Eucharist is the remission of sins, or, that other effects do not result therefrom; let him be anathema.
>
> If any one saith, that in the mass a true and proper sacrifice is not offered to God; or, that to be offered is nothing else but that Christ is given us to eat; let him be anathema.[1]

The worshipers present, however, needed no such assurance or warning. They believed and put their hope in the priest who was about to become an *Alter Christus*—another Christ—in that he would call the real Christ down from heaven and sacrifice Him again for the salvation of the faithful and for the deliverance of souls in purgatory.

As the ritual unfolded, it was a drama to behold, a pageant that reenacted the experiences of Christ beginning at the Last Supper in the upper room and culminating with the Ascension. It was mesmerizing to watch the priest perform this drama. His bowing and genuflecting were supposed imitations of Christ in His agony and suffering. The various articles of clothing he wore represented those worn by Christ: the seamless robe, the purple coat, the veil with which His face was covered in the house of Caiaphas, a girdle representing the cords with which he was bound in the Garden, other cords that bound Him to the Cross, and other vivid reminders.

While the liturgy would be simplified in the mid-twentieth century, and would then be said in the colloquial language, in that day it was more theatrical and was conducted wholly in Latin. The mesmerized observers simply could not look away as the spectacle developed. In all, the priest made the sign of the cross sixteen times, turned toward the congregation six times, lifted his eyes to heaven eleven times, kissed the altar eight times, folded his hands four times, struck his breast ten times, bowed his head twenty-one times, genuflected eight times, bowed his shoulders seven times, blessed the alter with the sign of the cross thirty times, laid his hands flat on the altar twenty-nine times, prayed secretly eleven times, prayed aloud thirteen times, covered and uncovered the chalice ten times, walked back and forth twenty times, and performed other acts.

The priest had studied endlessly to be able to perform all this perfectly from memory, for to forget one element was to commit a great sin and invalidate the Mass.

But most important of all, the act that all present waited for, was the moment the priest declared, "We offer unto Thee, the living, the true, the eternal God." The people, of course, could not understand Latin, but it did not matter. They had been taught about what had just happened. With those words, the priest ate a large wafer and drank the wine on behalf of the congregation, and then each worshiper partook. In turn, each worshipper knelt before the altar with eyes closed. With a wafer in his hand, the priest made the sign of the cross and then placed it on the worshipper's tongue, saying, "The Body of Christ."

We recount all that to emphasize that the principle of *solus Christus*, Christ alone, therefore, plunged even deeper into heart of the Reformation debate, even driving "a stake," if you will, through its very heart. The Mass, the re-crucifying of Christ, was the focal point of the entire system. The Reformers, however, rejected this perverted spectacle and utterly blasphemous re-crucifixion of Christ. It was (and still is) a blatant departure from our text in Hebrews 10, where we read that Christ was offered **once** (10:10) for sin and is now seated **on the right hand of God** (10:12), not called by a human priest to die again. Our Lord does not **offer himself often, as the high priest [went] into the holy place every year with other blood**, the blood of animals (9:25). He was the perfect Lamb of God who **was once offered to take away the sins of many** (9:28), that is, His elect from the foundation of the world. *That once-for-all sacrifice is the only sufficient payment for our sin.* As Hebrews goes on to say, it was that one and only sacrifice on the cross that ushered Christ "into the holy place" where He "obtained eternal redemption for us" (9:12). Verse 15 goes on to declare with no ambiguity: "And for this cause he is the mediator of the new testament, that by means of death, for the redemption of the transgressions that were under the first testament, they which are called might receive the promise of eternal inheritance."

Regardless of those clear statements of Scripture, however, the Council of Trent responded to the Reformers' accusation of blasphemy by stating: "If any one saith, that, by the sacrifice of the mass, a blasphemy is cast upon the most holy sacrifice of Christ consummated on the cross; or, that it is thereby derogated from; let him be anathema."[2]

We are compelled here to emphasize once again just how anti-Christian the Roman system is. The Mass is the most wicked, blasphemous, and horrific act of the whole system. This doctrine, by itself, condemns the entire system as pagan. We lovingly submit that it is no less than reprehensible for a true evangelical to have any complicity whatsoever with this Satanic system.

Also at issue was the whole concept of the priesthood, that is, a priest as the mediator between God and the people. The Church of the 1st-century had no priests. Nowhere in the New Testament do we read that this is an office in the Church. It was a position in Mosaic Judaism alone and was replaced by the finished work of Christ. Rome's priesthood, in fact, resembles more of paganism than it does the Old Testament priesthood. Hebrew 7:12 clearly declares, "For the priesthood being changed, there is made of necessity a change also of the law," and verse 17 adds that Christ alone is our "priest for ever." Verses 18–27 go on to settle the matter:

> For there is verily a disannulling of the commandment going before for the weakness and unprofitableness thereof. For the law made nothing perfect, but the bringing in of a better hope did; by the which we draw nigh unto God. And inasmuch as not without an oath he was made priest: (For those priests were made without an oath; but this with an oath by him that said unto him, The Lord sware and will not repent, Thou art a priest for ever after the order of Melchisedec:) By so much was Jesus made a surety of a better testament. And they truly were many priests, because they were not suffered to continue by reason of death: But this man, because he continueth ever, hath an unchangeable priesthood. Wherefore he is able also to save them to the uttermost that come unto God by him, seeing he ever liveth to make intercession for them. For such an high priest became us, who is holy, harmless, undefiled, separate from sinners, and made higher than the heavens; Who needeth not daily, as those high priests, to offer up sacrifice, first for his own sins, and then for the people's: for this he did once, when he offered up himself.

The whole idea, then, of the so-called "Christian priesthood" is a totally Roman Catholic invention and a blasphemous one at that. It maintains, according to Trent, that Jesus Himself "constituted [the apostles as] priests of the New Testament; and by those words, Do this in commemoration of me [Lk. 22:19; 1 Cor. 11:24–25], He commanded them and their successors in the priesthood to offer" Jesus' "body and blood under the species of bread and wine,"[3] while Scripture, of course, says no such thing.

In addition to the Lord Jesus as our High Priest, which is repeatedly emphasized in Hebrews (3:1; 4:14–15; 5:10; 6:20; 7:26; 8:1; 9:11; 10:21), every believer is a priest, as 1 Peter 2:9 declares: "But ye are a chosen generation, a royal priesthood, an holy nation, a peculiar people; that ye should shew forth the praises of him who hath called you out of darkness into his marvellous light." Revelation 1:6 likewise says that we are all "kings and priests unto God." This is why, while only priests could enter God's presence in the tabernacle and temple, we all now have "boldness to enter into the holiest by the blood of Jesus, By a new and living way, which he hath consecrated for us, through the veil, that is to say, his flesh" (Heb. 10:19–20). We need no earthly priest to mediate for us, because now "there is one God, and one mediator between God and men, the man Christ Jesus" (1 Tim. 2:5). We all have direct access to the Holy of Holies because Christ alone is our Mediator.

Catastrophically, all this today is progressively being reversed. In spite of the overwhelming proof of Rome's blasphemies, many professing evangelicals not only want to *embrace* Rome but even *return* to it. As far back as 1982, **Robert Schuller** planted the seed for what has today become the wholesale undoing of the Reformation. In his apostate book, *Self Esteem: A New Reformation*, he attacks the very core of "Reformation Theology" by saying that it "failed to make clear that the core of sin is a lack of self-esteem" (p. 98),[4] and that the Reformers were "rampantly reckless in assaulting the dignity of the person" (first paragraph of fly-leaf). Instead, Schuller insists, "What we need is a Theology of salvation that begins and ends with a recognition of every person's hunger for glory" (pp.

Robert Schuller

26–27). Neither is hell a literal place in Schuller's theology, rather, "A person is in hell when he has lost his self-esteem (pp. 14–15), and salvation "means to be permanently lifted from sin (psychological self-abuse . . .) and shame to self-esteem (p. 99)." Such apostasy is almost beyond comprehension. If all that is not shocking enough, Schuller later wrote in 1984:

I don't think anything has been done in the name of Christ and under the banner of Christianity that has proven more destructive to human personality and, hence, counterproductive to the evangelism enterprise than the often crude, uncouth, and unchristian strategy of attempting to make people aware of their lost and sinful condition.[5]

Think of it! It is actually unchristian to tell people of their sin and need for salvation in Christ! Nevertheless, countless millions are following this apostate.

Some ten years later, that seed spawned another movement, this one within Evangelicalism itself. With the signing of a document titled *Evangelicals and Catholics Together: The Christian Mission in the Third Millennium* (ECT) in March 1994, the Reformation was directly attacked like never before. Co-written by **Charles Colson** (director of Prison Fellowship Ministries and a widely known author and speaker) and **Richard John Neuhouse** (a former Lutheran minister who converted to Catholicism in 1990 and has since been ordained to the priesthood, and is also a noted author and speaker and editor-in-Chief of *First Things*), ECT was a way to bring together Roman Catholics and Evangelicals for the purpose of evangelism and a "betterment of life in America." Several notable evangelicals signed this document, including: Pat Robertson (Christian Broadcasting Network), Bill Bright (Campus Crusade), Mark Noel (Wheaton College), Thomas Oden (Drew University), *and most shockingly of all*, J. I. Packer, the noted author, professor at Regent College, and for years a strong defender of the biblical doctrines of the Reformation.

At the very beginning of the document, we read, "We [Evangelicals and Catholics] together confess our sins against the unity that Christ intends for all His disciples." The fallacy of this statement, of course, is that Catholics are *not* disciples of Christ, as is made clear in this statement about salvation in ECT: "We affirm together that we are justified by grace through faith because of Christ. Living faith is active in love that is nothing less than the love of Christ." On the surface, that statement sounds good, and has, in fact, been applauded as a great unifying truth of Catholicism and Evangelicalism. But a discerning look reveals that it flatly denies the biblical truth that became the material principle of the Reformation, namely, that faith *alone* brings justification, not just faith. *Sola fide* nowhere appears in ECT, because it is nowhere found in Catholicism. It was evangelicals who compromised theology in this document; the Roman Catholic signers of ECT compromised not a single teaching of the Roman system, while evangelicals "gave up the ship."

Some fifteen years later (2009), Evangelicalism drifted even further from the truth of Christ alone. One example is **Rick Warren**, who by his own admission, was greatly influenced by Schuller's philosophy of appealing to unbelievers, is a graduate of Schuller's "Institute for Church Growth," and shuns preaching on sin and repentance. Warren's own Semi-pelagianism, which elevates man, is quickly making him the new Charles Finney.

As if all that were not bad enough, there is **Joel Osteen**, who should grieve the heart of every true child of God. Did you know that the word "sin," along with its other forms (sins, sinner, sinners, sinful) appears some 900 times in Scripture? It would seem, therefore, that sin is a pretty important theme, right? In spite of that, however, in a building that holds 16,000 people and with three services, Osteen proudly *never* preaches on sin, calling himself an encourager, not someone who condemns anyone. When asked by Larry King on live television (10/17/07) about the Gospel, he said, "The Gospel is translated 'good news,' and to me good news is letting people know that God loves them, Jesus came, that we can overcome any obstacle, that we can be forgiven for our mistakes. I don't see how beating people down [obviously by preaching about sin] . . . helps them grow closer to God." No, Mr. Osteen, that is *not* the Gospel! You are not even close!

When then asked who will go to heaven, whether an atheist, Muslim, or Jew, he answered, "I don't know; I just think only God can judge a person's heart. . . . I've spent a lot of time in India with my father and I don't know everything about their religion, but I know they love God. I don't know, I've seen their sincerity. I don't know." No, he most certainly does not know! Here is, indeed, perhaps the worst false teacher of our time who seldom opens a Bible, whose message is just prosperity teaching, and who refuses to preach the Gospel, assuming he even knows what it is.

Additionally, as has been recently reported by several sources, University of Virginia sociologist James Hunter reports that 35% of evangelical seminarians deny that faith in Christ is absolutely necessary for salvation. It has also been reported in polls conducted by George Gallup and George Barna that 35% of the entire adult Evangelical population agrees with the statement: "God will save all good people when they die, regardless of whether they have trusted in Christ." Do you see what has happened? We have jettisoned the very core of Scripture, Christ Himself. One poll goes on to conclude:

> Many committed born again Christians believe that people have multiple options for gaining entry to Heaven. They are saying, in essence, "Personally, I am trusting Jesus Christ as my means of gaining God's permanent favor and a place in Heaven—but someone else could get to Heaven based upon living an exemplary life." Millions of Americans have redefined grace to mean that God is so eager to save people from Hell that He will change His nature and universal principles for their individual benefit. It is astounding how

many people develop their faith according to their feelings or cultural assumptions rather than biblical teachings.[6]

How many people today have a false sense of security? How many are depending upon a warm feeling they had when they walked the church aisle? How many are depending upon a prayer they said at Vacation Bible School when they were seven years old? How many are depending upon the nebulous "commitment to Christ" they professed at a Billy Graham crusade? Among the most frightening verses of Scripture are these words from our Lord Himself:

> Not every one that saith unto me, Lord, Lord, shall enter into the kingdom of heaven; but he that doeth the will of my Father which is in heaven. Many will say to me in that day, Lord, Lord, have we not prophesied in thy name? and in thy name have cast out devils? and in thy name done many wonderful works? And then will I profess unto them, I never knew you: depart from me, ye that work iniquity. (Matt. 7:21–23)[7]

Another shocking, though not surprising, statistic is that 77% of American evangelicals believe that human beings are basically good by nature. This is certainly understandable; after all, salvation is not really a big issue if sin isn't a big problem. This underscores again how Pelagianism and Arminianism, while defeated and shown to be heresy several times in church history, have imbedded themselves deep into Christian thinking. No longer is salvation by faith alone in Christ alone, but comes by many means, which is nothing but the old teaching called Universalism.

One other crucial development in our day is "inclusivism," lead by theologian **Clark Pinnock** and others. Inclusivism is the teaching that, although salvation comes through Jesus, it is not necessary to possess specific

Billy Graham

knowledge concerning Jesus as Savior. Other religions, in fact, can be vehicles of salvation for people who never heard of Jesus Christ, but "finally" (ultimately) are included because of their sincerity and positive response to general revelation. One could, for example, look at the beauty of the Rocky Mountains as they drive through Estes Park, "see God in it all," and therefore go to heaven. Did you know that both Robert Schuller and **Billy Graham** agree that it is not necessary to hear of or believe in Jesus Christ or His Gospel to go to heaven? Billy Graham has openly stated that Muslims, Hindus, and others can all make it to heaven without Jesus. In an interview by Robert Schuller on his program "Hour of Power" in 1997, Billy Graham stated:

. . . you know, I think there's the Body of Christ. This comes from all the Christian groups around the world, outside the Christian groups. I think everybody that loves Christ, or knows Christ, whether they're conscious of it or not, they're members of the Body of Christ. And I don't think that we're going to see a great sweeping revival, that will turn the whole world to Christ at any time. I think James answered that, the Apostle James in the first council in Jerusalem, when he said that God's purpose for this age is to call out a people for His name.

And that's what God is doing today, He's calling people out of the world for His name, whether they come from the Muslim world, or the Buddhist world, or the Christian world or the non-believing world, they are members of the Body of Christ because they've been called by God. They may not even know the name of Jesus but they know in their hearts that they need something that they don't have, and they turn to the only light that they have, and I think that they are saved, and that they're going to be with us in heaven.[8]

Where is the Gospel? It most clearly is not there. Graham's position is not new, in fact. He maintained this view as far back as 1960 in an article he wrote for *Decision* Magazine. When we dig further, we find moderate forms of inclusiveness are also to be found in C. S. Lewis[9] and even Arminian John Wesley.

We have mentioned all this to emphasize that the Reformation tenet of *solus Christus* returned to the biblical mandate that salvation comes by Christ *alone*, that Christ *alone* is our Mediator. The modern idea that says, "I found God" or "I found Jesus" is a misnomer to say the least. Jesus was never lost and didn't need finding. It is man who is lost, and it is Jesus who seeks (Lk. 19:10) and finds those who the Father gave Him before the foundation of the world (Jn. 6:37, 39; cf. Eph. 1:4). He is the only way to God, the only way of salvation, not only according to John 14:6, but also Acts 4:12: "Neither is there salvation in any other: for there is none other name under heaven given among men, whereby we must be saved." And as Paul added in his letter to the Romans, "How then shall they call on him in whom they have not believed? and how shall they believe in him of whom they have not heard? and how shall they hear without a preacher?" (Rom. 10:14). Sin is, indeed, an important issue, and Christ *alone*, the Author and Finisher of our faith (Heb. 12:1), is the answer. The Apostle John adds:

Who is a liar, but he that denieth that Jesus is that Christ? the same is that Antichrist that denieth the Father and the Son. Whosoever denieth the Son, the same hath not the Father. Let therefore abide in you that same which ye have heard from the beginning. If that which ye have heard from the beginning, shall remain in you, ye shall also continue in the Son, and in the Father (1 John 2:22–24, Geneva Bible).

The Geneva Bible note on this passages is challenging, indeed, in our day:

> The whole preaching of the Prophets and Apostles is contrary to that doctrine [of denying Christ]: Therefore it is utterly to be cast away and this wholly to be holden and kept, which leadeth us to seek eternal life in the free promise, that is to say, in Christ alone, who is given to us of the Father.

It adds elsewhere: "There is no true knowledge of God, nor quietness of mind, but only in Christ alone" (note on Matt. 11:27). And still again it rightly declares: "all the parts of our salvation consist in Christ alone" (chapter summary of Col. 1).

In his book, *Whatever Happened to the Gospel of Grace?* **James Montgomery Boice** reminds us of the centrality of *Solus Christus*. After discussing three essential words for understanding what the Cross was about—*satisfaction*, *sacrifice*, and *substitution*—he then concludes:

> It has been a popular idea in some theological circles that the Incarnation is the important truth of Christianity . . . and that the Atonement is something like an afterthought. . . . To focus on the birth of Jesus apart from the Cross leads to false sentimentality and neglect of the horror and magnitude of sin. . . . Any "gospel" that talks merely about the Christ-event, meaning the Incarnation without the Atonement, is a false gospel. Any gospel that talks about the love of God without showing that love led him to pay the ultimate price for sin in the person of his Son on the Cross, is a false gospel. The only true gospel is the gospel of the "one mediator" who gave himself for us (1 Tim. 2: 5, 6). If our churches are not preaching this gospel, they are not preaching the gospel at all, and if they are not preaching the gospel, they are not true churches. Evangelicalism desperately needs to rediscover its roots and recover its essential biblical bearing . . .[10]

James Boice

So, we would again close with a statement in The Cambridge Declaration of the Alliance of Confessing Evangelicals on April 20, 1996. Concerning *solus Christus*, it boldly declares:

> We reaffirm that our salvation is accomplished by the mediatorial work of the historical Christ alone. His sinless life and substitu-

tionary atonement alone are sufficient for our justification and reconciliation to the Father.

We deny that the gospel is preached if Christ's substitutionary work is not declared and faith in Christ and his work is not solicited.

Oh, that this would be a new call to each of us to understand like never before that it's all about Christ *alone*. If we abandon that, we have indeed given up the ship.

NOTES

[1] Session 13, Canons 1, 2, 5; session 22, canon 1.

[2] Session 22, canon 4.

[3] Session 22, Chapter 1.

[4] Robert H. Schuller, *Self-Esteem: The New Reformation* (Word Books, 1982), 98.

[5] *Christianity Today*, October 5, 1984, 12.

[6] The Barna Update, "Americans Describe Their Views About Life After Death," October 21, 2003 (www.barna.org/FlexPage.aspx?Page=BarnaUpdate&BarnaUpdateID=150).

[7] For a detailed exposition and application of this passage, see chapter 48, "The Most Terrifying Words in the Bible," in the author's *Truth on Tough Texts: Expositions of Challenging Scripture Passages* (Sola Scriptura Publications, 2012), 468–477.

[8] "Hour of Power," program #1426 entitled, "Say 'Yes' To Possibility Thinking," originally broadcast May 31, 1997.

[9] E.g., "There are people in other religions who are being led by God's secret influence to concentrate on those parts of their religion which are in agreement with Christianity, and who thus belong to Christ without knowing it. . . . For example a Buddhist of good will may be led to concentrate more and more on the Buddhist teaching about mercy and to leave in the background (though he might still say he believed) the Buddhist teaching on certain points. Many of the good Pagans long before Christ's birth may have been in this position" (*Mere Christianity*, 176–177).

[10] James Mongomery Boice, *Whatever Happened to the Gospel of Grace* (Crossway Books, 2001), 105.

It is a destructive addition to add anything to Christ.

Richard Sibbes
Puritan Golden Treasury

8

Soli Deo Gloria: Our Only Motive

1 Chronicles 16:23–36; Revelation 5:12

Sing unto the Lord all the earth: declare his salvation from day to day. Declare his glory among the nations, and his wonderful works among all people. For the Lord is great and much to be praised, and he is to bee feared above all gods. For all the gods of the people are idols, but the Lord made the heavens. Praise and glory are before him: power and beauty are in his place. Give unto the Lord, ye families of the people: give unto the Lord glory and power. Give unto the Lord ye glory of his Name: bring an offering and come before him, and worship the Lord in the glorious Sanctuary. Tremble ye before him, al the earth: surely the world shall be stable and not move. Let the heavens rejoice, and let the earth be glad, and let them say among the nations, The Lord reigneth. Let the sea roar, and all that therein is: Let the field be joyful and all that is in it. Let the trees of the wood then rejoice at the presence of the Lord: for he commeth to judge the earth. Praise the Lord, for he is good, for his mercy endureth for ever. And say ye, Save us, O God, our salvation, and gather us, and deliver us from the heathen, that we may praise thine holy Name, and glory in thy praise. Blessed be the Lord God of Israel for ever and ever: and let all people say, So be it, and praise the Lord. (Geneva Bible)

Worthy is the Lamb that was killed to receive power, and riches, and wisdom, and strength, and honor, and glory, and praise. (Geneva)

In the final "sola" of the Reformation, we discover that our only *motive* in all we have seen is to bring God, and God *alone*, glory. All our theology, all our preaching, all our teaching, all that we do and say, is to bring glory to God *alone*. Ephesians 1:6 declares: "To the praise of the glory of his grace, wherein he hath made us accepted in the beloved." *The Geneva Bible* note on that verse reads:

Soli Deo Gloria

The uttermost and chiefest final cause is the glory of God the Father, who saveth us freely in his Son. That as his bountiful goodness deserveth all praise, so also it should be set forth and published.

We turn first to a little history once more. In the days prior to the Reformation, it was only popes, priests, cardinals, monks, and nuns who were considered to be those who honored God. The Reformation shattered that illusion and called such spiritual elitism the lie that it is. The Reformers, for example, cherished marriage and child rearing, which flew in the face of the supposed superiority of celibacy. The people were taught, in fact, that *everything* they did could glorify God, just as Paul wrote to the Corinthians, "Whether therefore ye eat, or drink, or whatsoever ye do, do all to the glory of God" (1 Cor. 10:31) and then to Colossians, "whatever you do in word or deed, do all in the name of the Lord Jesus, giving thanks to God and the Father by him" (Col. 3:17).

What was the result of such revolutionary teaching? The effects on society were astounding. Art, for example, was transformed from merely pictures of saints to ones that celebrated creation and ordinary life, using people, landscapes, flowers, birds, and people at work and play.

Music was also transformed. For 1,000 years, Latin hymnody was devoid of truth, filled with Mariolatry as well as many praises written to the martyrs. The Council of Laodicea (343–381) decreed that only specially appointed singers, usually choirs of monks, could present music sung in Latin. Think of it! *For over a thousand years, the Church did not sing.* It was held that "average people" could not understand or appreciate such holy music and, therefore, could not participate. What an appalling tragedy! They could not even understand what was sung because the common people could not understand Latin. That was a wholesale departure from the obvious fact of congregational singing in the early church.

We should interject here that while music has become the central aspect of worship today, it is extremely significant that it is not even mentioned in the Book of Acts. Yes, we see it referred to later in the Epistles, but it was clearly not central. Sadly, "style of music" is also at the forefront of many churches, but all this has missed the centrality of the pulpit ministry and elevated music to a place to which it has no right to be.

We also note that not only was there the *elevation* of Mary, but also the apostate *lowering* of the nature of God. While God was pictured as an angry, intolerant, and unlovable kind of deity, the Virgin Mary was portrayed as the embodiment of the kindness, humanity, and sympathy, and all that came out in the hymnody of the day.

The Reformation, however, replaced the worship of Mary with the Christian message of the person and work of Christ alone. It improved some of the Latin hymns and produced many new ones. The Reformation brought back congregational singing and replaced the cold, hollow chanting of priests. Because of the Reformation, for example, we have the music of Bach and Mendelssohn. The words *Soli Deo Gloria*, in fact, were carved into the organ at Bach's church in Leipzig, and Mendelssohn penned his *Reformation Symphony* (Symphony No. 5 in D Major) in 1832 in honor of the 300th anniversary of Luther's Augsburg Confession.

The study of science was also a product of the Reformation. Because Roman Catholicism was based more on Aristotle's dualistic view of the universe instead of Scripture, it stifled scientific discovery. The Reformers, however, taught that God has written two books, the book of Nature and the book of the Word and that these two complement the other and are never contradictory. Just one example is, "The heavens declare the glory of God; and the firmament showeth his handiwork" (Ps. 19:1). Here the physical universe (Nature) declares and praises the very God of the Word who made it all.

But once again, our day has spawned a new attack. And once again **Robert Schuller** is at the forefront of this apostasy: "Classical [i.e., Reformation] theology has erred in its insistence that theology be 'God-centered,' not 'man-centered.'"[1] Did you get that? In other words, in his unimaginable arrogance, Schuller clearly states that all those godly Reformers were wrong in starting with God while he is right in starting with man and building a "theology" with man's self-esteem at the core. Of course, to say that theology is man-centered is not only blasphemous but is an oxymoron, the height of contradiction. How in the world can theology (*theos*, God) have anything to do with man? But once again, that is the norm of our day, a fact that was spawned by the Humanism of the Renaissance.

Another example is that instead of self-esteem, other leaders, such as **Rick Warren** and **Bill Hybels**, have decided that "personal fulfillment" is the greatest need and have built their churches on that sandy foundation. As a result, gone today are the truths of sin, wrath, and repentance, and in their place are "felt-needs," love, acceptance, and personal fulfillment. Addressing these issues is also radically different. Doctrine, absolute truth, and expository preaching are out, while entertainment, psychology, motivational "sermons," and other man-centered methods are in.

To summarize the matter, Truth has simply vanished. As a magician performs slight of hand by keeping your attention on one hand while his other does something else, that is what has happened today. While one hand has been mesmerizing the crowds with all kinds of eye-pleasing, flesh-satisfying feats, Truth has been discarded.

Worse, other movements continue to arise. Open Theism, led by **Clark Pinnock** and others, maintains that God does not actually know everything, that He is Himself learning and adjusts His plan and purpose as He goes along. There is also the Emerging Church Movement, which rejects all certainty. It dismisses the possibility of a sure and settled knowledge of

Truth. In fact, to say that we can know anything for sure is actually arrogant to Emergent leaders such as **Rob Bell**, **Mark Driscoll**, **Brian McLaren**, and others.

I would interject here that during final preparation of this book for publication, I came across still another form of such relativism. A noted evangelical sent out a discussion question to the readers of his email network:

> I have received several emails from organizations that want to destroy all other Christianities that differ from them in doctrine. . . . They don't seem to understand that there has never been one monolithic Christianity. At the beginning, in the first century there were great differences in the several Christianities. [There were] Jewish Christians . . . Gnostic Christians . . . Marcion Christians . . . and Roman Imperial Christians. . . . None of the earliest Christianities believed in the virgin birth of Christ. And none believed that Jesus was God. It was not important to them. Even the apostle Paul did not mention the virgin birth or the teachings of Jesus. Anyone that says that they have the true gospel and all others are completely false are very presumptuous. . . . [Likewise today there are] Gay Christians . . . [and] Zionist Christians.

While I usually do not weigh in on such email or Internet discussions, I was so appalled that I felt compelled to do so this time. As I shared with the group, the term "Christianities" is troubling in the extreme. *There is only one Christianity*; it views Christ as God in the flesh who came to save the elect by grace alone, through faith alone, in Christ alone. Many use the term "Christian" when they are nothing of the sort, as in America being a "Christian nation," which nowadays is absurd. There is no such thing as a Gnostic that is a true Christian, much less the idea that Marcion was one or that there are "Gay Christians." And as we have repeatedly demonstrated here in these studies, Catholicism is not biblical Christianity. Yes, many call themselves "Christian" today, but calling a horse a cow, regardless of how loud, passionate, and convinced you might be, does not make it so. Further, to say, "Anyone that says that they have the true gospel and all others are completely false are very presumptuous," is troubling indeed (Gal. 1:8–9). That is clearly Post-Modernism, a "theology" of relativism, doubt, and uncertainty and is apostasy plain and simple.

So, why has the truth vanished? Because, and please get this, *the Reformation has been abandoned*. When that happened, as mentioned in our last study, we gave up the ship. As we will see, these doctrines are the only ones that truly give God glory.

What, then, was the Reformers' point in *Soli Deo Gloria*? Was it man's "felt-needs"? Was it entertainment? Was it man's self-esteem? No! Their driving motive was God's glory. Their point was two-fold.

God *Alone* Must Be Glorified

First Chronicles 16:7–36 is a psalm of thanksgiving and celebration and is actually a compilation of three passages in the Book of Psalms: verses 8–22 are from Psalm 105:1–15; verses 23–33 (quoted earlier) are from Psalm 96:1–13; and verses 34–36 (also quoted earlier) are from Psalm 106:1, 47–48. This repetition suggests the importance of the truths presented here, namely, giving glory to God for what He alone has accomplished, that is: **his deeds** (v. 8), **his wondrous works** (v. 9), **his judgments** (v. 14), and His **word** (v. 15). The whole passage is filled with praising God alone: **Declare his glory** (v. 24), **much to be praised** (v. 25), **Praise and glory are before him** (27), **Give unto the Lord ye glory of his Name** (v. 29), **worship the Lord in the glorious Sanctuary** (v. 29), **Let the heavens rejoice, and let the earth be glad** (v. 31), **Let the sea roar** (v. 32), **let the field rejoice** (v. 32), **the trees . . . rejoice at the presence of the Lord** (v. 33), **Praise the Lord** (v. 34), **that we may praise [His] holy Name** (v. 35), and **glory in [His] praise** (v. 35). Verse 36, therefore, concludes: **Blessed be the Lord God of Israel for ever and ever: and let all people say, So be it, and praise the Lord.**

That is not only what drove the *Reformers* but also the *Early Church*. Throughout Acts and the Epistles, it is God's glory that is preeminent. We defy any modern teacher to cite a single example of the modern concepts of ministry we have referred to several times. Why are there no such precedents? Because they are *man-elevating*, not *God-glorifying*. Scripture is not *anthropocentric* (man-centered), rather *Theocentric* (God-centered), even Christocentric (Christ-centered).

As our second text (Rev. 5:12) then declares, only the **Lamb** is **worthy . . . to receive power, and riches, and wisdom, and strength, and honour, and glory, and blessing.** One does not have to read the Reformers very long to notice how they were virtually obsessed with giving God alone glory, that this was their driving *motive*. While glory today goes to the newest method of ministry, the biggest church, the most book sales, and even the most baptized converts, the Reformers recognized that God *alone*—not the Church, popes, images, saints, Mary—was to receive glory. Even worse in our day is that instead of *God* being *glorified*, it is *people* who are *entertained*. We have become, just as Robert Schuller insists we should, *man*-centered instead of *God*-centered. That truly sums up a large portion of the Church today. We do whatever appeals to people's flesh; we simply give them what they *want* instead of what they *need* and what God *demands*.

God Alone is Glorified Only Through the Other *Solas*

The only way God alone *can* be glorified, the Reformers insisted, is through the other *solas*. To fail in any one of these, in fact, is to rob God of glory. God receives glory only when *Scripture alone* is our authority; popes, councils, and priests, are robbers. God receives glory only when *grace alone* is acknowledged; so-called free will and those who espouse such humanistic rubbish are robbers. God receives glory only when *faith alone* is established; works and human effort are robbers. God receives glory only when *Christ alone* is recognized; sacraments are robbers.

With that firmly entrenched in our minds, let us briefly summarize the glory of the Doctrines of Grace, the only doctrines of salvation that give God alone *all* the glory for salvation.[2] We submit, Arminianism is a robber. To conclude our series, let us note five ways the Doctrines of Grace alone give glory to God alone.

Man's Depravity Gives God Glory

Arminianism, which as we have seen is thoroughly Roman Catholic and has been rejected repeatedly through the ages as heresy, teaches that although human nature was seriously affected by the fall, man has not been left in a state of total spiritual helplessness. Man's will has not been en-slaved in his sinful nature, rather he has a free will, which is free to choose good over evil in spiritual matters. While the sinner does need the Spirit's help to be *saved*, he does not need the Spirit's help for *believing*, for faith is man's act only and is man's contribution to salvation. Is God glorified by such teaching? Certainly not.

What Scripture teaches is man's total depravity and inability to turn to God, which demands God's intervention. As stated in an earlier study, "To speak of a sinner as totally depraved does not mean that he is as bad as he could possibly be, but rather that sin contaminates the totality of his be-ing."[3] The reason is because he is spiritually dead, as Ephesians 2:1–3 clearly states. A dead man cannot do anything, including believe. As we have noted, while many teachers insist on running to the term "free will," the irrefutable fact is that this term appears in the New Testament only in the context of stewardship (e.g., 2 Cor. 8:1–4); it *never* appears in the con-text of coming to Christ in faith. The Scripture's entire emphasis regarding the will is its *bondage*, not its freedom. Romans 3:11–18 clearly shows that man runs from God, in no way ever seeks God, and does nothing to please God.

What must happen, therefore, for man to receive the Gospel? The answer is simple: *salvation is all of grace*. When His disciples asked Him who can be saved, Jesus answered: *"With men it is impossible*, but not with God: for with God all things are possible" (Mk. 10:27). If that does not emphasize man's total inability, nothing does. Man contributes absolutely nothing to his salvation. As Luke tells us: "For the Son of man is come to seek and to save that which was lost" (Lk. 19:10). Can a lost item find itself? No, it takes an outside power to find it.

The Apostle John also makes it clear that salvation comes totally from outside man:

> No man can come to me, except the Father which hath sent me draw him: and I will raise him up at the last day. . . . And he said, Therefore said I unto you, that no man can come unto me, except it were given unto him of my Father (Jn. 6:44, 65).

Additionally, after writing of man's spiritual death and inability in Ephesians 2:1–3, Paul then writes in verses 4–6 about God's intervention:

> *But God*, who is rich in mercy, for his great love wherewith he loved us, Even when we were dead in sins, hath *quickened us* [i.e., made us alive, and here is the doctrine of regeneration] together with Christ, *(by grace* ye are saved;) And *hath raised us up* together, and made us sit together in heavenly places in Christ Jesus: That in the ages to come *He might show* the exceeding riches of his grace in his kindness toward us through Christ Jesus (emphasis added).

We submit, therefore, it is in only in this view that God *alone* is glorified.

The Full Grace of Salvation Gives God Glory

Arminianism teaches that God chose certain individuals for salvation before the foundation of the world based on His foreknowledge that they would believe. He chose for salvation those whom He knew would, of their own free choice, choose to believe in Christ. This view says, therefore, that election is not based on God choosing us but us choosing God. In the final analysis, then, salvation is not based solely on God's grace but on our faith. But is God glorified in such an idea? Certainly not.

What Scripture teaches, as we just read in Ephesians 2:4–6, is that salvation is the work of God *alone*. Man is nowhere to be found in that passage, nor is man anywhere to be found in Romans 8:29–30, which speaks *only* of what God has done: "foreknow," "predestinate," "called," "justified," and "glorified." Only God is doing something here, and it is for this reason we say that the Doctrines of Grace are the real heart of Christianity, Christianity in its purest form but have repeatedly been attacked because men simply do not like them. Throughout the history of the Church these doctrines have been the real power of Christianity. Why? Compare the Doctrines of Grace to *any* religion. Not one of them speaks this way because they are all of man. Only the Doctrines of Grace emphasize that *salvation is all of God.*

The word "chosen" in Ephesians 1:4 is pivotal. It is the Greek *eklegō*, which carries the basic meaning "to pick out, choose, select for one's self." Most importantly, however, is the fact that this is in a construction in the Greek (middle voice) that indicates that God did the choosing independently in the past and did so *primarily* for His own interest, that is, His glory. While modern Arminian evangelism is based on what "God will do for you," the biblical truth is our salvation is primarily for *God's* glory, not ours. Why don't we preach that today? The answer is obvious: because it doesn't serve man, address his felt needs, or make him feel good about himself. Verses 6, 12, and 14, however, bear this out with full force, for they all emphasize the words "*His* glory" (emphasis added). Foreseen faith is *not* the basis for election ("foreknowledge," *prognōsis*, in 1 Pet. 1:2, simply does *not* mean merely precognition, regardless of who insists it does[4]). Election speaks *only* of an action done by God in the *past*, not on man's faith in the *future*.

Woven into the very fabric of Scripture, in fact, is this principle of God's election for His glory. To list only a few: Deuteronomy 10:14–15; Psalm 33:12; 65:4; Matthew 11:27–28; 22:14; Luke 4:25–27; John 15:16; 17:6; Colossians 3:12; and we could go on. It is only in this view that God *alone* is glorified.

The Result of the Cross Gives God Glory

Arminianism teaches that the atonement of Christ provided *potential* salvation that becomes effective only to those who believe. Christ died for all men without *exception*, but only those who believe are saved. Jesus' death, then, didn't really accomplish salvation, rather its power is only potential. But is God glorified in such an idea? Certainly not.

What was the result of the cross? What did it actually accomplish? Did it actually do anything? *The cross accomplished our redemption.* While it is obvious that Christ died in the past, what is the depth of that truth? Did His death simply make redemption *possible*, that is, possible if we believe? If that is true, then the *cross* itself did not actually save us, rather it was our *believing* that saved us. This, of course, cannot be. The truth is that Christ's death did not provide *potential* redemption, rather *actual* redemption. *It was the cross that saved us.*

Ephesians 1 bears this out with irresistible force. As we can see, all three members of the Godhead are present. The Father chose us before the foundation of the world (vs. 3–4), a choice that was not *potential* but *actual.* Second, the Son's death redeemed us from our sins (v. 7), again a redemption that was not *potential* but *actual.* Third, the Holy Spirit applies the death of Christ (vs. 13–14), once again an application that is not *potential* but *actual.* Therefore, at all three points the work of the Godhead is *effectual*, that is, *each actually does something.* The work of each is not something that is *virtual*, but something that is *real.*

Now ponder the outworking of this. First, was the sinner saved when the Father chose him? *Yes*, though not yet in the sinner's personal experience. Second, was the elect sinner saved when Christ died? *Yes*, though not yet in the sinner's personal experience. Third, is the elect sinner saved when the Holy Spirit applies the merits of Christ's death? *Yes*, and this time it *did* happen in the sinner's personal experience. It is only in this view that God *alone* is glorified.

The Power to Believe Gives God Glory

Arminianism teaches that man's will is free, he is the deciding factor in salvation. The matter is totally up to him. Faith is man's contribution to salvation and is what makes salvation possible. The Holy Spirit can draw to Christ only those who allow Him to do so. But is God glorified in such an idea? Certainly not. **James Montgomery Boice**, in fact, once again makes a very strong statement. He submits that one

> category of people who cannot say "to God alone be glory" are Arminians. Unfortunately, they are the vast majority of those who call themselves evangelicals in our day, which is a major cause of the problems that beset the evangelical church. Arminians believe in grace. They want to glorify God. Indeed, they can and do say "to God be glory," but they cannot say "to God *alone* be glory," because they insist on mixing human will power or ability with the human response to gospel grace.[5]

What Scripture teaches is that there are two calls of God to men. The first call is the *general* call (or *external* call). It is to this our Lord refers in Matthew 22:14: "For many are called, but few are chosen." While there is a call to all men to believe, however, it is equally clear that the majority of people reject this call. In fact, as we preach and witness, the Gospel often hardens a person even more.

The second call of God, however, which we find primarily in the Epistles, is the *effectual* call (or *inward* call). This call is the inward call of the Holy Spirit that draws the elect one to God. Our Lord alludes to this in John 6:44: "No man can come to me, except the Father which hath sent me draw him."

Why is this effectual call necessary? Because of man's depravity, this drawing follows of necessity. As we have seen, man is in darkness and even in death, so God had to call us in a *very special way*. After all, how can a dead man hear a call at all? God had to create the ability for us to respond. What is this effectual call? It is this: the Word of God comes with such power of the Holy Spirit that God's chosen ones are brought to life and drawn to God. God effectually draws to Himself those who belonged to Him from before the foundation of the world. It is only in this view that God *alone* is glorified.

The Security of Grace Gives God Glory

Arminianism teaches that those who believe and are truly saved can lose their salvation when they sin. But we ask one more time, is God glorified in such an idea? Certainly not.

What Scripture teaches is that man is secure in God's grace. There is probably no other picture concerning the Holy Spirit's work in salvation that is more graphic than that of *sealing*. Turning to Ephesians 1 once again (which is only one reason Ephesians is my passion), we read, "In whom ye also trusted, after that ye heard the word of truth, the gospel of your salvation: in whom also after that ye believed, ye were sealed with that holy Spirit of promise, Which is the earnest of our inheritance until the redemption of the purchased possession, unto the praise of his glory" (vv. 13–14).

The concept of sealing is quite ancient. In fact, we can trace this concept back a millennium or more before Christ. Herodotus (c.484–525 B.C.), the first of the great Greek historians, wrote in his *History* that ancient man possessed not only his staff but his seal. The Greek verb used here is *spragizō*, "to set a seal; mark with a seal," and comes from the noun *spragis*, which refers to a signet ring that had a distinctive mark. There are many illustrations of sealing. We can see many of these by looking at four pictures that this term provides. While space doesn't permit examining *acquisition*, *absolute ownership*, and *authenticity*, let us look briefly at *assurance*.[6]

The spiritual parallel is staggering. The Holy Spirit's sealing seals us *eternally* in Christ. The verb tense is past in all three New Testament references that refer to sealing. Ephesians 4:30 declares, that we are "sealed [in the past] for the day of redemption" (see also 2 Cor. 1:21–22). Does this say, "God sealed us temporarily until we sin our way out?" No, it says, "God sealed us in the past until the day we are redeemed into glory." It is only in this view that God *alone* is glorified.

Conclusion

I cannot emphasize strongly enough how pivotal these doctrines are. To reject them is to reject the very core, heart, and soul of Christianity. Here is the typical view of our day, which comes from a reviewer one of **Steven J. Lawson's** books on this subject. Please be warned—we are going to encounter that really "scary" term that upsets so many people nowadays, *Calvinism*:

> Dr. Lawson's work makes frequent use of the same fallacious language which, again, is all too characteristic among those of his persuasion. At various points in the book, he uses terms such as "sound doctrine" and "Biblical truth" as if they are automatically synonymous with Calvinism, which they are certainly not! Similarly, he describes the modern church as being "spiritually bankrupt" and a "whitewashed tomb." While the Church certainly does have its problems, such broad generalizations are both unfair and inaccurate.[7]

That well summarizes the attitude of much (if not most) of today's church. Most people are clueless that our Christian heritage has all but vanished. In stark contrast, here is what **Charles Spurgeon** preached almost 150 years ago when introducing his Bible conference on "Exposition of the Doctrines of Grace," held on April 11, 1861:

> It may happen this afternoon that the term "Calvinism" may be frequently used. Let it not be misunderstood, we only use the term for shortness. That doctrine which is called "Calvinism" did not spring from Calvin; we believe that it sprang from the great founder of all truth. . . . We use the term then, not because we impute any extraordinary importance to Calvin's having taught these doctrines. We would be just as willing to call them by any other name, if we could find one which would be better understood, and which on the whole would be as consistent with fact.[8]

It is for that very reason that I personally prefer the term Doctrines of Grace, for that is what they are, and they are, indeed, true, biblical Christianity. Spurgeon himself made this clear when he, in no uncertain terms, preached that these doctrines are biblical truth and Arminianism is the heresy:

> I have heard it asserted most positively, that those high doctrines [of grace] which we love and which we find in the Scriptures, are licentious ones. I do not know who has the hardihood to make that assertion, when they consider that the holiest of men have been believers in them. I ask the man who dares to say that [these Doctrines of Grace are] a licentious religion, what he thinks of the character of Augustine, or Calvin, or Whitfield, who in successive ages were the great exponents of the system of grace; or what will he say of those Puritans, whose works are full of them? Had a man been an Arminian in those days, he would have been accounted the vilest heretic breathing; but now we are looked upon as the heretics, and they the orthodox. *We* have gone back to the old school, *we* can trace our descent from the Apostles. It is that vein of free grace running through the sermonising of Baptists, which has saved us as a denomination. Were it not for that, we should not stand where we are. We can run a golden link from hence up to Jesus Christ himself, through a holy succession of mighty fathers, who all held these glorious truths; and we can say to them, where will you find holier and better men in the world? We are not ashamed to say of ourselves, that however much we may be maligned and slandered, ye will not find a people who will live closer to God than those who believe that they are saved not by their works, but by free grace alone.[9]

Charles Spurgeon

If that is not clear enough, in his autobiography, Spurgeon viewed these doctrines as the very heart of the Gospel, the one and only *true* Gospel. He wrote "that there is no such thing as preaching Christ and Him crucified, unless we preach what nowadays is called Calvinism." He went on to comment on the words "salvation is of the Lord" in Jonah 2:9:

> That is an epitome of [the Doctrines of Grace]; it is the sum and substance of [them]. If anyone should ask me what I mean by a Calvinist, I should reply, "He is one who says, Salvation is of the Lord." I cannot find in Scripture any other doctrine than this. It is the essence of the Bible. "He only is my rock and my salvation." Tell me anything contrary to this truth, and it will be heresy; tell me a heresy, and I shall find its essence here, that it has departed from this great, this fundamental, this rock-truth, "God is my rock and my salvation." What is the heresy of Rome, but the addition of something to the perfect merits of Jesus Christ—the bringing in of the

works of the flesh, to assist in our justification? And what is the heresy of Arminianism but the addition of something to the work of the Redeemer? Every heresy, if brought to the touchstone, will discover itself here.[10]

We submit that it is only in these doctrines is God *alone* glorified. While these doctrine upset (and even anger) some Christian teachers, it is hard to understand why. Why get upset when it is God alone who is getting the glory? With that in mind, we close with this statement on *Soli Deo Gloria*, as stated in The Cambridge Declaration of the Alliance of Confessing Evangelicals on April 20, 1996:

> We reaffirm that because salvation is of God and has been accomplished by God, it is for God's glory and that we must glorify him always. We must live our entire lives before the face of God, under the authority of God and for his glory alone.
>
> We deny that we can properly glorify God if our worship is confused with entertainment, if we neglect either Law or Gospel in our preaching, or if self-improvement, self-esteem or self-fulfillment are allowed to become alternatives to the gospel.

That statement challenges not only Arminians, as mentioned earlier, but even strong adherents to the Doctrines of Grace, to do all for God's glory *alone*. We can get so caught up in our methods, programs, personal success, and even our loyalty and defense of our denomination, that we get the credit for ourselves instead of God alone. All we do must be to that end. As Paul wrote to the Corinthians, a proud, self-confident group:

> For ye see your calling, brethren, how that not many wise men after the flesh, not many mighty, not many noble, are called: But God hath chosen the foolish things of the world to confound the wise; and God hath chosen the weak things of the world to confound the things which are mighty; And base things of the world, and things which are despised, hath God chosen, yea, and things which are not, to bring to nought things that are: *That no flesh should glory in his presence.* But of him are ye in Christ Jesus, who of God is made unto us wisdom, and righteousness, and sanctification, and redemption: That, according as it is written, *He that glorieth, let him glory in the Lord.* (1 Cor. 1:26–31 emphasis added)

In closing this part of our study, oh, that the five *solas* of the Reformation would be burned into the hearts and minds of God's people today! These are not just the tenets of the Reformation; they are the very pillars of Christianity itself. My dear Christian Friend, without them, we are doomed; not only is salvation impossible, but the Church has no foundation. Let us embrace them, defend them, and proclaim them. Why? For only they give God *alone* glory.

As we close, then, let us each ask ourselves this question: Do I want to be a product of the Reformation, or just a casualty of innovation?[11]

NOTES

[1] Robert H. Schuller, *Self-Esteem: The New Reformation*, 64.

[2] For a deeper study of the Doctrines of Grace, see the author's two books: a basic study in *The Doctrines of Grace from the Lips of Our Lord: A Study in the Gospel John* (Wipf & Stock Publishers, 2012); and a deeper study in *Salvation is of the Lord: the Doctrines of Grace Expounded By a Former Arminian* (Sola Scriptura Publications, to be released 2013).

[3] Robert Spinney and Justin Dillehay, *Not the Way I used to Be: Practical Implications of the Bible's Large doctrine of Regeneration* (Tulip Book, 2007), 2

[4] First Peter 1:1–2 declares: "Peter, an apostle of Jesus Christ, to the strangers scattered throughout Pontus, Galatia, Cappadocia, Asia, and Bithynia, Elect according to the foreknowledge of God the Father, through sanctification of the Spirit, unto obedience and sprinkling of the blood of Jesus Christ: Grace unto you, and peace, be multiplied." Arminians insist that "foreknowledge" simply means "precognition," that God simply knew who would believe and elected them accordingly.

It is, however, a fact of the language that that is not what the Greek *proginoskō* ("foreknowledge") means. To argue otherwise is foolish. The root *ginoskō* means "to know by experience" and is practically synonymous with love and intimacy. Joseph, for example, "did not know" Mary before Jesus was born, that is, they had not yet been physically intimate (Matt. 1:25). The prefix *pro*, when used of time, adds the ideas of before, earlier than, or prior to. The fact that it does not mean precognition is beyond all doubt when we read another verse in this same chapter, one often either overlooked or ignored: "[Christ] verily was foreordained [*proginoskō*] before the foundation of the world, but was manifest in these last times for you" (v. 20). Obviously this doesn't mean that God simply foresaw that Christ would be manifested. Rather, He was, as we are, foreordained and foreknown by an intimate relationship before the foundation of the world. In other words, foreknowledge is not to *foresee* but to *"fore-love."* This is exactly what we see when we read what God said to Jeremiah: "Before I formed thee in the belly I *knew* thee; and before thou camest forth out of the womb I sanctified thee, and I *ordained* thee a prophet unto the nations" (Jer. 1:5, emphasis added). What a thought that is! Christ knew us in the elective and saving sense before we even existed.

[5] James Mongomery Boice, *Whatever Happened to the Gospel of Grace* (Crossway Books, 2001), 167.

[6] For a detailed study, see chapter 22, "The Sealing of the Holy Spirit," in the author's *Truth on Tough Texts: Expositions of Challenging Scripture Passages* (Sola Scriptura Publications, 2012), 220–233.

[7] James H. Boyd in a reader review of Steve Lawson's book *The Expository Genius of John Calvin* (Orlando: Reformation Trust, 2007), Amazon.com.

[8] *The Metropolitan Tabernacle Pulpit*, Vol. 7, Sermon #385, 546 (*Ages Digital Library, Spurgeon Collection*).

[9] *The New Park Street Pulpit*, Vol. 1, sermon #22, p. 312–313 (*Ages Digital Library, Spurgeon Collection*).

[10] Charles Spurgeon, *C.H. Spurgeon's Autobiography* (Passmore and Alabaster, 1897), vol. 1, 172.

[11] For deeper study, see the author's *The Doctrines of Grace From the Lips of Our Lord: A Study in the Gospel of John* (Wipf & Stock, 2013) and *Salvation Is of the Lord: The Doctrines of Grace Expounded by a Former Arminian* (Sola Scriptura Puvblications, 2013).

We also highly recommend the following: James Boice, *Whatever Happened to the Gospel of Grace?* (Crossway Books, 2001); Boice, *The Doctrines of Grace: Recovering the Evangelical Gospel* (Crossway, 2002); Stephen J. Lawson, the "A Long Line of Godly Men" series (Reformation Trust, 2006, 2011, etc.); Tom Nettles, *By His Grace and For His Glory*, Revised and Expanded 20th Anniversary Edition (Founders Press, 2006).

We glorify God when we are God admirers; admire His attributes, which are the glistening beams by which the divine nature shines forth.

Thomas Watson
Body of Divinity

Part III:

Other History Lessons

9

Target: Historical Evangelical Christianity*

Jude 3

Beloved, when I gave all diligence to write unto you of the common salvation, it was needful for me to write unto you, and exhort you that ye should earnestly contend for the faith which was once delivered unto the saints.

The previous section is actually a precursor to this chapter. There we considered the Reformation and the five tenets of that pivotal event in Church History, that is, the five "*solas,*" which can be summarized thusly:

> It is *Scripture* alone that declares that salvation comes by *grace* alone, through *faith* alone, in *Christ* alone, by which *God* alone is glorified.

As we also noted, so pivotal, so essential, so axiomatic are these truths that neither the Reformation nor Christianity itself can in any way be understood apart from them. These are, in fact, the very pillars of Christianity.

Jude 3 **exhort[s]** us to **earnestly contend for the faith which was once delivered unto the saints.** The word **faith** is not a verb here; that is, it is not describing the *action* of faith. Rather, it is a noun referring to the body of revealed truth that constitutes *Historical Evangelical Christianity.* This does not mean an entire system of theology on which we all can agree; that would be impossible. Rather it refers to the unique revelation of God through Christ. Specifically, this body of truth is the very essence of the Gospel, the redemption by blood and salvation by grace alone, through faith alone, in Christ alone (cf. Rom. 1:16–17), and it is upon that we *must* agree.

First, and foremost, this faith is *historical*. The words **once delivered** demonstrate this historical aspect. Literally translated this phrase reads,

---

* This chapter was originally TOTT issue #62, September 2010. While parts of this reprint have been deleted because such material appears elsewhere in this book, some new material has been added.

"Once-for-all delivered" and, of course, is referring to the preaching and teaching of the apostles as the historical base of our faith (Acts 2:42).

Even more instructive is the meaning of the word **delivered**. The Greek *paradidōmi* carries the basic meaning "to hand over; deliver up," but when used in a context such as Jude, it means "to hand down, pass on instruction from teacher to pupil" and also "conveys the idea of handing down tradition."[1] Other examples of this idea are found elsewhere in Scripture (1 Cor. 11:2; 11:23; 15:3).

So our faith is historical. We can look at many religions, cults, systems, and "faiths," but not one of them is truly historical, that is, based on historical fact and historical event, except Christianity. Our faith is not mystical, hypothetical, or philosophical. It is historical! It is based upon the historical event of the death, burial, and resurrection of Jesus Christ.

Second, this faith is *evangelical*. This term refers to believing in what we call the "evangel," a word that describes "the Gospel message." "Gospel" is *euangellion*, which literally means "good message" (or good news; English "evangelism" and "evangel"). W. E. Vine defines it perfectly, "The good tidings of the Kingdom of God and of salvation through Christ." It is also interesting to observe that even though Jude did not write about salvation *directly* (as he intended), he nonetheless writes about it *indirectly*. He writes about contending for the **faith**, but which faith? The Gospel message, the glorious salvation in Jesus Christ.

Third, this faith is *Christianity*. This is self-explanatory. Christianity is not only *implied* here in verse 3 but it is *stated* in verse 4, "The only Lord God, and our Lord Jesus Christ."

Jude, therefore, declares that we must **earnestly contend** for this historic faith. Those two words are a single word in the Greek, *epagōnizomai*, which appears only here in the New Testament. The root *agōn* (English *agony*) means "strife, contention, [a] contest for victory."[2] It, along with the verb *agōnizomai*, originally referred to the fighting and struggle involved in the Greek games. By adding the prefix *epi* ("for"), Jude is telling us that we must fight *for* the faith. Like Paul in Ephesians 6:10–20, Jude uses graphic imagery to show us the spiritual war in which we are engaged, an all-out agonizing war that gives no quarter to error or those who propagate it.

Why does Jude **exhort** (*parakaleō*, the act of comforting and encouraging, as well as addressing someone with exhortation, entreaty, and instruction) us to **earnestly contend for the faith**? *Because of apostasy*, which sets the stage for the remainder of the letter. Likewise, as never before, Christians today need to **contend for the faith**.

With this text ever on my mind, I recently began considering various trends within the Church that have occurred since the Reformation. I began to wonder what each of those movements actually attacked and found something very interesting, not to mention disturbing. I discovered, in fact, that through the centuries it has consistently been those very doctrines of the Reformation that have been repeatedly attacked by trend after trend, movement after movement, heresy upon heresy. I also realized that this fact makes perfect sense, for these pillars must be torn down before any false teaching can begin building its imitation.

With that in mind, let us again observe a little history and note some of those trends and how they attacked the foundation of **the faith which was once delivered unto the saints.**

The Council of Trent

On the very heels of the Reformation came the first attack upon its doctrines at the Council of Trent, which met in three sessions (1545–47, 1551–52, and 1562–63). One historian puts it well: "*Everything* the Protestant Reformation stood for was vigorously—one could almost say violently—rejected at Trent" (emphasis added).[3] As noted in the quotations we cited in our earlier studies, *sola fide* was especially targeted by Trent, *sola gratia* was redefined, and *Solus Christus* was blasphemously perverted in the Mass. As we have irrefutably demonstrated, to insist that Roman Catholicism is Christianity, as many do today, is ludicrous in the extreme.

The Roman Inquisition

If Trent was the *roar* of the beast, The Inquisition was its *teeth*. Actually beginning before Trent, any open profession of Protestantism in Italy was suppressed. Those who did not flee were subject to imprisonment, torture, and death. While Catholic apologists have often tried to minimize the significance and severity of the Inquisition, insisting that very few were actually directly affected, the evidence overwhelmingly proves otherwise. From such straightforward torments as strangulation and burning to unspeakably sadistic and creative tortures, thousands, in fact, were so treated. It would nauseate some readers to even describe some of them here.

The Inquisition also introduced an "Index" listing prohibited books, which included every word the Reformers wrote, as well as all Protestant Bibles. "There was no appeal to the Word of God," writes one historian, "no turning to the old paths, no repentance from dead works, and no belief in the basic doctrine of justification by faith."[4] The tenets of the Reformation, and biblical Christianity itself, were an enemy to be banned, burned, and buried. And that has not essentially changed to this very day.

A common torture during the Inquisition

James Arminius

As we have also detailed in previous studies, **Pelagius** (c. 360–420), **John Cassianus** (c.360–435), and **James Arminius** (1560–1609) all attempted to soften what they viewed as harsh. Feeling that viewing man as fallen in every respect, including the will, was too radical an idea, they each adjusted this doctrine to better conform to human sensitivities. They all said basically the same thing, namely, man's will is free.

So serious is such error that preacher and hymn writer **Augustus Toplady**—best known for his hymn "Rock of Ages"—pulled no punches in his condemnation of it.

> "Our God is in the heavens: he hath done whatsoever he pleased" [Ps. 115:3]. This is not the Arminian idea of God: for our free-willers and our chance-mongers tell us, that God does not do whatsoever he pleases; that there are a great number of things, which God wishes to do, and rags and strives to do, and yet cannot bring to pass. They tell us, as one ingeniously expresses it: "That all mankind He fain would save, But longs for what He cannot have. Industrious, thus, to sound abroad, A disappointed, changing God."
>
> Is their god the Bible-God? Certainly not. Their god "submits" to difficulties which he "cannot help" himself out of, and endeavors to make himself "easy" under millions and millions of inextricable embarrassments, uncomfortable disappointments, and mortifying defeats. . . . This said scheme ascends, on the ladder of blasphemy, to the mountain top of atheism; and then hurls itself from that precipice, into the gulch of blind, adamantine necessity, in order to prove mankind free agents![5]

John Owen

One can hardly mention these issues without turning to **John Owen** (1616–1683), the greatest of the Puritans. *A Display of Arminianism* was Owen's first publication (1642) in which he challenges us to "proclaim 'a holy war' to such enemies of God's providence, Christ's merit, and the powerful operation of the Holy Spirit." Strong language? Yes, but unlike the majority of the Church today, Owen recognized the true nature of such doctrine. He went on to outline in detail that Arminians

> exempt themselves from God's jurisdiction . . . deny the eternity and unchangeableness of God's decrees . . . depose the all-governing providence of this King of nations . . . deny the irresistibility and uncontrollable power of God's will . . . deny original sin and its demerit . . . deny the efficacy of the merit of the death of Christ . . . [and even] grant some to have salvation quite without [Christ], that never heard so much as a report of a Savior.[6]

So it has been that in each era there were those who rose up against error, those who did **earnestly contend for the faith which was once [for all] delivered to the saints**. It is not the doctrine of Arminius and his followers that is Historic Christianity. *It is the doctrine of Sovereign Grace that has stood through the ages as the core truth of the Christian Faith.*

In spite of all the biblical and historical evidence, however, it is happening once again! Sadly, proving something wrong doesn't make it go away, and the same was true of Arminianism. On the contrary, Arminianism entrenched itself into theological thought. In his Introduction to Luther's classic, *The Bondage of the Will*, J. I. Packer wrote: "The present-day Evangelical Christian has semi-Pelagianism in his blood."[7] Indeed, countless evangelicals hold the Arminian view because they fail to stop and just think what the words "for by grace are you saved" really mean. Arminianism (historically and today) is nothing but warmed-over Roman Catholicism, with which we can have absolutely no compromise, regardless of what many "evangelicals" are saying to the contrary. While there are a few who are standing and condemning this fourth attack, their voices are being overpowered by the sheer mass of Arminian preachers and teachers who sell Jesus like they sell shoes, tell people to "walk the aisle" and "say this prayer," elevate man's "self-esteem," and have turned the Gospel into just another commodity to market.

The Age of Reason

While also referred to as The Enlightenment, the title "Age of Reason" better summarizes the era from 1648–1789. While the noted philosopher **Immanuel Kant** (1724–1894) was not one of its early pioneers, he was nonetheless a major proponent and provides us with what is probably the best definition of that age:

Immanuel Kant

> Enlightenment is man's emergence from his self-imposed immaturity. Immaturity is the inability to use one's understanding without guidance from another. This immaturity is self-imposed when its cause lies not in lack of understanding, but in lack of resolve and courage to use it without guidance from another. *Sapere Aude!* [Dare to know!]—"Have courage to use your own understanding!"—that is the motto of enlightenment.[8]

In a key turning point in the history of philosophy, and even theology itself, *reason* ultimately trumps *revelation*. Commenting on Kant's definition, Harold O. J. Brown puts it well:

Inasmuch as Christianity is by its very nature a religion of divine revelation, one that presupposes that human reason needs guidance and in fact is guided by God's revelation, it is apparent that Kant's principle is totally incompatible with Christianity.[9]

So, which tenet of the Reformation was at stake here? *Sola Scriptura*, the "formal principle," of course. No longer was the *revelation* of the *Creator* our starting point and authority, rather the *reason* of the *creature* was now the beginning and end of all things. Once revelation is thrown out, game over.

Now, we might be tempted here to think, "Ah, well, that was just the world; the Church was a different matter." Oh, if only that were true! As **Francis Schaeffer** (1912–1984) writes:

Francis Schaeffer

> The teachings of the Enlightenment became widespread in the various faculties of the German universities, and *theological* rationalism became an identifiable entity in the eighteenth century. Then gradually this came to full flood through the German theological faculties during the nineteenth century. Thus, though the Reformation had rid the Church of the humanistic elements which had come into the Middle Ages [via the Renaissance, *ed.*], a more total form of humanism entered the Protestant church, and has gradually spread to all the branches of the Church (emphasis in the original).[10]

As the Enlightenment continued, the doctrines of Historical Evangelical Christianity were diluted, denied, and denounced wholesale in venue after venue. One of the first casualties of German rationalism was the doubting of the historical text of Scripture. Led by one German rationalist after another—Johann A. Bengel (1687–1752), Johann J. Griesbach (1745–1812), J. S. Semler (1725–91), Samuel P. Tregellas (1813–1875), etc.—Lower (Textual) Criticism rejected the historic (providentially preserved) text and went in search of the "authentic text," which could only be discovered by reason, not revelation. For these men, and many others who followed, *sola Scriptura* was an outdated idea of the Reformation and certainly not relevant in the Age of Reason. So persuasive were those teachers, that even that great defender of the faith, **B. B. Warfield** (1851–1921), was swayed after studying textual criticism under German rationalists.[11]

With its *text* successfully challenged, the next casualty was Scripture's *historicity*. This was the full-blown Higher (Historical) Criticism, fueled again by the Enlightenment's German rationalism and helmed by such men as: Heinrich Paulus (1761–1851), Karl Graf (1815–1869), Abraham

Kuenen (1828–1891), Julius Welhausen (1844–1918), and others. Miracles were now denied, historical facts were challenged, and even something as easily verifiable as the Mosaic authorship of the Pentateuch was rejected. By now *sola Scriptura* was barely even a memory from the long ago days of "naïve and childish authoritarianism." Man was now "enlightened" and could think for himself.

Most tragic of all, however, *Christianity has never escaped the Age of Reason*. Just as the Renaissance tried to blend together Aristotle with Christianity (via **Thomas Aquinas**; see pages 17–19, 52), so others blended together the rationalism of the Enlightenment, and once that batter was mixed, there was no separating the ingredients.[12]

Charles Finney

The 19th-century so-called "revivalist" **Charles Finney** (1792–1875), has become virtually the "patron saint" of modern evangelism and founder of Pragmatism. His errors, however, are almost unimaginable. Finney was, in fact, no less than a full-blown Pelagian; he rejected the Doctrines of Grace in their entirety, along with any semblance of orthodoxy; he denied original sin, the substitutionary atonement, justification, and the need for regeneration by the Holy Spirit. In his *Autobiography*, in fact, he wrote:

Charles Finney

"Instead of telling sinners to use the means of grace and pray for a new heart, I call on them to make themselves a new heart and spirit." Further, as one historian recounts, while Scripture clearly indicates that revival comes down from heaven by the sovereign bestowing of the Spirit of God, and in that sense "prayed down," Finney taught that it could be "worked up."[13]

Finney also invented the modern staple of evangelism that we call the "altar call," in which he would pressure people to "make a decision for Jesus," "a commitment to Christ," and other clichés we have adopted as though they were based on Scripture. "Finneyism" is, in fact, one of the major contributors to today's predominantly Arminian theology. Since doctrine always works itself out in practice, the practice of Arminianism demonstrates its serious doctrinal errors. In the end, Finney's methods were an abject failure. Out of thousands of "conversions," by his own admission, true conversions were very few. And again, the sad fact is that Evangelicalism is still suffering from Finneyism.

Modern Trends

It goes without saying that every cult and false religion in the world rejects the foundational doctrines of the Reformation. Without a single exception, the five *solas* and the historical Doctrines of Sovereign Grace are nowhere to be found in any such false system. When those pillars are removed, no truth remains, and anything goes.

Nothing has changed on that note right to our present day. We have seen this several times already in previous studies, noting false teachers of our day who have joined the ranks of those who came before them. It would require a separate book to outline the scores of other false prophets, heretical doctrines, and apostate teachings that inundate the Church today. We have touched on only a few.

For the rest we resubmit part of a statement by Charles Spurgeon quoted in a previous study. He insisted that the Doctrines of Grace, the historical truths we have been emphasizing here, are "the essence of the Bible. Every heresy, if brought to the touchstone, will discover itself here."[14] Indeed, every heresy through the ages and today is rooted right there. Look at any false teaching, examine any unorthodox doctrine, consider any so-called "innovation," and at its foundation you will find a rejection of the historic doctrines of Christianity. When man has a wrong view of God, a wrong analysis of man, and a wrong way of salvation, literally anything is possible. We see error everywhere we look, and it is all because of the same reason: the rejection of the Truth.

Conclusion: Christianity's Core

As Ephesians 2:4–10 declares, salvation is the work of God *alone*. Man's input is nowhere to be found in that passage, as is also true of Romans 8:29–30. God *alone* is acting, and it is for this reason that we say the Doctrines of Grace are the very core of Christianity, Christianity in its purest form, but have repeatedly been attacked because men simply don't like them. Throughout the history of the Church these doctrines have been the real power of Christianity. Why? Compare the Doctrines of Grace to *any* religion. Not one of them speaks this way because they are all of man. *Only the Doctrines of Grace emphasize that salvation is all of God, and are always the first doctrines to be jettisoned by the false teacher.*

At the risk of being redundant, the pivotal nature of these doctrines simply cannot be overstated. To reject them is to reject the very core, heart, and soul of Christianity.

Postscript: Error, Schism, and Heresy

By Puritan Thomas Adams

"There is difference betwixt error, schism, and heresy. Error is when one holds a strong opinion alone; schism when many consent in their opinion; heresy runs further, and contends to root out the truth. Error offends, but separates not; schism offends and separates; heresy offends, separates, and rageth. . . .

"Error is weak, schism strong, heresy obstinate. Error goes out, and often comes in again; schism comes not in, but makes a new church; heresy makes not a new church, but no church. . . . Error untiles the house, schism pulls down the wall, but heresy overturns the foundation. . . .

"Error will hear reason, schism will wrangle against it, heresy will deny it. . . . Error is reproved and pitied, schism is reproved and punished, heresy is reproved and excommunicated. Schism is in the same faith, heresy makes another faith. . . . Though they be thus distinguished, yet without God's preventing grace, one will run into another. . . . The heretic exceeds the schismatic; the one hates only peace, the other hates truth."[15]

NOTES

[1] Colin Brown, *The New International Dictionary of New Testament Theology* (1975, 1986), Vol. 3, 772–773.

[2] Spiros Zodhiates, *The Complete Word Study Dictionary: New Testament* (AMG Publishers, 1992), entry #73.

[3] Bruce Shelly, *Church History in Plain Language*, 3rd Edition (Thomas Nelson, 2008), 277.

[4] S. M. Houghton, *Sketches from Church History* (Banner of Truth Trust, 1980), 61.

[5] From "The Golden Idol of Freewill " and "The 'god' of Arminianism."

[6] John Owen, *A Display of Arminianism* (Still Water Revival Books, 1989 reprint), 7, 12–14.

[7] "Historical and Theological Introduction," *The Bondage of the Will*, p.58.

[8] *Was ist Aufklärung* ["What is Enlightenment"]?—the title of Kant's 1784 essay in the December 1784 publication of the *Berlinische Monatsschrift* [*Berlin Monthly*].

[9] Harold O. J. Brown, *Heresies: Heresy and Orthodoxy in the History of the Church* (Hendrickson, 1998), 397.

[10] *How Should We Then Live?* (Fleming H. Revell, 1976), 175.

[11] See chapter 8, "What's *Really* At Stake in the Textual Issue," in the author's *Truth on Tough Texts: Expositions of Challenging Scripture Passages* (Sola Scriptura Publications, 2012).

[12] Still another casualty of The Enlightenment is Bible prophecy by way of the popular eschatological view called Preterism (Latin *preater*, "past" and *ire*, "to go," that which has gone past or belongs to the past), which places many or all prophetic events in the past, especially during the destruction of Jerusalem in AD 70. While *never* the historical view of the Church, mild forms arose in the 16th-century but were actually rejected by more orthodox teachers, such as the Huguenots. It was then in the 1800s that full Preterism emerged as just one more product of German rationalism. The same movement that rejected supernatural revelation and hatched the eggs of both Lower Criticism and Higher Criticism, also gave birth to Preterism. Why? Because it fit their model. Preterism was a perfect way to avoid predictive prophecy and give a naturalistic interpretation to the Book of Revelation by comparing it with the apocalyptic literature of the Aprocypha and Pseudepigraphra. As it then spread from Europe to Britain to the United States, it began influencing men such as J. Stuart Russell (1816–1895) and Moses Stuart (1780–1852), whose works delineated the modern forms of Preterism. By the 1970s, it gained enough momentum to form the foundation of the Christian Reconstruction movement. (For a more detailed analysis of Preterism, see issue #82 ["The Perils of Preterism"] in the author's monthly publication, *Truth on Tough Texts*, at www.TheScriptureAlone.com).

[13] Houghton, 219.

[14] Charles Spurgeon, *C.H. Spurgeon's Autobiography* (Passmore and Alabaster, 1897), vol. 1, 172.

[15] Thomas Adams, *Exposition Upon Second Epistle General of St. Peter*, (Henry G. Bohn, York Street, Covent Garden, 1633), 211.

We don't need to be in the novelty shop, as much as we need to be in the antique shop, where we find the old truths of God's Word. We don't need something new today half as much as we need something so old that it would be new if anybody tried it.

Vance Havner
Interview with Dennis Hester

10

"Once More Unto the Breach" (1)*

Ephesians 6:11 & 13

Put on the whole armour of God, that ye may be able to stand against the wiles of the devil. . . . Wherefore take unto you the whole armour of God, that ye may be able to withstand in the evil day, and having done all, to stand.

To introduce and illustrate our theme, I would like to recall a scene from what has gradually become my favorite of Shakespeare's plays, the historically accurate *Henry V*. While one famous scene is Henry's rousing speech at Agincourt (Act V, Scene 3), there is another earlier in the play that more than equals that drama.

In the Prologue to Act III, Henry sails from England with a large fleet of warships, lands in France, and lays siege to the port city of Harfleur on the northern coast (very near, in fact, the shores where five centuries later the allies would land in Normandy). The cannons roar as the terrifying battle rages against the city walls. To make peace, the anxious King Charles offers Henry his daughter Katherine in marriage, along with a few insignificant dukedoms (small sub-regions within France) as part of her dowry. Henry rejects the offer out of hand and the siege continues, ultimately leading to a staggering victory. As the English army prepares to storm the city, Henry's words ring out, part of which are as follows:

> Once more unto the breach, dear friends, once more;
> Or close the wall up with our English dead.
> In peace there's nothing so becomes a man
> As modest stillness and humility:
> But when the blast of war blows in our ears,
> Then imitate the action of the tiger;
> Stiffen the sinews, summon up the blood,
> Disguise fair nature with hard-favored rage.
> . . .
> . . . Let us swear
> That you are worth your breeding, which I doubt not,
> For there is none of you so mean and base

---

* This chapter was originally TOTT issue 77 (May/June 2012).

> That hath not noble luster in your eyes.
> I see you stand like greyhounds in the slips,
> Straining upon the start. The game's afoot.
> Follow your spirit, and upon this charge
> Cry "God for Harry, England, and Saint George!"[1]

While that's pretty clear English even for our day, for those who still struggle with Elizabethan prose, here's a modern "translation":

> Attack the breach in the city wall once more, dear friends, attack it once more—or else let's close it up with English corpses. In peacetime, nothing looks better in a man than restraint and humility. But when the battle trumpet blows in our ears, then it's time to act like the tiger. With muscles taut and blood stirred up, hide your civilized nature under the guise of [hard-featured] rage. . . . Prove you are worthy of your birth, which I do not doubt for a moment. For there isn't one of you so low-born that your eyes don't shine with noble luster. I see you're standing like greyhounds on a leash, straining for the moment when you'll be let loose. The hunt is on! Follow your spirit, and as you charge cry, "God for Harry, England, and Saint George!"[2]

Now, while I am in no way trying to glorify war (or English history for that matter), this does vividly illustrate the war that Christians are, in fact, engaged in and how we should respond to that chilling reality.

Turning to our text, in these well-known verses about spiritual warfare, Paul first instructs us, **Put on the whole armour of God, that ye may be able to stand against the wiles of the devil**. The words **stand against** are *stēnai pros*, a military expression that means to stand in front of with a view to holding a critical position, to hold one's ground. Further, **able** is *dunamai* (Eng. "dynamic"), which can be defined as "that which overcomes resistance." By putting on God's armor, we are **able** to defeat any resistance Satan offers and overcome any obstacle he puts in our path, whether it be moral, spiritual, or even doctrinal.

The idea here, then, is a primarily defensive tone, that we just face the enemy and hold our ground. This is further indicated by the fact that God has given us five pieces of *defensive* armor (vs. 14–17a) while giving only one *offensive* weapon, the sword (v. 17b).

There is something else here, however. It's extremely significant that Paul not only says that the armor makes us able to *stand* against Satan's attacks (v. 11), but he adds in verse 13: **Therefore take up the whole armor of God, that you may be able to *with*stand in the evil day, and having done all, to stand** (emphasis added). The Greek is actually different here. The root behind "stand" is *histemi*, while the word for **withstand** is *anthistemi*, which means "to set oneself against, oppose, resist." This is the same word used in James 4:7, "Resist the devil, and he will flee from you." In light of the defensive word we saw earlier, this word is more offensive in tone. Not only must we be *defensive*, holding our present ground, but we must also be *offensive*, landing blows of our own on the enemy. Militarily speaking, no battle, no war, can be won by defense alone. God not only wants us to stand our ground, but He wants us to resist and oppose and land blows of our own with the Word of God.[3]

How we need men today who will, indeed, cry, "Once more unto the breach," and then lead the attack! Why? Because "the game's afoot"! The parallels here, in fact, are amazing. How many men today are willing to end up a corpse in the rubble in the fight for Christianity? We are not in peacetime, so we cannot afford stillness and restraint. The trumpet has sounded for war and we have to wage it with tenacity, for after all, we wield not just "a sword" but the Sword of the Spirit, which is the Word of God! Taking prisoners, in fact, is not an option. While our nature remains civilized, and we certainly speak the Truth in love, this is still in the "the guise of [hard-featured] rage" against untruth. Further, how many men today truly "are worth [their] breeding," that are fulfilling the demands God has set forth for leaders? How many are, indeed, "stand[ing] like grey-hounds in the slips, straining upon the start"? And what should be our cry as we charge into the breach by the power of the Holy Spirit? *Soli deo Gloria*!

Let us contemplate history once again. Have there been men who have stood in that breach? Indeed there has. Here are just six that immediately come to mind.

Charles Spurgeon & Robert Shindler

I can think of no better illustration to begin with than what **Charles Spurgeon** (1834–1892) faced in his day, namely, the Down-Grade Controversy. The Controversy began in 1887 as a result of several articles that appeared in Spurgeon's magazine, *The Sword and the Trowel*, which referred to the Modernism that had crept into the Baptist Union. Spurgeon was deeply troubled by the Higher Criticism,[4] the deemphasis on preaching, the decline of the historic doctrines of salvation,[5] the resultant diluting of the faith, and the general attitude of Pragmatism of the age.

In the March and April issues, **Robert Shindler**, a fellow Baptist pastor and close friend of Spurgeon, wrote two articles about these trends. In the first article, he cited how numerous liberal beliefs, such as Rationalism,[6] Unitarianism,[7] Socinianism,[8] Arianism,[9] and Arminianism,[10] had replaced the pure Gospel preached and lived by the Puritans. He also cited the coldness and lifelessness of preaching even among evangelicals, as well as their willingness to fellowship with those who were teaching false doctrine.

Even more important was Shindler's second article. He continued his outline of the decline of Christianity, but even more critical was *the reason he offered that such a decline occurred.* He submitted that the Down-Grade was being caused by the same thing that caused similar declines throughout history. It was not due to doubting some particular doctrine or calling into question some principle of orthodoxy; rather *the first step astray is a want of adequate faith in the divine inspiration of the sacred Scriptures.*

Shindler hit the proverbial nail on the head. Historically, the Word of God is the first casualty in any war on Christianity. It must be this way, for once the authority of any system is destroyed, whether it be a religious system, political system, or any other system, then that system will crumble. In a very real sense, Christianity has never recovered from the Down-Grade. It resulted in attack after attack: Lower (Textual) Criticism, Higher (Historical) Criticism, Modernism, Neo-Evangelicalism, Pragmatism, Relativism, Open Theism, and the Emergent Church. Where are we headed next?

Spurgeon went further to lay the blame for this departure from the faith at the feet of the same ones who are to blame today, namely,

Charles Spurgeon

preachers, men who, for whatever reason, refuse to preach the Truth, the whole Truth, and nothing but the Truth. He wrote: "Too many ministers are toying with the deadly cobra of 'another gospel,' in the form of 'modern thought.'" As a result, he was criticized and ostracized as one who was "unloving," "narrow-minded," and "divisive," words we often hear today about anyone who preaches doctrinal purity. In response to the criticism, Spurgeon gathered even more proof and wrote in the September issue, "A chasm is opening between the men who believe their Bibles and the men who are prepared for an advance upon Scripture." After many appeals to the Baptist Union for reform, and after careful thought and much prayer, Spurgeon withdrew.

Instead of that being the end of the matter, the Baptist Union sent a delegation of four doctors of divinity who met with Spurgeon on January 13, 1888 to ask him to rethink his withdrawal and to seek a way to maintain unity. Spurgeon boldly replied that he would do so if an evangelical statement of faith were drawn up, unlike the existing statement that required a member to believe only in baptism by immersion. The Union flatly refused to do so, and five days later not only voted to accept

Spurgeon's withdrawal, but also voted on a resolution to condemn what he had done. The resolution passed by a vote of 2,000 to 7! Friends and even students in his Pastor's College turned against him, once again illustrating that the majority is often wrong and that people *will* become our enemies simply because we tell them the truth (Gal. 4:16).[11]

Neither Spurgeon nor Shindler hesitated for a moment to go "once more unto the breach." Are we willing? How many pastors today agree with these words from Spurgeon?

> I sometimes think if I were in heaven I should almost wish to visit my work at the Tabernacle, to see whether it will abide the test of time and prosper when I am gone. Will you keep in the Truth? Will you hold to the grand old doctrines of the Gospel? Or will this church, like so many others, go astray from the simplicity of its faith, and set up gaudy services and false doctrines? Methinks I should turn over in my grave if such a thing could be. God forbid it![12]

Athanasius

Returning to the Arianism mentioned above, most Christians (and sadly many preachers) are totally unaware just how crucial the 4th-century was for Christianity. Arius, a parish priest in Alexandria, taught that Jesus was not coequal with God and was, in fact, a created being. Upon proclaiming his views concerning Christ's Deity in 313, Arius' teaching ignited controversy in Alexandria. By 318, the conflict had grown hostile and bitter. While Arius and his followers were condemned at a local church council in Alexandria in 321, the fight was far from over. False teaching is never so easily defeated. From Alexandria, their teaching spread all over Christendom. As well-known church historian Philip Schaff put it:

> Bishop rose against bishop, and province against province. The controversy soon involved, through the importance of the subject and the zeal of the parties, the entire church, and transformed the whole Christian East into a theological battle-field.[13]

The Roman Emperor Constantine badly wanted the conflict to end, probably more for the strength of the empire than for any spiritual reason. To that end, he called the famous church-wide Council of Nicea in 325, where over 300 bishops convened to settle the controversy. Constantine read several letters from bishops about the issue and urged everyone to find a way to unify. Many were willing to compromise on the nature of Christ, but one man was not, a man whom God, in His eternal providence, strategically placed there for that very moment. That man's name was **Athana-**

sius (293–373), a young 23-year-old theologian, also from Alexandria, who fiercely debated Arius, a man 40 years his senior. It was, indeed, David taking on Goliath. In the end, Athanasius was triumphant, which lead to the most basic of all the creeds of the Church, the Nicene Creed, which reads in part:

> We believe in . . . one Lord Jesus Christ, the only-begotten Son of God, begotten of the Father before all worlds; God of God, Light of Light, very God of very God; begotten, not made, being of one substance with the Father . . .

But again, the war had only begun. While only three men (Arius and two followers) refused to sign the creed, many others who did sign were still tolerant of Arians, not wanting to call anyone a "heretic." Some even

twisted the language of the Creed to say that Arianism really could fit into the wording. As a result, Athanasius was mercilessly persecuted. During his 46 years as bishop of Alexandria and his tireless and inflexible opposition to Arianism, he spent a total of 20 of those 46 years on the run, being exiled five times, usually because Arians were in political control, and enduring false charges that ranged from witchcraft to murder. It was because of all that, in fact, that the phrase *Athana-*

Athanasius

sius contra mundum (against the world) arose. He stood virtually alone against almost overwhelming defection from orthodoxy. It is not an exaggeration to say that were it not for Athanasius, who has been dubbed "The Father of Orthodoxy," we might all be Arians today.

Like Spurgeon, Athanasius also provides another challenge for us today. He refused to compromise the Truth for any reason. He rejected such ideas that we today have dubbed "Post-modernism," the "Emerging Church," "Post-evangelicals," and other terms. He would have grieved over popular platitudes as: "Christ unites us, but doctrine divides us." Or, "It's not *propositions* that matter but *people* that matter." All such things are nothing but a smoke screen that hides error.

So, while the vast majority of Christians today have never heard of Athanasius, he is one of the great illustrations of the *providence* of God, the *power* of Truth, and the *perseverance* of courage. He was not afraid for a moment to go "once more unto the breach." Are we?

J. Gresham Machen

Princeton Seminary (founded in 1812) was once a pillar of Christianity, where men such as Archibald Alexander, Charles Hodge, and A. A.

Hodge championed the historical faith. Another great warrior, who taught New Testament literature and exegesis for 15 years (1914–1929) was **J. Gresham Machen** (1881–1937).

J. Gresham Machen

Like a virus, however, Modernism crept into Princeton via German Rationalism. As we have noted before, even the celebrated B. B. Warfield (1851–1921), another Princeton giant, was infected.[14] Like Warfield, Machen went to Germany, spending a year studying the New Testament under German scholars. It was there that he was exposed to the virus of destructive biblical criticism and was almost infected, especially by the strong influence of theologian Wilhelm Herrman.

Thankfully, however, Machen came out on the other side stronger for his struggle. So it was that when Princeton was reorganized in 1929 according to modernistic influences, Machen departed, along with three other powerful warriors—Robert Dick Wilson, Oswald T. Allis, and Cornelius Van Til—and founded Westminster Theological Seminary. Why? Because he felt compelled to fight the blatant unbelief that had crept into the Church, for Princeton Seminary was, in fact, the flagship of the General Assembly of the Presbyterian Church (PCUSA). His two books—*Christianity and Liberalism* (1923) and *What is Faith?* (1925)—were a devastating critique of Protestant Modernism.

What was the Church's response? The same reaction that always results when Truth is leveled against error. He was put "on trial" and ejected from the Church. Undaunted, however, he went on to become the principal figure in the founding of the Orthodox Presbyterian Church (OPC).

What does Machen's example say to us today? Plenty! One does not have to be a Presbyterian to recognize the threat of Modernism or its descendent that plagues us today—*Post-modernism*. Because of the abject failure of the rationalistic approach of Modernism, Post-modernism throws all that off and dismisses the possibility of a sure and settled knowledge of Truth. It is a sad commentary on the Church today when men who call themselves evangelicals not only tolerate but embrace the Relativism of the so-called Emergent Church. Machen fearlessly went "once more unto the breach." Do any of us have such conviction to do likewise?

John Huss

Dying, ironically, in the same year that Henry V landed in France, **John Huss** (1369–1415) has rightly been called a "Pre-reformer." The same is true of John Wycliffe (c.1328–1384), "The Morning Star of the Reformation."

What Wycliffe had been to England, Huss became to Bohemia (what we today call the Czech Republic). Educated at the University of Prague, he was ordained a priest in 1401 and occupied the most influential pulpit in the city, Bethlehem Chapel. While a loyal Roman Catholic, he had the same desire for doctrinal purity and church reform that Wycliffe had championed in England. He even translated Wycliffe's famous work *Trialogue* into Bohemian, which boldly declared that

> holy Scripture was the highest authority for every believer, the standard of faith and the foundation for reform in religious, political and social life. . . . In itself it was perfectly sufficient for salvation, without the addition of customs or traditions such as canon law, prayers to the saints, fastings, pilgrimages or the Mass.[15]

This electrified Bohemia, and the masses rallied around Huss. By 1410, Pope Alexander V issued a papal bull ordering the surrender and burning of all Wycliffe's writings. Huss refused to relinquish his copies and was summarily excommunicated but continued writing and preaching in Bethlehem Chapel. With pressure steadily growing and the threat of a horrible death ever looming, he refused to be deterred.

John Huss

In his two memorable books, *De Ecclesia* (*On the Church*) and *De Sex Erroribus* (*On the Six Errors*) he attacked transubstantiation, subservience to the pope, the popular belief in saints, the efficacy of the absolution by a priest, unconditional obedience to earthly rulers, and simony.[16] In 1414, he was summoned to the Council of Constance with the solemn promise from King Wenceslaus, Emperor Sigismond, and the Pope of safe passage and treatment to and from the council. Within a month, however, he was arrested and cast into the dungeon in the Dominican convent—such are the promises of Satan and his minions. After months of "investigations," the final trial came. Upon being confronted with his "heresies" and demands that he recant, Huss replied that he could do so only if he could be proven wrong from Scripture. As the flames burned around him he sang out, "Christ thou Son of the Living God, have mercy upon me."

One more historical note is significant. In the Prague Library, there is a hymn to Huss' memory, dating from 1572, with three medallions pictured. On the first medallion is a picture of Wycliffe striking sparks against a stone. On the second, Huss kindles a fire from the sparks. The third depicts Luther holding aloft a flaming torch. Are we not thankful for these three men who courageously went "once more unto the breach"? We are left to ask: as future generations look back on our era, will they see any such men?

The burning of John Huss

Thomas Cranmer

While we could fill many more pages with examples,[17] one more will have to suffice for now. We end with a study in contrast, a man who was actually quite different from our other pictures. Were it not for such contrast, in fact, he would be little more than a footnote in history.

Thomas Cranmer (1489–1556), while an English Reformer, was also a man of compromise. King Henry VIII wanted to divorce Catherine of Aragon—since she had failed to give him a male heir—and marry Anne Boleyn, but the Pope would not give him permission to do so. In desperation, Henry broke with the Pope and the Roman Catholic Church and looked for someone who was willing to accept his claim that he had never been married to Catherine according to God's Law. The man he found was Cranmer, who he ultimately appointed Archbishop of Canterbury.

Thomas Cranmer

While Henry was never a true Protestant—he opposed Luther, for example, and continued to defend Catholicism—he was not without a merit or two. For one, he was instrumental in stripping the Church of the secular powers it had wielded for centuries. For another, William Tyndale's dying prayer—"Lord open the eyes of the King of England"—was answered through Henry. To improve his image and lift his dignity, he was persuaded by Cranmer, as well as Thomas Cromwell, to publish *The Great Bible*, which in-turn was the result of the labors of Miles Coverdale, was 70-percent Tyndale's genius, and was the forerunner of both the Geneva Bible[18] and the King James Version.

Sadly, in addition to the above compromise, Cranmer, also sanctioned Henry's further marriages and divorces, as well as secretly taking a wife for himself and keeping her in seclusion until late in his life. There was a positive side, however. He greatly aided the Reformation in England. He welcomed other Reformers from Europe, cooperated in removing images from churches, renounced the authority of the pope, replaced the Roman Catholic Missal (Service Book) with the English *Book of Common Prayer*, and introduced Coverdale's Bible to the churches and encouraged its circulation, even writing the Preface, urging everyone to read, memorize, and live by Scripture. He also spoke out against masses for the dead, prayers to the saints, pilgrimages, and celibacy.

It was when Mary Tudor (Bloody Mary) ascended the throne in 1553, however, that compromise again overtook Cranmer. While Mary hated all Protestants—she burned nearly 300 at the stake, including children—she hated Cranmer in particular. She had never forgiven him for his part in annulling the marriage of her mother Catherine and Henry VIII, as well as his preference of Protestant Lady Jane Grey, a distant relative of the Royal line, for the throne instead of her. He was arrested and imprisoned in the tower in London. In the hope of leniency, Cranmer signed seven documents recanting most of his Protestant views and accepting the doctrines of Catholicism.

But, thankfully, one final reversal lay ahead. On the morning of Saturday, March 21, 1556, wood was piled in the middle of Broad Street in Oxford. Cranmer was bought forth and allowed to make a statement to the crowd, no doubt to further humiliate him. While no one doubted for an instant that he would use his last moments to recant his "heresies" and return to the "Holy Mother Church," he stunned all present by announcing that in signing a recantation of his former beliefs, his hand had "offended in writing contrary to his heart." He then continued, "Therefore, my hand shall first be punished, for if I may come to the fire it shall be first burned. And as for the Pope, I refuse him as Christ's enemy, and Antichrist, and all his false doctrines." He then actually ran to the stake. As the flames rose around him, he kept his vow. He thrust his right hand into the flames, leaving it there until it charred, and repeated the following words as long as he was able: "This unworthy right hand. This hand hath offended."

So, while Thomas Cranmer faltered and compromised, in the end he did, indeed, go "once more unto the breach." His martyrdom—along with Nicholas Ridley and Hugh Latimer six months earlier—solidified the Reformation in England.

This prompts us again to ask, *What of us today?* How many evangelicals have signed documents in recent years that are nothing but compromises with Rome and other errors equally heinous? How many continue to falter, waver, and hesitate concerning the historic truths of the Faith? How many are "reevaluating" and "renegotiating" the very truths on which Christianity stands?

Well, like Cranmer, it is not too late for any of us to go "once more unto the breach."

A Closing Request

I would close with a humble request. If you agree with the message presented in this chapter and are likewise burdened, I would deeply appreciate hearing from you.[19] My reason is simple: that we might pray for one another (Job 42:10) and then encourage one another (1 Thes. 5:11; Heb. 3:13) to go "once more unto the breach, dear friends, once more." As David prayed: "He hath delivered my soul in peace from the battle that was against me: for there were many with me" (Ps. 55:18).

NOTES

[1] *Henry V*, III.1.1–8, 27–34

[2] *No Fear Shakespeare: Henry V* (Spark Notes), 89–90. I inserted "hard-featured" instead of "ugly." Webster's 1828 dictionary defines "hard-favored" as, "Having coarse features; harsh of countenance."

[3] The three preceding paragraphs are from the author's book, *A Word for the Day: Key Words from the New Testament* (AMG Publishers), 276.

[4] An attack on the authority of the Bible by denying its historical accuracy.

[5] In contrast to Arminianism, recognizes man's total depravity and helplessness in sin and God's total sovereignty in salvation.

[6] The belief that reason, apart from any outside authority, such as the Bible, is the only guide.

[7] Holds that Jesus was merely human, human character can be perfected, the Bible has a natural not supernatural origin, and all souls will ultimately be saved.

[8] Rejected the pre-existence of Christ, the propitiatory view of atonement, and puts a limitation on God's omniscience.

[9] Denies the full deity of Christ.

[10] In contrast to Calvinism, elevates man's "free will" over God's sovereign choice in salvation. Teaches that God chose people for salvation based on His foreseeing that they would believe.

[11] For a deeper study of the Down-Grade, see Iain Murray's excellent book, *The Forgotten Spurgeon* (The Banner of Truth Trust).

[12] *Metropolitan Tabernacle Pulpit*, Vol. 23, 514.

[13] *History of the Christian church*, Vol. 3, Ch. IX, § 119.

[14] See chapter 8, "What's *Really* At Stake in the Textual Issue?" in the author's *Truth on Tough Texts: Expositions of Challenging Scripture Passages* (Sola Scriptura Publications, 2012), 99–112.

[15] G. H. W. Parker, *The Morning Star* (The Paternoster Press, 1965), 43.

[16] *Simony* is the act of paying for sacraments and consequently for holy offices or positions in the hierarchy of a church; named after Simon the Sorcerer (Acts 8:9–24).

[17] We would recommend the book, *A Treasury of Evangelical Writings*, compiled and edited by David Otis Fuller (Institute for Biblical Textual Studies).

[18] It is common knowledge that Shakespeare used the Geneva Bible in his plays. In fact, there are numerous echoes from Isaiah in *Henry V*. It appears that he actually used "the text of the Geneva Isaiah and its [annotations] to create a medieval backdrop for his Renaissance drama." See this interesting study, "Shakespeare's *Henry V* & the Geneva Bible," by John Knoeple, at: http://www.illinoismedieval.org/ems/VOL6/knoepfle.html.

[19] Email: sspmail1521@gmail.com. USPS: PO Box 235; Meeker, CO; 81641.

11

"Once More Unto the Breach" (2)*

Ephesians 6:11 & 13

Put on the whole armour of God, that ye may be able to stand against the wiles of the devil . . . . Wherefore take unto you the whole armour of God, that ye may be able to withstand in the evil day, and having done all, to stand.

At the risk of belaboring the point made in the previous chapter—but actually at the request of some readers—I would dare remain here for one additional installment. As we noted, Henry V's cry, "Once more unto the breach," as offered by Shakespeare, vividly illustrates the war in which we too are engaged, as a study of the language in Ephesians 6:11 and 13 indicates. Using six great figures from Christian history, we then demonstrated the challenge that lies before us to stand for biblical truth, whatever the cost.

To demonstrate that those are not just a few isolated incidents, I would share five more, the last of which is very close to home, indeed, for it happened within the first decade of this century.

Gottschalk of Orbais

Our first mini-biography is of a man we dare say very few Christians today have ever heard of. It was the age of **Charlemagne** (Charles the Great) but also a period known as the Dark Ages in the Mediterranean world because of 400 years of darkness under the Goths. When Pope Leo III crowned Charlemagne "Emperor of the Romans," however, light began to filter in. Under his leadership—he reigned from 800–814—culture was reborn, including fair government, art, literature, education, and even scholarship. While his empire declined after his death due to his weak son and warring

Augustine

grandsons, Charlemagne actually laid the foundation stones for the Renaissance that would come 500 years later.

---

* This chapter was originally TOTT issue 78 (July/August 2012).

Interestingly, while Charlemagne professed to be Christian, his morals would seem to indicate otherwise. He did, however, greatly enjoy **Augustine's** works, especially *City of God*. Such great works came into new focus during this period of renewal.

A man who was forever changed through his own study of Augustine was German **Gottschalk of Orbais**[1] (c. 808–869). As one might imagine, with the rebirth of intellectual pursuit introduced by Charlemagne, controversy was inevitable, and this age brought several great theological debates, including: images, the Trinity, the nature of the soul, the virginity of Mary, the Eucharist, and others. No doubt the greatest storm of all, however, raged around the question of God's sovereignty in salvation, and it was Gottschalk who brewed the storm.

Gottschalk of
Orbais

Born in Mainz, his parents dedicated him early to a monastic life, insisting he take such vows. While he tried to get released from his vows upon reaching maturity, he was denied. As a concession, he was allowed to relocate from the then famous monastery in Fulda to the one in Orbais in northeast France. It was there he devoted himself to the study of not only Augustine but also another North African bishop, Fulgentius of Ruspe. Both had strongly taught the doctrine of God's sovereignty over all things, including man's salvation.

As joy overcomes every believer who embraces the Doctrines of Grace, it seized Gottschalk as well, compelling him to excitedly and passionately begin preaching and teaching them. As is also always the case, men by nature rebel against the absolute sovereignty of God. The attack upon Gottschalk came first from theologian **Rabanus Maurus**, who had actually been the head of the monastery school in Fulda and Gottschalk's teacher. He was thoroughly Semi-Pelagian in his theology, which is still at the core of Roman Catholic theology today.[2] Maurus did everything he could to defame, discredit, and denounce Gottschalk. In response, Gottschalk emphasized Maurus's Semi-Pelagianism (a doctrine condemned at the Synod of Orange in 529) and accused him of denying the sovereignty of God in saving grace. Further, Maurus propagated the view that election is based upon God foreseeing a person's faith, which clearly makes man the determining factor in salvation, not God. The firestorm was thus ignited.

Called upon to appear before two Synods (one at Mainz and another at Chiersy), Gottschalk was interrogated and required to give an account of his teachings. While accused of heresy, he never wavered. He was then publicly flogged to the point of death, his books were burned, and he was imprisoned in the monastery of Hautvillierss near Rheims. It was there he spent the last 20 years of his life. Why? Think of it! Just because he believed in the absolute sovereignty of God.

Please consider this: Is it not appalling, indeed, that because of the Arminianism (Semi-Pelagianism) that permeates Christianity today, many evangelicals would actually find themselves siding with Roman Catholicism against Gottschalk? Are there any who will, with Gottschalk, go "once more unto the breach?"

John Wycliffe

In a passing reference to **John Wycliffe** (c. 1328–1384) in part 1, we noted he has rightly been called a "Pre-reformer" and dubbed with the title, "The Morning Star of the Reformation." No truer words have ever been spoken. More than 100 years before Luther nailed his 95 Theses to the church door at Wittenburg—the act that ignited the Reformation—it was Wycliffe who struck the spark. In fact, he anticipated Luther's teaching and was, like Luther, a doctrinal Reformer.

John Wycliffe

While born in Yorkshire, Wycliffe was educated and spent most of his life in Oxford, beginning in his sixteenth year. Possessing a brilliant mind, he mastered liberal arts as well as theology, ultimately earning a Doctor of Divinity degree and teaching at Oxford for 40 years. Called upon to serve the crown, first as a diplomat and then a polemicist against French interests, his flawless logic led him to argue for limitations on any institution, secular or religious, and that none should overstep boundaries established by God. Particularly at issue were taxes levied by the Papacy and the temporal authority of the Pope. Also, as Augustine had taught centuries before, Wycliffe declared that the true church was comprised of all elect believers, not just the Pope and bishops, and that true believers' lives will produce fruit, a fact not evident in the lives of many bishops and even the Pope himself.

Additionally, Wycliffe maintained that Scripture is the authoritative center of Christianity (note a quotation from his *Trialogue* in the John Huss section of part 1), the claims of the papacy unhistorical, monasticism irredeemably corrupt, and that the immorality of priests invalidated their office.

As controversial as all that was, however, the most notable issue for Wycliffe was transubstantiation. The real fury came against him when he publicly repudiated the doctrine that the bread and wine miraculously turned to the body and blood of Christ, even writing a list of theses of why this was unscriptural. Just as **Athanasius** stood alone in the 4th-century on the Deity of Christ (see part 1), so Wycliffe was a solitary voice a millennium later on another pivotal doctrine. While he was popular with the common people—this fact kept his enemies from physically attacking him—he was abandoned by the heads and fellows of various colleges at Oxford and even by the king himself, who had once greatly admired him.

Escaping persecution by retiring to his parish in Lutterworth, Wycliffe lived out his days in relative peace. It was also there that he undertook his famous work of translating the Latin Vulgate into Middle English. But Rome's hatred for him never abated. As one Roman Catholic historian ranted about him: "that instrument of the devil, that enemy of the Church, that author of confusion to the common people, that image of hypocrites, that idol of heretics, that author of schism, that sower of hatred, that coiner of lies."[3]

So deep was this hatred, in fact, that he was physically attacked *after* his death. While he died of a paralytic stroke late in 1384, the Council of Constance declared him in May of 1415 to have been a stiff-necked heretic and decreed that his books not only be burned, but that his remains be dug up and burned and the ashes cast into the River Swift. Such is the hatred towards those who are willing to go "once more unto the breach."

Girolamo Savonarola

While Italian explorer Christopher Columbus was sailing the high seas in search of a passage to India, another Italian was sailing a very different sea and heading for a far more important destination. In contrast

to Wycliffe and Huss, who were concerned with the *doctrinal* apostasy in the Church, another "Pre-reformer," **Girolamo Savonarola** (1452–1498), more directly attacked its *moral* apostasy. Though an obscure and little remembered figure in history, Savonarola was one of the greatest reformers, teachers, preachers, politicians, and philosophers in the history of Christianity.

Girolamo
Savonarola

Born in Ferrara about 30 years before Luther, Savonarola's family planned that he would enter the medical field, but he entered the monastic life instead. Becoming noteworthy for his zeal and piety in the monastery in Bologna, he moved on to Florence at the age of 38. There he developed into a powerful speaker, drawing large crowds that heard his pointed criticism of the corruption among both clergy and laity. His "sermons were like the flashes of lightning and the reverberations of thunder," historian Philip Schaff writes. "It was his mission to lay the axe at the root of dissipation and profligacy."[4] While Florence was the center of Renaissance science, art, literature, and philosophy, it was also a den of vice and spiritual darkness. Through Savonarola's preaching on sin, repentance, and turning to Christ, Florence became a place of revival, although Romanism still maintained a strong grip.

A significant figure at that time was Lorenzo the Magnificent, the head of the famous House of Medici and ruler of Florence. The Medici family had no love for Savonarola's teaching and high morals, so Lorenzo tried to silence his preaching with favors and gifts, but to no avail. Upon Lorenzo's death, his son succeeded him, but the people overthrew the Medici family and chose Savonarola as their ruler. He set out to wholly reform the city, but many resented the strictness that went along with his vision of a truly Christian commonwealth. New laws were passed against gambling, improper dress, adultery, homosexuality, and public drunkenness. In a great "bonfire of vanities," cards, dice, immoral books and pictures, carnival costumes, and even jewelry, dresses, wigs, mirrors, and cosmetics were stacked in a pyramid 60 feet high and 240 feet in circumference at its base and set ablaze.

As one can imagine, such extremes invited opposition, not only from some of the people but the Pope himself, Alexander VI. A man with no moral values or scruples, he tried to bribe Savonarola into silence by offering him the "red hat" of a cardinal, to which he responded by saying the only red hat he wanted was that of a martyr, "a hat reddened with blood." He was, in fact, passionate in his accusations against the Pope. He wrote letters to the kings of England, France, Germany, Hungary, and Spain in which he charged the Pope with scandal, sacrilege, simony, and other sins, including even atheism, and asked the kings to help him in reform.

Upon intercepting the letter addressed to Charles VIII, the Pope denounced Savonarola and excommunicated him. After extensive plotting, a mob seized him, bound and beat him, and then turned him over to the civil authorities. The city fathers pressed him to withdraw his charges against the Pope, but he refused and was subjected to sadistic torture with the full approval of Alexander. As Schaff describes it, "Savonarola was bound to a rope drawn through a pulley and, with his hands behind his back, was lifted from the floor and then by a sudden jerk allowed to fall. On a single day, he was subjected to 14 turnings of the rope." Delirious with pain, he once confessed but quickly recovered his senses and reversed himself.

Finally, while no credible charges could be brought against him, letters from Rome stated that the commission had instructions "to put Savonarola to death, even if he were another John the Baptist." A mock trial was convened and the execution set. The sentence was death by hanging, after which his body was to be burned and the ashes thrown into the River Arno.

Now, while we do not deny Savonarola's extremes—he claimed the gift of prophecy, condoned wives leaving their husbands for the convent, and even dreamt that the city might reach such perfection that all marrying would cease—we nonetheless recognize him, as did Luther, as a pioneer of the coming Reformation. No one in his day stood as he did for righteousness and against hypocrisy. He refused any course other than the one leading "once more unto the breach."

A. W. Tozer

Like many Christian readers who have heard of **A. W. Tozer** (1897–1963)—who preferred to be addressed simply as "Tozer"—I first became acquainted with his writing through his classic book, *The Knowledge of the Holy*. While there have been many books on the attributes of God, none blends theology and spirituality together better than Tozer's.

Other than that classic work, however, I read almost nothing else of Tozer in my first two and a half decades of full-time ministry. I have since

A. W. Tozer

made up for that deficiency. One day one of the lambs under my care handed me a copy of *God Tells the Man Who Cares* and said, "After reading this I thought it might be an encouragement and maybe even a challenge to you." Well, it was both of those. What I read positively astounded me! I had no idea that Tozer, decades ago, not only faced but courageously addressed most of the same issues that are diluting Christianity and undermining the Church today. I became so fascinated by this that about a year of research resulted in a book, *The Forgotten Tozer: A.W. Tozer's Challenge to Today's Church*, which is scheduled for publication in 2013.

As I read more and more of Tozer, two verses kept coming to mind: Isaiah 40:3 and Matthew 3:3—"The voice of one crying in the wilderness." Like **Charles Spurgeon** during the Down-Grade (see part 1), Tozer said and wrote much about what was going on in contemporary Christianity. He said so much, in fact, that he was once quoted as saying to Martyn Lloyd-Jones, that great expositor and 30-year pastor of Westminster Chapel in London, "I have preached myself off every Bible conference platform in the country."[5] While he never desired to offend, Tozer knew that the Word of God *does* offend (Matt. 15:12–13), and that when you tell people the Truth, they often become your enemy (Gal. 4:16).

I view Tozer, as well as Spurgeon and others, as "the voice of one crying in the wilderness" because people seem to consider such men crackpots, troublemakers, or simply opinionated critics whom we can easily dismiss. It greatly distresses me when even those who love Tozer seem to dismiss many of the things he said as being mere opinion and therefore unworthy of serious consideration. One author, for example, who loves Tozer's preaching and writing, nonetheless comments: "This does not mean I always agree with Tozer. There were times when I felt he was leading a parade of one down a dead-end street, such as when he vigorously opposed Christian movies. His sometimes acid criticisms of new Bible translations and of churches that 'majored in counting noses' were but small defects in an otherwise straight and sturdy wall."[6]

While I certainly do not agree with Tozer in every "jot and title," I must take issue with the listed observations being labeled "defects." There are, indeed, legitimate points to challenge in all three of those. Tozer was committed to the authority of Scripture and quickly (and rightly) condemned that which did not conform to it. "I guess my philosophy is this," he wrote: "Everything is wrong until God sets it right."[7]

It is this very dismissal of much of Tozer's contemporary comment that again reminds me of John the Baptist (Isa. 40:3; Matt. 3:3). Seven hundred years before John preached, Isaiah foretold of the herald's coming to "prepare the way" for Christ. When the herald arrived, he announced (or "heralded") the arrival of the King. Such heralding was a common practice in ancient times. The herald would travel far ahead of the monarch and prepare the way. He, along with a group of servants, would repair the roadway and make sure it was as neat as possible. The herald would then arrive and proclaim the coming of the monarch to everyone he met.

I have often pondered the scene of John thundering out the truth of the Living God to the people of his day. I often imagine the shocked look on the faces of the self-righteous Jews when John pointed his finger at them and said that they, the covenant people of Abraham, needed to repent. Nowhere do we see John compromise, cower, or capitulate his message. In reading Tozer, I see the same attitude. I see a man who stood firmly for the Word of God and thundered forth its truth. For example:

> Within the circles of evangelical Christianity itself there has arisen in the last few years dangerous and dismaying trends away from true Bible Christianity. A spirit has been introduced which is surely not the Spirit of Christ, methods employed which are wholly carnal, objectives adopted which have not one line of Scripture to support them, a level of conduct accepted which is practically identical with that of the world—and yet scarcely one voice has been raised in opposition. And this in spite of the fact that the Bible-

honoring followers of Christ lament among themselves the dangerous, wobbly course things are taking.

So radical is the essential spirit and content of orthodox Christianity changing these days under the vigorous leadership of undis-
cerning religionists that, if the trend is not stopped, what is called
Christianity will soon be something altogether other than the faith of
our fathers. We'll have only Bible words left. Bible religion will
have perished from wounds received in the house of her friends.[8]

So thorough was he in addressing modern Christianity, in fact, that in
my own research of Tozer I cannot think of a single stone he left unturned:
biblical authority, worship, entertainment, preaching, apologetics, the para-
church, competition, humor, leadership, money, prosperity teaching, psychology and counseling, lordship, spirituality, revival, tolerance, discern-
ment, unity, pragmatism, worldliness, the Charismatic Movement, and the
list goes on.

As Warren Wiersbe comments, "To listen to Tozer preach was as safe
as opening the door of a blast furnace!"[9] Is there any wonder that he
preached himself off every Bible conference platform in the country? In
contrast, have you been to a Bible Conference lately? I fear you saw something quite different. Indeed, if any man in recent history went "once more
unto the breach," it was Tozer.

Dr. Henry

This will date me, but some readers no doubt will also remember the
old *Dragnet* television series. Every episode of the long-running (1952–70)

police drama began: "The story you are about to see is
true. The names have been changed to protect the inno-
cent," followed by a thespian theme song that still rings in
my ears. Well, that is the case with our final story. What
you are about to read actually happened just a few short
years ago, but to protect our protagonist, and in the spirit
of Henry V, we will just call him **Dr. Henry**.

Dr. Henry was a tenured professor at a well-known Christian university. Upon the retirement of a president who had served faithfully for 25
years, the new president, along with others from the board, administration,
and faculty, saw a golden opportunity "to broaden the theological base of
the institution." And what was that broadened theological base? *Postmod-
ernism.* In Dr. Henry's words, these men were "applauding doubt rather
than certainty in interpreting biblical teaching." While flying the flag of

conservatism over the flagship school of the denomination, they were deliberately steering the vessel into the waters of uncertainty.

It did not take long for the dispute to escalate. While the liberals hid behind the cloak of "humility and openness," they absurdly labeled the conservatives as Cartesians (followers of philosopher René Descartes).[10] The clash became even more personal when more than 200 students signed a letter to the board expressing concern as to where the institution was heading. Wrongly assuming faculty members were behind the letter, the president retaliated by axing the chair of the Bible department and one non-tenured faculty member. In protest, the Dean—who was only three months from retirement after 40 years of service—as well as a couple of faculty members, resigned.

As the dispute continued to intensify, two tenured professors, Dr. Henry being one of them, were dismissed without any previous warning, reprimand, or disciplinary action and with no talk of a severance package (all blatant violations of tenure). But that was not enough; the school posted statements on its websites that were not only untrue but also character assassinations of both men. While one settled behind closed doors, Dr. Henry chose to stand. Himself a graduate of the school years before, he was most concerned about what was happening, so he filed a grievance, an action explicitly permitted by the Faculty Handbook. Despite several tactics by the liberals to rig the proceedings, including denying Dr. Henry's request for a third-party (the American Association of University Professors) to be present at the hearings, the Grievance Panel actually ruled in Dr. Henry's favor, due in no small part to the more than 1,000 pages of documentation he presented demonstrating his innocence. But evil ignores such formalities. The President, the board, and the school lawyer seized the documentation, overturned the decision, and ultimately forced out the two Bible faculty members who had testified on Dr. Henry's behalf!

It should also be noted, that while all this (and much more) was transpiring, the school hired private investigators to go through these men's lives and even seized their computers. Worse, their vehicles were "keyed" and particular files were stolen. So low did this conduct sink that graffiti was sprayed on the home of Dr. Henry's in-laws.

So, since the decision was ignored, there was no recourse but legal action, though everything was done to avoid this step. The goal was not money—they could have gotten that by settling behind closed doors. Rather, the "desire," Dr. Henry states, "was to expose the evil and pray that this would change the course of the institution" (Dr. Henry didn't even ask for his job back!). Throwing out the lawsuit for "breach of contract because the school was a religious institution," the only charge the judge allowed to be tried was fraud. Dr. Henry found out after the trial that the jury would have ruled in his favor, but the judge had stated he would have vetoed their decision. (Makes one wonder what else transpired behind closed doors, does it not?) "The most troubling thing of the five-day trial," Dr. Henry adds, "was seeing various board members take the stand and lie under oath!"

If I may interject, while some might (and did) criticize Dr. Henry for this, citing the precedent of not taking believers to court in 1 Corinthians 6, it would behoove us to ask a question: Are lies, deceit, theft, character assassination, and vandalism of property—not to mention the core issue of rejecting truth and even the possibility of knowing truth—the actions of true believers? Yes, I know some will criticize *me* for asking such a "judgmental question," but such critics refuse to recognize what is happening to Christianity today. That was why even Paul himself appealed to Caesar when necessary (Acts 25:11). Knowing that a trial would not be impartial if conducted by Festus in Jerusalem, Paul appealed to Rome for justice. When the "religious crowd" is unjust, what is left?

Dr. Henry, therefore, did the same, but alas, like others before him when they stood for truth, justice did not prevail. When the smoke cleared, he was left with settling anyway. He received a $300,000 settlement (though his legal fees were app. $440,000), an endorsement letter from the school, and no gag order. "The process was horrific," Dr. Henry recounts:

> The worst was probably the depositions that lasted one week. During three days of interrogation by five lawyers from the school, I was accused of being a fundamentalist, homophobic because I did not support the visit of a pro-gay "Christian" group to the campus, ungodly because I took legal action (even though the school hired lawyers and came after me), a woman-hater (because I hold to a complementarian view), etc. Almost the entire time was addressing issues irrelevant to our case. It was an attack of my character and my theology. Thankfully, the Lord allowed me to share the Gospel three times during that event, explaining why I believe God's Word and will stand strong by His grace.

On top of all that, there is also concrete evidence that Dr. Henry and others have been blackballed at other institutions. No, like Tozer, Dr. Henry did not lose his life, nor even threatened with that fate, but he, his family, and others most certainly suffered for Christ all the same. Why? Simply because they had the temerity, the impudence, the unmitigated gall to insist that there *is* Truth and that it *matters*. I feel honored and blessed to have met him face-to-face and corresponded with him on these matters. I also appreciated his reluctance in my telling his story. He wrote: "I would never equate myself with such spiritual giants as Zwingli and Wycliffe." That is a humble man. But as I shared with him, part of Webster's definition of *giant* is "a living being of great size . . . something unusually large or powerful." Spiritually speaking, it seems to me that all it really takes to look liked a giant nowadays is the willingness to *stand* while everyone else is *sitting*.

On that count, Dr. Henry qualifies. Like those we have noted, and many others we could examine, he was willing to go "once more unto the breach," whatever the cost.

A Closing Plea

Christianity is in trouble. In the name of "cultural relevance," "tolerance," "open-mindedness," and other pious sounding platitudes, we go out of our way to compromise the Truth. We redefine terms, deny historical realities, and dilute doctrine. In ignoring the precedents of Scripture (the prophets, the apostles, and our Lord Himself), as well as those we have noted from history, we continue to drift farther away from shore and into troubled waters that are too deep for an anchor to touch bottom, even if we had one. I greatly appreciated Dr. Henry's last word on his ordeal: "We mourn for the school; and pray for another 'parting of the Red Sea.'" Likewise, let us mourn and pray for Christianity.

If I may also interject, one other common expression we increasingly hear nowadays should also trouble us. On any given issue (just pick one), we hear: "Oh, well, that's not a hill to die on." Granted, some issues are more critical than others, but it is sad, indeed, that it seems that few today are choosing *any* hill to die on.

So, I end by renewing the plea I made in part 1. If you agree with the message presented here and are likewise burdened, I hope to hear from you.[11] (I thank those who have already responded.) We need to be praying for one another (Job 42:10) and then encouraging one another (1 Thes. 5:11; Heb. 3:13) to go "once more unto the breach, dear friends, once more."

NOTES

[1] Picture by Kent Barton, from Steven J. Lawson, *Pillars of Grace* (Reformation Trust, 2011).

[2] While Semi-Pelagianism views all men as sinful because of the fall, and views the will as *weakened*, it rejects the idea that the will was *totally corrupted*, that it is, in fact, partially free and can, therefore, cooperate with divine grace in salvation. Its maxim is: "It is mine to be willing to believe, and it is the part of God's

grace to assist." This unbiblical view was condemned at the Synod of Orange in 529.

[3] Cited in Philip Schaff, *History of the Christian Church* (Charles Scribner's Sons, 1910), Volume 6, Chapter 5, "Reformers before the Reformation," § 40. John Wyclif.

[4] Ibid, § 76. Girolamo Savonarola.

[5] Cited in *A Treasury of A. W. Tozer* (Baker, 1980), 8.

[6] Warren Wiersbe, *Walking With the Giants* (Baker, 1976), 163.

[7] Cited in *A Treasury of A. W. Tozer*, 7.

[8] *The Price of Neglect*, 6–7.

[9] Wiersbe, 163.

[10] Cartesianism is the school of philosophy of René Descartes, best known for his statement, "I think, therefore I am." It is a type of Rationalism because it insists that knowledge can be derived through reason, but in this case from "innate ideas" (ideas inborn in the human mind, in contrast to those received from experience). His system is often contrasted with Empiricism, in fact, which asserts that knowledge comes only, or at least primarily, from sensory experience.

[11] Email: docwatson3228@gmail.com. USPS: POB 235; Meeker, CO; 81641. Dr. Watson is available to speak on these and other issues.

12

400 Years of Biblical Truth: The Legacy of the King James Version*

Isaiah 40:8

May 5, 2011 marked the 400th anniversary of the publication of the King James Version of the Bible. Many organizations and groups are observing this landmark and giving this magnificent translation the recognition it so well deserves.

I would like to begin by quoting Isaiah 40:8: **The grass withereth, the flower fadeth: but the word of our God shall stand for ever.** While that beautiful verse is obviously not talking about Bible translations, it does illustrate, using graphic prose, what has occurred in history. Since the appearance of the King James Version in 1611, more than 150 either complete or partial English translations have been produced (nine from just 2001–2005), but most have, in fact, vanished from use. These have sprung up and blossomed for awhile but ultimately just withered like the **grass** and faded like a **flower.** The few that have endured have done so mostly because of millions of dollars of marketing. *Nothing has endured on its own merits like the King James Version.*

There are several reasons for this. I would like to take a few minutes to show you these reasons through three points: a brief history of the English Bible; the development of the King James Version; and why we should retain the King James Version.

Before doing so, a word is in order for those who might consider this just another peroration from a "King James Only" advocate. That, however, is *not* our platform. There are some in that camp who are an embarrassment, not only because of their lack of scholarship but also because of their often unchristian manner. That said, this book is about Christian history and the loss of such history, and the textual/translation debate is actu-

---

* This essay was originally a lecture delivered on December 9, 2011 in commemoration of the 400th anniversary of the King James Version of the Bible. A few small additions have been made to this reprint. The author is available to speak on this and other topics.

ally far more about history than many people realize and many scholars are willing to admit. So, like other historical matters in the Church, it is our desire here to demonstrate that historical texts are equally critical.

A Brief History of the English Bible

As early as the 8th-century AD, several attempts were made to bring the Scriptures into both the Anglo-Saxon and early English languages. Much happened in the next few centuries as English evolved, going from Old English, which was a Western Germanic language, to Middle English.

Overshadowing all those early attempts was **John Wyclif's** (c.1328–1384) translation into Middle English, the New Testament being completed in 1380 followed by the Old Testament in 1382. Since he didn't know either Greek or Hebrew, he translated the Latin Vulgate. His work, in fact, demonstrated how far from biblical truth the Vulgate was in some instances, which in turn resulted in him being accused of heresy and excommunicated. As noted in chapter 11, so deep was this hatred for Wycliff that he was physically attacked even *after* his death. While he died late in 1384, The Council of Constance declared him in May of 1415 to have been a stiff-necked heretic and decreed that his books not only be burned, but that his remains be dug up and burned and the ashes cast into the River Swift. Such is the hatred of Truth.

The next scene in the story is even more captivating and fascinating. In the annuals of history, there are few men who can be considered a focal point in time. One such man, however, was **William Tyndale** (1494–1536), a brilliant linguist who mastered six languages besides his native

William Tyndale

English (French, German, Italian, Greek, Hebrew, and Latin). He understood that the Roman Catholic Church's allegorical method of biblical interpretation enabled it to isolate itself from the common people. Since the meaning of the Bible was hidden in such allegory, the people couldn't possibly understand it. This was made all the worse by the Bible being written in Latin. He also discovered that even most of the clergy knew nothing of the Bible, only what was quoted in the Missal (Mass Book). The story has been told often that in a heated argument one day with a priest, who said, "It was better to be without *God's* laws than the *Pope's*," Tyndale responded, "I defy the Pope and all his laws; if God spares my life, I will cause a young farm boy to know more of the Scriptures than you do."

In defiance of the Roman Church, which would never allow an English translation of the Bible, as Wyclif had experienced, or any other vernacular language for that matter, as Martin Luther discovered about German, Tyndale defied Rome, went into exile in Europe, and evaded his pursuers for a decade to carry on his work. It was in 1525, in the German city of Worms—where Luther had taken his stand just four years earlier—that Tyndale completed the New Testament and then had it printed but with great difficulty. Bibles were then smuggled into England in bales of merchandise, but the Roman Church burned every copy it could find. Finally, Tyndale was betrayed, accused of heresy, and imprisoned, which included a winter of severe cold for which he had almost no protection in his cell. After 17 months of cold, lonely misery, Tyndale was tied to a stake and burned in 1536 at the age of 42.

At his martyrdom, Tyndale cried out, "Lord, open the King of England's eyes."

There is a portrait of Tyndale that remains in Hertford College, Oxford. Beneath that portrait one will find two lines written in Latin. They have been translated into English thusly:

> *That night o'er all thy darkness, Rome,*
> *In triumph might arise,*
> *An exile I freely become,*
> *Freely a sacrifice.*

As we observed in chapters 10 and 11, many have stood "once more unto the breach," and William Tyndale is one more among them. Sadly, unlike Tyndale, many in Evangelicalism today continue to compromise with Rome instead of recognize the darkness it continues to spread.

The primary reason we say Tyndale was a focal point is that his true genius is seen in his "translation theory," a theory that has completely vanished in our day. He took the English and molded it around the Hebrew and Greek, even going so far as replicating idioms and expressions from those languages into English. Modern thinking is just the opposite, where translators foolishly mold the biblical languages into English vernacular, however sloppy that ends up being. This was so critical that almost a century later the King James Bible translators (themselves outstanding scholars) used Tyndale's work as part of their foundation and rarely touched what he had done. Ninety percent of the King James Bible, in fact, is actually identical to Tyndale's.

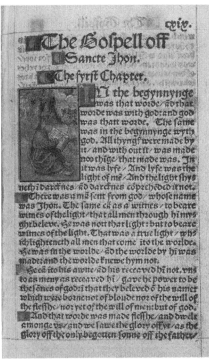

The first page of the Gospel of John in Tyndale's 1525 translation.

What was the immediate result of Tyndale's work? It spurred on more work. Tyndale's dying prayer—"Lord open the eyes of the King of England."—was soon answered. Less than three years later, King Henry VIII, to improve his image and lift his dignity, was persuaded to publish *The Great Bible*, the result of the labors of Miles Coverdale, and which was 70-percent Tyndale's work. This Bible became what could be called the first "authorized version," as it was the first be authorized for public use.

When Mary Tudor (Bloody Mary) ascended the throne in 1553, however, she was determined to put an end to the Protestant Reformation once-and-for-all and reestablish Roman Catholicism as the national religion. Almost 300 Protestants were burned at the stake and hundreds more escaped to Europe. Many of those godly exiles, among whom were some of the finest theologians and Bible scholars in history, found refuge in Geneva, Switzerland and were determined to translate a Bible into English, which they did from 1557 to 1560. The result was the famed *Geneva Bible*.

It is significant, indeed, that when the Pilgrims set foot on the New World in 1620, it was *The Geneva Bible* they held in their hands, and it continued to be the Bible of the home for 40 years after the publication of the King James Bible and went through 144 editions. It was *The Geneva Bible* from which the Scottish Reformer John Knox preached at St. Giles Cathedral in Edinburgh, and which was the Bible of William Shakespeare, John Milton, John Bunyon, and, of course, the Puritans.

While in the end, the King James Bible (which reads 90-percent the same as the Geneva) is a better and richer translation, the Geneva helped lay the foundation. In fact, even the preface to the King James Bible, titled "The Translators to the Reader," took its own quotations of Scripture from *The Geneva Bible*.

The Church of England responded to the Geneva by publishing *The Bishops' Bible* in 1568, a revision of *The Great Bible* commissioned by the great Queen Elizabeth I. While a stunning piece of work, a large folio with many beautiful engravings throughout, it was a rather poor translation and never achieved popularity. It did, however, also become part of the foundation for the King James Bible that was just ahead.

If I may interject, every time I think of Tyndale, I marvel at his endurance. His work remained the foundation for most English translations until the 20th-century. Sadly, however, much of that legacy of endurance has been lost in our day by the minimizing of the reliability and even value of that history of the English Bible.

That sets the stage for our second emphasis, which is indeed an astounding story.

The Development of the King James Version

King James VI became King of Scotland when he was just thirteen months old, succeeding his mother Mary, Queen of Scots, who had been compelled to abdicate in his favor. He was finally able to take full control in 1581. It was then in 1603 that he succeeded the last Tudor monarch of England and Ireland, Queen Elizabeth I, and became King James I of England.

In 1604, Puritan **John Rainolds**—President of Corpus Christi College, Oxford, and of whom it was said he was the most learned man in England—suggested to King James that a new translation of the Bible be considered. James liked the idea because he despised *The Geneva Bible*, specifically its marginal notes, which among other things sanctioned civil disobedience when rulers violate God's law (e.g. Ex. 1:19). The project would also unify the Church Bishops and the Puritans. So, as head of the project, Rainolds assembled a 47-man committee, which is truly hard to imagine could ever be duplicated, especially in today's post-modern world.

John Rainolds

Lancelot Andrews, for example, was so immersed in the original languages that he prepared his manual for his private devotions in Greek. He was also a genius of English prose. The amazing **John Bois** (or Boys) learned Hebrew at the age of five and elegantly writing it at the age of six. He likewise distinguished himself in Greek. By the time the translation of the King James Bible commenced, he had read sixty grammar texts of the ancient languages, was a Greek scholar by the age of fourteen, and for years spent more than twelve hours a day in the Cambridge library studying languages and manuscripts. In his excellent book about the King James Bible translators, Gustavus Paine writes that these men were not superb writers doing scholarly work, rather they were just "minor writers, though great scholars, doing superb writing."[1]

The group was divided into six smaller groups so that each could work on various portions of the task and then be checked by the other groups. The final draft was reviewed by one more committee of six and prepared for printing, thereby raising the level of academic excellence to a level never known before. The entire work was completed in less then seven years.

My Dear Christian Friend, it is sad, indeed, that the King James Bible has been under attack for decades, and this issue of translation is just one of many approaches. One writer, for example, asserts that these translators "may have harbored less than perfect motivations for their work. Some hoped to gain favor with the king and advancement in their positions through their work."[2] Such speculation is barely worthy of comment. No evidence whatsoever exists that this was true. The writer himself, in fact, proves this is conjecture by using the word "may."

Another popular attack is, "Well, which edition of the King James Bible are you using?" implying that it has dramatically changed through the years. Such is not the case. The King James Version has gone through four major revisions—1629, 1638, 1762, and 1769—and a few minor ones. None of these changed the text, rather they merely corrected early printing errors and updated spelling and punctuation.

One such famous misprint was Psalm 119:161 in the 1702 edition. Instead of reading, "Princes have persecuted me without a cause," it read, "Printers have persecuted me without a cause." The most infamous of all appeared in the 1632 edition, an error that earned it the nickname *The*

Wicked Bible because it omitted the word "not" from the commandment, "Thou shalt not commit adultery."

So, the 1762 revision, for example, greatly enhanced the use of italics (which indicated supplied words not in the original languages) and modernized most of the spelling. It was then the 1769 Oxford edition that included several additional revisions, including printing errors, spelling, and expanded marginal and introductory notes. This edition has become the standard for today's printed Bibles.

Another mocking attack on the King James Bible concerns its being referred to as the "Authorized Version," which it actually never was in the United Kingdom; indeed, only *The Great Bible* was ever recognized as "authorized." On the other hand, for all practical purposes it became the "authorized" version when the King's Printer produced no further editions of the *Bishops' Bible* and the 1662 *Book Of Common Prayer* replaced most of the text from *The Great Bible* with that of the King James Bible.

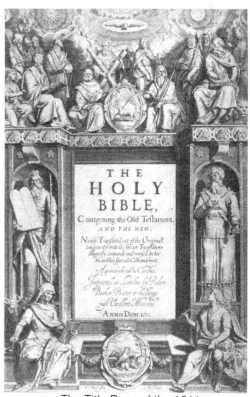

The Title Page of the 1611
King James Version

Technically, then, the King James Bible was *never* adopted as an Authorized Version, right? *Wrong*. No, it never was in the United Kingdom, *but it was right here in the United States.* **Robert Aitken** was the official printer of the Journals of the United States Congress. He was a great patriot and was deeply burdened about the shortage of English Bibles that existed in his country. In 1771, he produced the first English language New Testament printed in America, which was eagerly received and went through five printings to 1781. It was in that same year that Aitken petitioned Congress to authorize, and even fund if possible, the printing of the King James Bible. On September 10, 1782, he received that authorization, the only instance in history of the U.S. Congress authorizing the printing of a Bible. In fact, George Washington wrote a letter to Aitken in 1783 commending him for the Bible that is now known as the "Bible of the American Revolution." How many of us were taught *that* in school?

It is sad, indeed, that even in spite of its being at the roots of our country—our own "Authorized Version," if you will—some evangelicals today go out of their way to undermine the King James Bible in any way they can. This leads us to one other emphasis.

Why We Should Retain the King James Version

Why retain a translation of the Bible that is 400 years old? Why not replace it with one that uses today's language? Would not that be more relevant? Those questions actually lead us to the first of six reasons we should, in fact, retain *the Bible of the Renaissance and the Reformation*. We emphasize that phrase because this Bible is historic. It is of staggering significance and priceless value.

Its Superior Biblical Language

One of the most common and serious misstatements of our day on this subject goes like this: "Well, the King James Version was certainly good as the contemporary Bible of *its* day, but we need a contemporary Bible for *our* today." It is that kind of thinking that produces Bible translations such as, *the word on the street* (formerly *the street bible*) published in 2003 by Zondervan and described as a "'dangerously real' retelling of Scripture." Dragging the Bible down to the level of the urban style language of the street, it condenses the whole Bible story into less 500 pages. Here's how the first three verses of the Bible sound in this atrocity:

> First off, nothing. No light, no time, no substance, no matter. Second off, God starts it all up and WHAP! Stuff everywhere! The cosmos in chaos: no shape, no form, no function—just darkness . . . total. And floating above it all, God's Holy Spirit, ready to play. Day one: Then God's voice booms out, "Lights!" and, from nowhere, light floods the skies and "night" is swept off the scene.

Well, while that is certainly contemporary, it is precisely what the King James Bible was *not*. Neither was Tyndale's, as we saw earlier. Please get his: *The English used in both was NOT the contemporary language of the day*. Rather it was *biblical* language. As noted earlier, this is evident *first* and foremost in how Tyndale molded the English around the Hebrew and Greek.

Second, it is also evident in the use of the singular and plural second person pronouns, that is, the so-called "thees" and thous" that so many people abhor. Most people mistakenly say, "That's the way they talked then, but we don't talk like that anymore." But this again shows the misinformation that is propagated nowadays. The fact of the matter is that they did *not* talk like that. These pronouns were purposely used because they alone could accurately convey the singular and plural indicated in the Greek and Hebrew; modern English cannot. Tyndale knew all this and deliberately revived words that had already passed from common use for the sole purpose of *accuracy*.

For example, John 3:7 reads, "Marvel not that I said unto *thee, Ye* must be born again" (emphasis added), while new translations replace both "thee" and "ye" with "you."[3] But "you" does not indicate whether the second person pronoun is singular or plural. In contrast, "ye" is plural and "thee" is singular. In fact, this is 100% consistent throughout the King James Bible. Every pronoun that begins with "y" (ye, you, and your) is plural, and every pronoun that begins with "t" is singular (thou, thee, thy, and thine).

While the King James Bible is accused of not being "accurate," such an attack is patently false and absurd. The inarguable fact is that because of the Old English pronouns, it is fundamentally more accurate than modern translations in more than 19,000 instances.[4]

Another example of the importance of this is how the King James Version uses "you" and "thee" *in the same verse* literally hundreds of times. Just one of these is Romans 1:11, where Paul writes: "For I long to see *you*, that I may impart unto *you* some spiritual gift, to the end *ye* may be established" (emphasis added). In other words, "I long to see *all of you as a group*, that I may impart unto *all of you* some spiritual gift, to the end that *each one of you individually* may be established." To say that these pronouns are not important is simply foolish.[5]

Third, the biblical language of the King James Bible is also demonstrated in the words the translators chose to use. One graphic example is the often mentioned verse 2 Timothy 2:15: "Study to show thyself approved unto God, a workman that needeth not to be ashamed, rightly dividing the word of truth." "Study" is the Greek *spoudazō*, which speaks of being diligent or eager. Many think, therefore, that newer translations are better, such as: "Be diligent" (NASB, NKJB) or "Do your best" (NIV and ESV). Commentators often insist that "study" is too narrow because it refers to studying books. But if we may lovingly submit, no, it does not. That's an *application*, but not the basic *meaning*. The first meaning, in fact, given in Webster's 11th Collegiate Dictionary for the noun "study" is: "a state of contemplation." Webster then says of the verb: "to engage in study [i.e., contemplation] . . . meditate, reflect . . . to consider attentively or in detail." Deeper still, the first entry in Webster's current Unabridged Dictionary for the verb is: "To fix the mind closely upon a subject; to dwell upon anything in thought; to muse; to ponder." If we may lovingly ask, who is actually being "too narrow" here, the King James Bible or modern translations and commentators? Let's be honest: is not a word that speaks of fixed contemplation and meditation better than the ideas of diligence or the atrocious translation of doing our best?

There is a second reason we should retain the Bible of the Reformation and the Renaissance.

Its Superior English and Literary Wealth

As an avid student of the Apollo space program, I am always struck by Apollo 8. While orbiting the Moon in 1968, Bill Anders, Jim Lovell, and Frank Borman each in-turn read and broadcast to the world the first 10 verses of the Creation story. Did they read from the Revised Standard Version, or the New English Bible, or the Berkeley Version, or the Amplified Bible, or Phillip's Translation, all of which existed in that day? No. While gazing at that magnificent blue ball, the only color in the universe hanging in a sea of blackness nearly a quarter of a million miles away, they read the beauty, majesty, and dignity of the King James Bible, which Borman had reproduced on fireproof paper and placed in the back of the mission flight plan book.

My Dear Christian Friend, my point here is that not only does the King James Version reflect biblical language, its English is so far above contemporary language that the two are not much closer than distant cousins several times removed. The richness of the Elizabethan Period was the pinnacle of English, unequalled before or since. Is this simply the opinion of so-called "King James Only" advocates? No, it is not! In *The Story of English*, for example, the companion book to the PBS television documentary of the same name, the authors write concerning the extraordinary quality of the English language in the days of Shakespeare and the reigns of Queen Elizabeth and King James I (1558–1625):

> The achievements of these astonishing years are inescapably glorious. During their reigns, about seventy-five years, the English language achieved a richness and vitality of expression that even contemporaries marveled at.[6]

It is utterly fascinating that, setting religious matters aside for a moment, the King James Bible has molded the English language more than any other book in the history of western civilization. Did you know, in fact, that it would be almost impossible to get through a single day without consciously or unconsciously using language from either the King James Bible or Shakespeare? The King James Bible alone accounts for some 257 idioms that we use every day. Here are but a few:

> My brother's keeper (Gen. 4:9)
> A land flowing with milk and honey (Ex. 3:8 and 19 others)
> Fell flat on his face (Deut. 22:31)
> Apple of his eye (Deut. 32:10; Zech. 2:8)
> A howling wilderness (Deut. 32:10)
> Know for a certainty (Josh. 23:13)
> A man after his own heart (1 Sam. 13:14)
> With the Skin of my teeth (Job 19:20)
> All the days of my life (Ps. 23:6; 27:4)
> At their wits' end (Ps. 107:27)
> Nothing new under the sun (Ecc. 1:9)
> A time and a place for everything (Ecc. 3:1)
> Set thine house in order (Is. 38:1)
> The leopard cannot change his spots (Jer. 13:23)
> Feet of clay (Dan. 2:41)
> The writing on the wall (Dan. 5:25)
> Reap the whirlwind (Hosea 8:7)
> Salt of the earth (Matt. 5:13)
> An eye for an eye (Matt. 5:38)
> Turn the other cheek (Matt. 5:39)
> Walking the straight and narrow (Matt. 7:14)
> A house divided against itself shall not stand (Matthew 12:25)
> The blind leading the blind (Matt. 15:14)
> Signs of the times (Matt. 16:3)
> Kicking against the pricks (Acts 9:5)
> A law unto themselves (Rom. 2:14)
> The powers that be (Rom. 13:1)
> Becoming all things to all men (1 Cor. 9:22)
> Suffer fools gladly (2 Cor. 11:19)
> A thorn in the flesh (2 Cor. 12:7)
> A fall from grace (Gal. 5:4)
> A thief in the night (1 Thes. 5:2)

My dear Christian friend, please consider this: Does it not grieve us even a little that this is the heritage we are running away from as fast as we can? Does it not bother us even the tiniest bit that the Bible is today brought down to even the basest levels of our language, often for the sole purpose of just selling the consumer another Bible? Do we really prefer something like the *Black Bible Chronicles*, which describes Cain getting "bent out of shape" and how God "busts" him because he killed his brother? Do we really prefer to render Leviticus 19:20, where God speaks of fornication, this way: "It's bad to do the wild thing without a blessing from the Almighty. You have to be hitched"? Is that how we should treat God's Holy Word? Again, let's be honest: Are Bible publishers really concerned about the *preservation* of God's *Word* or the *proliferation* of their own *wealth*? I don't want that to sound judgmental or unkind, but we need to realize that we are pulling the Bible down to the gutter.

Another factor here, contrary to popular belief, is the basic simplicity of the King James language. While Shakespeare has a 20,000 word vocabulary, and Milton 13,000, the King James Version has a modest 6,000. Additionally, research has revealed that the entire King James Version averages 1.31 syllables and only 3.968 letters per word. Here is a quick test of vocabulary. Comparing the KJV to the NIV, which word is more quickly understood?

VERSE	NIV	KJV
Genesis 19:1	gateway	gate
Ezra 6:2	memorandum	record
2 Samuel 21:5	decimated	destroyed
1 Kings 7:6	colonnade	porch
Proverbs 23:10	encroach	enter
Isaiah 40:23	naught	nothing
Ezekiel 13:22	disheartened	sad
Daniel 10:6	burnished	polished
Habakkuk 1:6	impetuous	hasty
Romans 2:20	embodiment	form
Revelation 4:3	carnelian	sardine
Jude 25	forevermore	for ever

And that is only a dozen examples out of more than 100.

The fact of the matter is that numerous reading tests have been done on the King James Bible, including the standard Flesch Readability test, as well as both the Flesch-Kincaid and Bormuth Grade Level tests. What were the results? The entire King James Bible, on average, can be understood by a fifth to tenth grade reader. As creationist Henry Morris puts it, "Apart from a few archaic words or words whose meaning has changed, which can easily be clarified in footnotes, it is as easy to understand today as it was four hundred years ago."[7]

Have you also ever noticed something even as commonplace as a greeting card that quotes Scripture usually uses the King James Version? It would seem that when we wish to speak with depth, dignity, and serious-ness, we defer to the dignified language of the King James. Which of these renderings of 1 Peter 5:7, for example, honestly touches your heart more: "Casting all your care upon him; for he careth for you," or "Give all your worries and cares to God, for he cares about what happens to you" (NLT)?

We should also note that all of this is why the King James Bible is the easiest translation to memorize, as countless people through the ages can attest. The translators not only stayed true to the original language, but also succeeded in producing a Bible that "sings" with power and beauty. British theologian and hymn writer Frederick Faber (1814–1863) once wrote, "It lives on the ear, like music that can never be forgotten, like the sound of church bells, which the convert hardly knows how he can forego."

Can we not also see how this has affected worship? Just as contempo-rary language is destroying the Bible, it is likewise destroying hymns that are based upon this old standard. We should also note that it is virtually impossible for many congregations to publicly read Scripture together be-cause there is a plethora of translations peppering the assembly.

One speaker eloquently makes the point of the English and literary wealth of the King James Bible: "It's a special Bible, written at a special time, a time when the language was actually molten, when the language could have gone any way, they shaped it thus."[8]

Please consider a third reason we should retain the Bible of the Reformation and the Renaissance.

Its Superior Textual Foundation

We have time for only brief mention of this, but we should not over-look it. It is a complex subject, but we will make it as simple as possible. Ponder the following scenario: Assume 100 people witness an accident and write down what they saw. The reports of 98 of the witnesses are very much the same. The other two, however, differ greatly with the 98, and even with each other at times, even though they wrote their statements a month before the other 98. Now, let's be honest: which story are we going to believe?

That is, in fact, exactly what we see between two distinct families of manuscripts: the Alexandrian and the Byzantine. The Alexandrian are tout-ed as being superior simply because they are older, which, as just illustrat-ed, any first year student of logic would recognize is illogical. Further, while the Alexandrian texts (the most "revered" of which are Sinaiticus and Vaticanus) are very few in number, 80–90% of the 5,360 Greek manu-scripts that still exist are in the Byzantine family. Additionally, the manu-scripts in the Byzantine family are essentially the same. So again, whose story should we believe?

The case for the Alexandrian family is made worse by the fact that Sinaiticus and Vaticanus differ with each other more than 3,000 times in the Gospels alone. Still worse, several eminent scholars have demonstrated the inferiority of these manuscripts. They have conclusively proved that Gnostic heretics—such as the infamous Marcion (c.85–160), Valentinus (c.100–160), and others—flourished in Alexandria and corrupted the New Testament text by deleting or altering passages. Just as Jehovah's Witnesses have corrupted the text in our day, heretics did so then.

How does all this relate to English translations? Simple: Virtually all modern translations are based upon this inferior text. In contrast, the King James Version is based on the pure Byzantine textual family.

Consider a fourth reason we should retain the Bible of the Reformation and the Renaissance.

Its Superior Translation Theory

The King James Bible is the quintessential example of the "formal equivalence" approach to translation, which renders the Greek and Hebrew words as closely as possible into English, even to the use of verb for verb, noun for noun, and so forth. Formal Equivalence is the only method of translation that is consistent with verbal inspiration, which focuses on the *words* of Scripture.

In stark contrast, the most common approach to translation in the last several decades has been "dynamic equivalence," in which *word-for-word* translation is replaced with *thought-for-thought* translation. In other words, as long as we get across the thought of the author, then the exact words aren't really important. The NIV is a typical example. Please get this: It is indisputable fact that 20–25% of its English words have been added without any support in the original language whatsoever. On the other side of that coin, about five percent of the Greek words have not been translated at all simply because the translating committee didn't think they were necessary.

Here is a dramatic example. Ephesians 1:3–14 is one of the most beautiful and powerful passages in the Word of God, but the NIV, to put it bluntly, butchers it. In one long sentence, Paul expresses several of the most profound truths in the Scriptures. The NIV committee, however, thought it would be better to chop it into eleven sentences, leave out some words, and add others. Of its 205 Greek words, in fact, 36 are not translated at all, while 87 of the English words have no backing from the Greek, nor are they warranted by the context for the sake of clarity. If I may be so bold, it continues to baffle me why Christians and their leaders want this kind of translation. If we are not concerned about the *words* of Scripture, how can we possibly know the *Truth* of Scripture?

Again, Formal Equivalence is the only method of translation that is consistent with verbal inspiration, and that was the foundation of Tyndale's work and the King James Bible.

This leads us right to a fifth reason we should retain the Bible of the Reformation and the Renaissance.

Its Superior Doctrine

It would take a separate lecture (if not 2 or 3) to deal with this adequately, but briefly, the King James Bible is far superior to modern translations in doctrine. There are literally dozens of examples. We could examine the removal of the clearest statement in Scripture about the Trinity in 1 John 5:7–8.[9] We could also examine 1 Timothy 3:16, a critical verse about the deity and incarnation of Christ. Instead of "*God* manifest in the flesh," modern translations read "*He*" or "*who*," with no clear reference in the text to who that actually is.[10] We have time for only one, however, one that troubles me deeply.

Instead of "only begotten son" in John 3:16 (and other verses: 1:14, 18; 3:18), several modern translations read "only son" (ESV, NRSV, NLT, CEV, GNB, GWT), or far worse, "one and only son" (NIV, NCV, MSG). Now, the word "son" is *monogenēs*, literally "only offspring." As Bible scholar Jacob van Bruggen well says, however, while it is true that *monogenēs* can refer to an only child, it does so only when this fact is actually true (Lk. 7:12; 8:42; 9:38).[11] Is it true that God only has an "only Son" or "one and only Son"? Of course not. As 2 Corinthians 6:18, and other verses, makes crystal clear, all believers are "sons and daughters." Christ is the only Son of God by *natural* means, while we are children by *adoption*. This phrase, in fact, is a wonderful summary of Psalm 2:7: "Thou art my Son; this day have I begotten thee," a glorious reference to coming Messiah, which in in-turn is quoted and applied to Christ in Acts 13:33 and Hebrews 1:5 and 5:5. Modern translations are, therefore, inarguably wrong, and to defend them is foolish at best and just plain prideful at worst.

If I may also add, while many today insist this is "no big deal," history rebukes their lack of wisdom. The framers of both the original *Nicene Creed* of 325 AD and the later 381 version recognized this fact, declaring Christ to be the "only begotten" son, as did *The Definition of Chalcedon* (451). This was also recognized by the great theological minds that penned *The Heidelberg Catechism* (1576), *The Canons of Dort* (1619), and the two greatest statements of all: *The Westminster Confession of Faith* (1646), and *The London Baptist Confession* (1689). So, we are compelled to ask: while the ancient church could recognize the unique sonship of Christ, why can't we today?[12]

I would submit with this single example that there is absolutely nothing ambiguous in the issue of Bible translations and doctrine. While many evangelicals passionately deny that modern translations have poor theology, and scoff at those who defend the King James Bible, the evidence is unimpeachable.

This brings us to one final reason we should retain the Bible of the Reformation and the Renaissance.

Its Longevity

This reason, in fact, is the force behind this lecture. How many people today have ever even *seen*, much less still *read*, the Revised Version (1881), or its American counterpart the American Standard Version (1901), or the Revised Standard Version, or the New English Bible, or the Good News Bible, or a hundred others we could list? How about the New Revised Standard Version? This was a publishing flop, an abysmal failure in the publishing world. It remained virtually stagnate until the publisher used it as the basis for *The Green Bible*, a so-called "Study Bible" for radical environmentalists with contributions from liberal clergymen such as Desmond Tutu and N. T. Wright as well as Emerging Church leader Brian McLaren. Or how long will the popularity of Zondervan's NIV stand against the growing influence of Crossway's ESV? Then again, what will be the next translation *du jour* that will burst onto the scene and then just fade away?

In contrast to the short "shelf life" of modern translations, the King James Bible has endured for *400 years*, and is still going strong in spite of wave after wave of attack that sweeps over it. We simply cannot help but wonder why there is so much resistance to this venerable translation.

Conclusion

The book *The Story of English* we quoted earlier calls the King James Bible a masterpiece of English.[13] Someone recently handed me a copy of the December 2011 issue of *National Geographic*, which said the same thing—the cover story was titled: "The King James Bible: Making a Masterpiece." Of this there can be no doubt. In contrast, I for one cannot imagine anyone honestly using this word to describe the rambling paraphrase of the NIV or the dry as dust prose of the NASB, or the cold rendering of the ESV. But we have nonetheless elevated these over a true theological and literary work of art. If we were to put all these in an art gallery, the King James Bible would be the center exhibit while all the others would be no more than a curiosity in one of the back rooms. It is, indeed, a masterpiece, of *form*, *function*, and *flavor*. But sadly again, we are today running away from this as fast as we can.

We often hear the argument, "Well, we must be concerned about readability. The easier the Bible is to read, the more people will understand it." But that is simply not true, as 1 Corinthians 2:14 makes clear: "The natural man receiveth not the things of the Spirit of God: for they are foolishness unto him: neither can he know them, because they are spiritually discerned." Understanding comes only by the Holy Spirit, not by a contemporary English translation of the Bible.

David Martyn Lloyd-Jones was probably the greatest expositor of the 20th-century, filling the pulpit of Westminster Chapel in London for 30 years. Speaking at the National Bible Rally in October of 1961, the addressed the modern philosophy of bringing the Bible down to everyone's level:

> . . . we are told [that the Bible] must be put in such simple terms and language that anybody taking it up and reading it is going to understand all about it. My friends, this is nothing but sheer nonsense! What we must do is to educate the masses of the people *up* to the Bible, not bring the Bible *down* to their level. One of the greatest troubles in life today is that everything is being brought down to the same level; everything is being cheapened. The common man is made the standard and the authority; he decides everything, and everything has got to be brought down to him. You are getting it on your wireless [radio], your television, in your newspapers; everywhere standards are coming down and down. Are we to do this with the Word of God? I say, No! What has always happened in the past has been this: an ignorant, illiterate people in this country and in foreign countries, coming into salvation, have been educated *up* to the Book and have begun to understand it, and glory in it, and to praise God for it. I am here to say that we need to do the same in this present time. What we need, therefore, is not to replace the Authorized Version with what, I am tempted at times to call, the ITV [the only British TV channel financed by advertising] edition of the Bible. We need rather to teach and to train people up to the standard and the language and the dignity and the glory of the old Authorized Version.[14]

Martyn Lloyd-Jones

Oh, how we need men today who will stand up and preach like that! How we need seminary professors and pastors who will train and educate people *up to God* instead of pulling God down to the man's level!

In the original Preface to our Authorized Version, Miles Smith wrote: "We never thought from the beginning that we should need to make a new translation, nor yet to make of a bad one a good one . . . but to make a good one better, or out of many good ones one principal good one."

And that is *exactly* what that unprecedented body of translators produced. I would, therefore, close with this: What should be our attitude toward the King James Version, the Bible of the Renaissance and the Reformation? I leave you with this. Let us:

- **Remember** its *posterity*,
- **Recognize** its *power*,
- **Rejoice** in its *prominence*, and
- **Reinvest** in its *permanence*.

Let us close in prayer.

Closing Prayer

Our Gracious Father, we thank you for this evening of fellowship. We thank you for each one who is present and their desire to be with others of like mind and like faith. We thank you for the Truth you revealed to the Scripture writers and now illumine to the minds of readers. We thank you for the absolutes you provide in your Word, for the certainty it gives us in light of the uncertainty and Relativism of our day.

And now, Father, we thank you for this time to look back upon that focal point of 400 years ago when the King James Bible was born. We thank you for your sovereign control in bringing to us a translation that is unequalled in accuracy, beauty, and dignity. Father, we pray that each of us here will, indeed, remember its posterity, recognize its power, rejoice in its prominence, and reinvest in its permanence.

And most of all we pray all this to the praise of your glory, in our Savior's name, Amen.

NOTES

[1] Gustavus Paine, *The Men Behind the King James Version* (Baker, 1982 reprint from 1959), vii.

[2] James White, *The King James Only Controversy* (Bethany House, 1995), 70–71.

[3] Note also: Matt 5:29; 21:5; 23:37; Lk. 5:24; 13:34; 22:11; Jn. 3:11; Acts 5:9; Heb. 13:5; Rev. 2:10.

[4] Using *QuickVerse* 4.0, the data for the appearance of the second person pronouns is as follows: "thee" (3,827 times); "thy" (4,604 times); "thyself" (214 times); "thou" (5,474 times); "thine" (937 times); and "ye" (3,983 times); total 19,039.

[5] Just a few other examples, picked at random, one from each NT book (except 2 and 3 John), are: Matt. 5:11; Mk. 16:7; Lk. 6:31; Jn. 16:12; Acts 3:22; Rom. 12:1; 1 Cor. 1:10; 2 Cor. 2:4; Gal. 1:6; Eph 4:11; Phil. 1:27; Col. 1:9; 1 Thes. 2:2; 2 Thes. 3:4; Heb. 5:12; Jas. 2:16; 1 Pet. 5:10; 2 Pet. 1:12; 1 Jn. 2:1; Jude 1:3; Rev. 2:10. Every instance plainly shows the difference between the singular and plural and provides better understanding of the verse.

[6] Robert McCrum, William Cray, and Robert McNeil, *The Story of English* (New York: Viking, 1986), 91.

[7] *A Creationist's Defense of the King James Bible*, 12.

[8] John Rhys-Davies (narrator), making a personal comment in the documentary film, *The Book That Changed the Word: The Amazing Tale of the Birth of the King James Bible* (Lionsgate, 2010), "Interview with John Rhys-Davies."

[9] For a thorough examination, see chapter 51, "1 John 5:7–8: Beyond a Reasonable Doubt," in the author's *Truth on Tough Texts: Expositions of Challenging Scripture Passages* (Sola Scriptura Publications, 2012), 497–509.

[10] Ibid, chapter 46, "GOD Manifest in the Flesh," 450–58.

[11] Jacob van Bruggen, *The Future of the Bible* (Institute for Biblical Textual Studies, 2003 reprint of the 1978 original), pp. 134–135.

[12] For a more detailed discussion, see chapter 45, "The 'Only Begotten' Son," in the author's *Truth on Tough Texts: Expositions of Challenging Scripture Passages* (Sola Scriptura Publications, 2012), 442–49.

[13] McCrum, 113.

[14] D. M. Lloyd-Jones, *Knowing the Times: Addresses Delivered on Various Occasions, 1942–1977* (Banner of Truth Trust, 1989), 112 (emphasis in the original).

Bless God for the translation of the Scriptures. The Word is our sword; by being translated, the sword is drawn out of its scabbard.

William Gurnall
The Christian in Complete Armour

Conclusion

As in the first volume,[1] it was during the final editing of this book for print that I again contemplated an appropriate conclusion. As I reflected on all this material, in fact, I felt that a suitable conclusion was even more critical than it was for the first volume. We, therefore, close with two emphases.

First, the *success* of the Reformation. As we have noted repeatedly, what the Reformation accomplished, and gloriously so, was bringing the Church out of 1,000 years of darkness and was the first major attempt to return to biblical Christianity. Its primary accomplishments were the bringing back of salvation truth and a return to the authority and sufficiency of Scripture. As also noted, however, there are some today who call themselves evangelicals but at the same time undermine Reformation (i.e., *biblical*) tenets and even try to undo the good it accomplished. We submit that even the slightest sympathy with Rome is a betrayal of biblical Christianity and that the principles of the Reformation are needed today like never before since the 16th-century.

Second, however, we also submit that there clearly was a profound *shortcoming* in the Reformation. We touched on this briefly back in chapter 3 (p. 54). Quoting Lehman Strauss again, "The Reformation raised up a group of men who came out from Romanism and who rescued much from the mortuary of Rome. But they did not go far enough."[2] Francis Scheaffer echoes, "The Reformation was not a golden age. It was far from perfect."[3]

We further submit, for example, it is sad that such terms as "sacrament," "means of grace," and several others have been retained by many in spite of the incontrovertible fact that they are firmly rooted in Catholicism's mysticism and spiritualizing. Yes, most have been somewhat redefined, but they are still not free of their mystic overtones and clearly unbiblical foundations.[4] Other things that have descended from the Reformers should also trouble us, such as: state churches, forms, ceremonies, traditions, liturgies, and church hierarchy.

I do not wish to offend, but another particularly disturbing holdover from Catholicism is infant baptism, which some Protestants practice with no biblical support whatsoever except spiritualizing Old Testament circumcision to now mean baptism, which begs the unanswerable question, of course: "Why baptize baby girls?" Again, while they have certainly redefined its significance, they have still retained an indisputable error. And speaking of baptism, the New Testament precedent was without question immersion, but that too changed by the will of man, being totally replaced by pouring in Catholicism and some Protestant denominations.

Now, while I do *not* intend to start (or even advocate) a new "Christian movement"—we already have too many of those—I would submit that instead of the emphasis on *reform* why not emphasize a *return*? The intent of the Reformers, in fact, was to *reform* the Church, that is, change it from within. As most of them ultimately realized, however, it was impossible to reform a corpse, so they *returned* more and more to Scripture and found themselves having to obey 2 Corinthians 6:17: "Wherefore come out from among them, and be ye separate, saith the Lord, and touch not the unclean thing; and I will receive you." We praise God that the Reformers returned to the Word of God in certain areas, but they simply did not go back far enough; they didn't go back to the New Testament standards of the Church. As a result, their systems were riddled with man's traditions, organization, and other weaknesses. Would not Luther, for example, have been far better off, as would we, if he would have just thrown out *everything* and, with an open Bible in front of him, started over? Does this mean we will all agree perfectly on every point? Of course not. But we do submit that while there will certainly be *minor* points of *difference*, that is far different than *major* points of *departure*. We also tend at times to glorify the *men* of the *Reformation* instead of the *God* of the *revelation*.

So, while *sola Scriptura* was, of course, the "*formal* principle" of the Reformation (see p. 64), in some ways it never became the "*functional* principle." It *alone* did not become the driving force in the precepts, principles, practices, and polity adopted by the very ones who championed reform. Like today, *tradition trumped truth*. Someone wisely said to me recently as we discussed these issues, "While we certainly came out of the darkness of Rome, it seems as though we still tend to huddle in its shadows." Indeed, if Church History teaches us anything—and it teaches us much if we will but learn—it primarily teaches us the error that occurs when we step out of the light of Scripture and into the shadows of human thinking.

If we may, therefore, ask in closing: shall we champion a new *Reformation* or a true *return*?

NOTES

[1] *Truth on Tough Texts: Expositions of Challenging Scripture Passages* (Sola Scriptura Publications, 2012), 543–44.

[2] Lehman Strauss, *Book of Revelation* (Loizeaux Brothers, Inc., 1964), 73.

[3] Francis Scheaffer, *How Should We Then Live* (Fleming H. Revell Company, 1976), p. 84.

[4] See a discussion of these two terms in *Truth on Tough Texts* (488–492).

Appendix

Is Romanism Christianity?

by

T. W. Medhurst; Glasgow, Scotland

Editor's Introduction

As noted in chapter 2, T. W. Medhurst was a Scottish pastor and the first student at Charles Spurgeon's Pastor's College; Spurgeon even officiated at Medhurst's marriage in 1859. The article reprinted here originally appeared in *The Fundamentals*, a 12-volume collection of 90 articles, completed in 1915, devoted to the exposition and defense of Evangelicalism. Their purpose was to present with crystal clarity the crucial, *non-negotiable* doctrines of the Faith. In the spirit of that purpose, this article unambiguously and unabashedly demonstrates the once universal view of evangelicals that *Roman Catholicism is not true Christianity*. We reprint it here in the hope that this reminder will encourage today's Church to recognize a truth that was once as obvious as the fact that rain is wet.

📖   📖   📖

I am aware that, if I undertake to prove that *Romanism is not Christianity*, I must expect to be called "bigoted, harsh, uncharitable." Nevertheless I am not daunted; for I believe that on a right understanding of this subject depends the salvation of millions.

One reason why Popery has of late gained so much power in Great Britain and Ireland, and is gaining power still, is that many Protestants look on it now as a form of true Christianity; and think that, on that account, notwithstanding great errors, it ought to be treated very tenderly. Many suppose that at the time of the Reformation, it was reformed, and that it is now much nearer the Truth than it was before that time. It is still, however, the same; and, if examined, will be found to be so different from, and so hostile to, real Christianity, that it is not, in fact, Christianity at all.

Christianity, as revealed in the Sacred Writings, is salvation by Christ. It sets Him before us as at once a perfect man, the everlasting God, the God-man Mediator; who, by appointment of the Father, became a Substitute for all who were given Him. It teaches that by Him God's justice was magnified, and His mercy made manifest; that, for all who trust in Him, He fulfilled the law, and brought in a *complete righteousness*; and that by this alone they can be justified before God. It teaches that His death was a perfect sacrifice, and made full satisfaction and atonement for their sins, so that God lays no sin to their charge, but gives them a free and full pardon; that He has ascended to the right hand of God, and has sent down the Holy Spirit to be His only Vicar and Representative on earth; that He is the only Mediator between the righteous God and sinful man; that it is by the Holy Spirit alone that we are convinced of sin, and led to trust in Jesus that all who trust in Him, and obey Him with the obedience of faith and love, are saved, and, being saved, are made "kings and priests unto God," and have "eternal life" in Him.

This is Christianity, the Christianity the apostles preached. But side by side with the Apostles, Satan went forth also, and preached what Paul calls "another gospel." Paul did not mean that it was *called* "another gospel;" but that as Satan "beguiled Eve through his subtlety" (2 Corinthians 11:3), so some, while professing to teach the Gospel, were turning men away "from the simplicity that is in Christ;" and by doing so, did, in fact, teach "another gospel." Paul, speaking of those who were thus deceived, said, "I marvel that ye are so soon removed from Him that called you into the grace of Christ unto another gospel which is not another; but there be some that trouble you, and would pervert the Gospel of Christ." He means, that there can be but *one Gospel*, though something else may be called the gospel; and he says of those who had thus perverted "the Gospel of Christ": "If any one preach any other gospel unto you . . . let him be accursed" (Galatians 1:6–9).

He calls those who did so "false apostles, deceitful workers, transforming themselves into the apostles of Christ;" and he adds, "no marvel; for Satan himself is transformed into an angel of light. Therefore, it is no great thing if his ministers also be transformed as the ministers of righteousness; whose end shall be according to their works" (2 Corinthians 11:13–15).

Let us consider well the meaning of these passages of Scripture. Paul says that there cannot be another Gospel; the conclusion, therefore, is evident, that these teachers were not teachers of Christianity, but of a *Satanic delusion*.

I submit that the teaching of Rome is at least as different from that of the Sacred Writings as that which Paul calls "another gospel;" and that, therefore, his words authorize us to say that Romanism is not Christianity.

First: Christianity consists of what Christ has taught and commanded in Scripture.

But Romanism does not even profess to be founded on Scripture only: it claims a right to depart from what is contained in it—a right to add to Scripture what is handed down *by tradition*; and both to depart from and add to Scripture by making *new decrees*. It forbids the cup to the people, for instance, in what it calls "the mass," and yet admits that it was not forbidden to them at "the beginning of the Christian religion" (Council of Trent, Session 21, chap. 2). It says that councils and the pope have been empowered by the Holy Spirit to make decrees by which, in reality, the doctrines delivered by Christ are entirely annulled. To show how extensively this has been done, let the reader endeavor to trace the full effect of what Rome teaches as to baptismal regeneration, transubstantiation, justification by means of sacraments and deeds done by us, the invocation of saints—things which are entirely opposed to the teaching of Christ.

The canons of the Council of Trent, which sat at intervals from 1545 to 1563, may be called the Bible of Romanism. They were translated into English, as late as 1848, by a Roman Catholic priest, under the sanction of Dr. Wiseman. The Council tells us that one end for which it was called was "the extirpation of heresies." What, then, according to it, is the standard of truth? It tells us that Rome receives The Sacred Scriptures and "The Unwritten Traditions . . . preserved in continuous succession in the Catholic Church, with *equal affection of piety and reverence*"(Session 4); also that "no one may dare to interpret the Sacred Scriptures" in a manner contrary to that "Church; *whose it is to judge respecting the true sense and interpretation* of the Sacred Scriptures;" nor may any one interpret them "in a manner contrary to the unanimous consent of the fathers"(Session 4).

Christ commands us to "prove all things" (1 Thessalonians 5:21); to "search the Scriptures" (John 5:39); to ascertain for ourselves, as the Bereans did, whether what we hear agrees with what we read in Scripture (Acts 17:11). He commands us to "hold fast the form of sound words," uttered by Himself and His apostles (2 Timothy 1:13); to "contend earnestly for the faith *delivered once for all* to the saints" (Jude 3). But Rome says, "Let no one dare to do so"—let all "*Christian princes . . . cause [men] to observe*" our decrees (Session 16), nor "permit" them to be "violated by heretics" (Session 25). The Romanist must not dare to have an opinion of his own; his mind must exist in the state of utter prostration and bondage; he must not attempt to understand the Scripture himself. And if others attempt it—if they dare to receive the teaching and do the will of Christ, instead of receiving fictions and obeying commands of men, which wholly subvert and destroy the Truth and will of Jesus, Rome commands the civil ruler to restrain them; and, by the use of fines, imprisonment, and death, to compel them, if possible, to renounce what God requires them to maintain and follow, even unto death.

The Bible, the whole Bible, nothing but the Bible, is the standard and the rule of Christianity. To know its meaning for ourselves, to receive its teaching, to rely on its promises, to trust in its Redeemer, to obey Him from delight of love, and to refuse to follow other teaching, is Christianity itself. But Romanism denies all this; and therefore, Romanism is not Christianity.

Secondly: Christ commanded us to show "meekness" towards those who oppose us (2 Timothy 2:25).

He says, "Love your enemies, bless those who curse you, do good to those who hate you, and pray for those who use you despitefully and persecute you" (Matthew 5:44).

But Romanism teaches men *to hate*, and, if they are able, *to persecute to the death all those who will not receive it.* Its deeds have been diabolical and murderous. It is "drunken with the blood of the saints." It has inscribed on the page of history warnings which appeal to the reason and the feelings of all generations. Such a warning is what is told of the 24th of August, 1572. On that day the Protestants of Paris were devoted to slaughter by members of the Papal Church. For the one offence of being Protestants, thousands were slain. The streets of Paris ran with blood; everywhere cries and groans, were mingled with the clangor of bells, the clash of arms, and the oaths of murderers. The king, Charles IX; stood, it is said, at a window, and, every now and then, fired on the fugitives. Every form of guilt, cruelty, and suffering, made that fearful night hideous and appalling. Never, in any city, which has professedly been brought under the influence of Christianity, was there such a reveling in blood and crime. You may say, "Why do you recall the atrocities of a time so remote?" I answer, Because this deed received the sanction of the Church of Rome as a meritorious demonstration of fidelity to Romish precepts and doctrines. When the tidings of this wholesale murder were received in Rome, the cannon of St. Angelo were fired, the city was illuminated and Pope Gregory XIII and his cardinals went in procession to all the churches, and offered thanksgivings at the shrine of every saint. The Cardinal of Lorraine, in a letter to Charles IX, full of admiration and applause of the bloody deed, said, "That which you have achieved was so infinitely above my hopes, that I should have never dared to contemplate it; nevertheless, I have always believed that the deeds of your Majesty would augment the glory of God, and tend to immortalize your name."

Some say that Rome has ceased to persecute. But this is not the fact; either as to her acts, or rules of action. *She asserts that she is unchanged, unchangeable; that she is infallible, and cannot alter*, except so far as necessity, or plans for the future, may require; and facts are often occurring which prove that persecution is still approved by her. Rome has little power now; her persecuting spirit is kept in abeyance for a time; but it is still there. When it is free from restraint, it knows no way of dealing with difference of opinion but by the rack, the stake, the thumbscrew, the iron boot, the assassin's dagger, or a wholesale massacre. Let all who value their liberty, all who love the Truth as it is in Jesus have no fellowship with such deeds of darkness, nor with those who work them. Let us show that we have no sympathy with such a cruel spirit; and that we love the names and memory of the noble army of martyrs of the Reformation; of those who sealed their faith with their blood; of those who died to release their country and their posterity from the bondage of Rome.

I agree with Dr. Samuel Waldegrave, when he says that, "The Convocation of the English clergy did wisely, when, in the days of Elizabeth, they enacted that every parish church in the land should be furnished with a copy of *Foxe's Book of Martyrs*;" and that it would be well if a copy of it were "in every house, yea, in every hand;" for "Rome is laboring, with redoubled effort, for the subjugation of Britain," and "the people have forgotten that she is a siren who enchants but to destroy."

Thirdly: As to *the sacrifice* of Christ, Christianity teaches that He was "offered *once for all*, to bear the sins of many" (Hebrews 9:28); that those who are sanctified by His sacrifice are so "by the offering of the body of Jesus Christ *once for all*" (Hebrews 10:10); that "*by one offering* He has *perfected forever* those who are sanctified," or made holy (Hebrews 10:14).

These passages declare that the sacrifice of Christ was offered once for all, never to be repeated. But Rome declares that Christ is sacrificed anew, every time that the Lord's Supper, which she calls "the mass," is celebrated; and that those who administer it are *sacrificing priests*.

The Council of Trent (Session 22) says,

> Forasmuch as in this Divine sacrifice, which is celebrated in the mass, that same Christ is contained, and immolated in an unbloody manner, who once offered Himself in a bloody manner, on the altar of the cross, the holy synod teaches that *this sacrifice is truly propitiatory*, and that, *by means therof*, this is effected that we obtain mercy and find grace in seasonable aid, if we draw nigh unto God, contrite and penitent, with a sincere heart and upright faith, with fear and reverence. For the Lord, *appeased by the oblation thereof*, and granting the grace and gift of penitence, forgives even heinous crimes and sins. For *the victim is one and the same*, the same now

offering by the ministry of priests, who then offered Himself on the cross, the manner alone of offering being different." The synod commands the use of lights, incense, and the traditional vestments; also that the priests "mix water with the wine.

In chapter 9, canon 1, the synod says, "If any one say that in the mass *a true and proper sacrifice is not offered* to God; or, that *to be offered*, is nothing else but that Christ is given us to eat; let him be anathema." In canon 3, it decreed that,

> If any one say that the sacrifice of the mass is only a sacrifice of praise and thanksgiving; or that it is *a bare commemoration of the sacrifice consummated on the cross, but not a propitiatory sacrifice*; or, that it profits him only who receives; and that it ought not to be offered *for the living and the dead for sins; pains, satisfactions*, and other necessities; let him be anathema.

The Christ of Romanism is one who is sacrificed again and again for the remission of the sins both of the living and the dead; for those alive, and for those in purgatory. *Is this the Christ of Christianity?*

In canon 1 of its 13th Session, the synod says, "If any one deny that, in the sacrament of the most holy Eucharist, are contained truly, really and substantially *the body and blood, together with the soul and divinity of our Lord Jesus Christ*, and consequently the whole Christ, but say that He is only therein as in a sign, or in figure, or virtue; let him be anathema."

The Christ of the Bible, and of Christianity, is in heaven "at the right hand of God," where "He ever lives to make intercession for those who come to God through Him" (Romans 8:34; Colossians 3:1; Hebrews 7:25); nor will He come in bodily form to earth again until He comes the second time, without sin, unto salvation, to be admired in all those who believe (Hebrews 9:28; 2 Thessalonians 1:10).

But the Christ of Romanism is upon the altars of Rome; He is said to be brought there by the magic spell of her priests, and to be there in the form and shape of a *wafer*. What a fearful blasphemy! The priest pronounces certain words, gives the solemn consecration, and then elevates the wafer. *Taste* it—it is a wafer; *touch* it—it is a wafer; *look* at it—it is a wafer; *smell* it—it is a wafer; *analyze* it—it is a wafer. But the priest affirms, the Council of Trent affirms, Romanism affirms, the poor victims of delusion affirm, as they bow down before it, *"This is our Christ—our God!"* Here is the climax of this superstition—it exhibits for the person of Christ a morsel of bread: Is that morsel of bread the Christ of the Bible? Is that system which declares it to be so, Christianity?

Fourthly: Christianity is in direct opposition to Romanism as to *the mode of a sinner's justification before God.*

What say the Scriptures?

"By deeds of law shall no flesh living be justified before God" (Romans 3:20).

"Therefore we conclude that a man is justified by faith, without deeds of law" (Romans 3:28).

"Even David describes the blessedness of the man to whom God imputes righteousness without works" (Romans 4:6).

Israel, "being ignorant of the righteousness of God, and seeking to establish their own righteousness, have not submitted themselves to the righteousness of God. For Christ is the end of the law for righteousness to every one who believes," or has faith (Romans 10:3, 4).

"God was in Christ, ... not imputing their trespasses unto them" (2 Corinthians 5:19).

"God has made Him to be sin for us, who knew no sin; that we might be made the righteousness of God in Him" (2 Corinthians 5:21).

"Therefore, being justified by faith, we have peace with God through our Lord Jesus Christ" (Romans 5:1).

The doctrine thus taught by Christianity is that all men are sinners; that without justification there is no hope for any sinner; that we are justified by the imputation of Christ's righteousness alone; and that His righteousness is received through faith.

Now, what says Romanism? It says that the righteousness by which men are justified is that which the Holy Spirit, by the grace of God, through Christ, makes them *work out for themselves*; that it is received by means of "the sacrament of baptism . . . without which no one was ever justified;" that it is received "in ourselves," when we are renewed by the Holy Spirit; that it is a righteousness "imparted," "infused," "implanted," and not imputed (Session 6, chapter 7). Among the declarations of the Council are these:

"If any one say that justifying faith is nothing else but confidence in the Divine mercy which remits sin for Christ's sake; or, that this confidence alone is that whereby we are justified; let him be anathema" (Session 6, canon 12).

"If any one say that... good works are merely the fruits and signs of justification obtained, but not a cause of the increase thereof; let him be anathema" (canon 24).

> "If any one say that he who is justified by good works, which are done by him through the grace of God and the merit of Jesus Christ, whose living member he is, does not truly deserve increase of grace, eternal life," etc. ... "let him be anathema" (canon 32).

Thus Romanism anathematizes the preaching of true Christianity! I will mention but one more proof that Romanism is not Christianity, though there are many others which might be given.

Fifthly: Christianity says "there is one Mediator between God and men, the man Christ Jesus" (1 Timothy 2:5),who is at the right hand of the Father (Ephesians 1:20), where He "ever lives to make intercession" for us (Hebrews 7:25).

Christianity says that there is but *one Mediator*; that we cannot draw near to God except through Jesus.

What says Romanism? I quote from "a book of devotion for every day in the month of May," published by Papal authority.

> Great is the need you have of Mary in order to be saved! Are you innocent? Still your innocence is, however, under great danger. How many, more innocent than you, have fallen into sin, and been damned? Are you penitent? Still your perseverance is very uncertain. Are you sinners? Oh, what need you have of Mary to convert you! Ah, if there were no Mary, perhaps you would be lost! However, by the devotion of this month, you may obtain her patronage, and your own salvation. Is it possible that a mother so tender can help hearing a Son so devout? For a rosary, for a fast, she has sometimes conferred signal graces upon the greatest of sinners. Think, then, what she will do for you for a whole month dedicated to her service!

Here you see that Mary is everything; that Jesus Christ is nothing. Romanism teaches also that it is right to ask the intercession of all departed saints (Session 25). How dreadful is it that sinners are thus kept back from Jesus, and are prevented from reaching God through Him.

Popery is emphatically *anti-Christian*: it is the adversary of Christ in all the offices which He sustains. It is the enemy of His *prophetic* office; for it chains up that Bible which He inspired. It is the enemy of His *priestly* office; for, by the mass it denies the efficacy of that sacrifice which He offered once for all on Calvary. It is the enemy of His *kingly* office; for it tears the crown from His head to set it on that of the Pope.

Can that be truly called Christianity, then, which is the reverse of it? Can that be fitly treated as Christianity which hates it, denounces it, and tries to destroy it? Can that be Christianity which forbids liberty of conscience, and the right of private judgment? Which commands the Bible to be burned? Which teaches the worship of saints and angels? Which makes the Virgin Mary command God? Which calls her the Mother of God, and the Queen of Heaven? Which sets aside the mediation of Christ, and puts others in His place? Which makes salvation depend on confession to man, and this is a confessional so filthy that Satan himself might well be ashamed of it? Can that be Christianity which condemns the way of salvation through faith, as a damnable heresy? Can that be Christianity which, by the bulls of its Popes, and decrees of its councils, requires both princes and people to persecute Christians? Which actually swears its bishops and archbishops to persecute them with all their might? Can that be Christianity which has set up, and still maintains, the Inquisition? That which has been so cruel, so bloodthirsty, that the number slain by it of the servants of Christ, in about 1,200 years, is estimated at fifty millions, giving an average of 40,000 a year for that long period? No, it cannot be! With a voice of thunder, let Protestants answer, "No!"

To aid such a system is to fight against God. He demands that we "resist the devil" (James 4:7), and have no fellowship with "works of darkness" (Ephesians 5:11). *"No peace with Rome,"* must be on our lips, and be in our lives. *"No peace with Rome,"* whether wearing her scarlet undisguised, or using the cloak of a Protestant name.

The voice from heaven (Revelation 18:4)—"Come out of her, My people, that ye be not partakers of her sins, and that ye receive not of her plagues"—is proof that there may be true Christians in the Roman body; but it is proof also that even while *in* it, they are not *of* it; and that they will strive to escape from it, so as not to share in its sins.

We are informed by God that this system is the work of Satan; that his ministers are "transformed as the ministers of righteousness, whose end shall be according to their works" (2 Corinthians 11:15); that it is he who turns men away "from the simplicity which is in Christ" (11:3); that it is he who is the author of that "mystery of iniquity" which was at work even while the apostles were still living, and which was to be further revealed, and to remain, till it should be consumed by Christ, and "destroyed by the brightness of His coming;" a system which is "according to *the working of Satan*, with all power, and signs, and lying wonders, and with all deceivableness of unrighteousness in them that perish; because they received not the love of the truth that they might be saved" (2 Thessalonians 2:7–10).

May those who love God, and yet have some connection with this system, listen to the command, *"Come out of her, My people."* May we in no degree partake of her sins: may we renounce, with a holy loathing, all her symbols; throw off, with righteous indignation, all allegiance to her corruptions. May we have nothing of Romanism in our doctrines, but contend earnestly for the pure faith of the Gospel of Jesus. May we have nothing of

Romanism in our *discipline*. May we be subject, in all matters of religious faith and practice, to the Word of God, and to that alone. May we have nothing of Romanism in our *services*, in our *buildings*, in our *forms*, in our *attire*. Because Israel burned incense to the brazen serpent which Moses had made, Hezekiah broke it in pieces. (2 Kings 18:4). For the like reason, let us cease to use, on person or building, that form of the cross which the Romanist treats with superstitious regard. "Come out of her."

Ye who seek salvation, go to Jesus. Him has God exalted to be a Prince and a Saviour. He is able to save to the uttermost those who come to God by Him. The Father is ready with out-stretched arms to clasp the penitent prodigal in His embrace. The Son is ready to give a free, full, complete forgiveness to: every redeemed sinner, and to justify all who come unto God by Him. The Holy Spirit is ready to sanctify, renew, instruct, and help all who call upon Him. The assembly of saved sinners on earth is ready to welcome you to partake of its fellowship and of its joys. Angels are ready with harps attuned, and fingers upon the chords, to give you a triumphant welcome, and to rejoice over you with joy. Come just as you are; come at once. "Him that cometh to Me," says Christ, "I will in no wise cast out" (John 6:37).

Editor's Conclusion

In our day of tolerance and open-mindedness, Medhurst's article appears scandalous and even hateful. The reason many view such speech as unloving, however, is because they simply are under the false impression that Roman Catholicism actually is a "branch of Christianity." But as Medhurst makes clear, such an idea is preposterous. As the "Editor's Introduction" also observed, this fact was once beyond even the slightest doubt in the discerning minds of true evangelicals. We are also reminded that Medhurst was the first student of Spurgeon's Pastor's College, which stood unapologetically for true Christianity, in contrast to many schools today that are leaders in compromise. So it is that until evangelicals today return to this obvious fact and realize that "to aid such a system is to fight against God," Christianity will continue its steady falling away from "the faith which was once [for all] delivered unto the saints" (Jude 3).

Subject Index

Person Index

Scripture Index

Foreign Words Index

Greek, Hebrew (H), and Latin (L)

About the Author

D r. J. D. "Doc" Watson (ThD, DRE) entered the ministry in 1974, serving in several capacities including 29 years in the pastorate, 26 of which at Grace Bible Church in Meeker, Colorado. He also speaks at Bible Conferences and other venues.

In addition to his other published books, he continues to write and edit the monthly publication *Truth on Tough Texts*, on which both the present book and its predecessor are based. His driving passion is the exposition of the Word of God as the sole and sufficient authority in all matters. This is demonstrated in no better way than in his 3-1/2 year (500,000 word) exposition of the Epistle to the Ephesians, which he hopes to publish in 2014.

Dr. Watson also serves on the board of On Target Ministry (www.ontargetministry.org), which is committed to international education. He has had the opportunity to serve overseas in this capacity, including teaching at the Haiti Bible Institute, which was founded by OTM in 2009. He likewise serves on the board of the Institute for Biblical Textual Studies, which is committed to defending the Traditional Text of the New Testament.

Dr. Watson has also contributed articles to other publications, including a weekly column in his local newspaper based upon his pulpit ministry. He also maintains three blogs:

- *Expositing Ephesians: The Christian's Wealth and Walk* (http://expositingephesians.blogspot.com).

- *Tas Membranas* (http://tas-membranas.blogspot.com/), which is dedicated to book reviews.

- *John Calvin for Today*, a devotional site based upon Calvin's expositions (http://johncalvinfortoday.blogspot.com/)

The other three loves of his life are his wife, Debbie (since 1974), his son, Paul (since 1988), and golf (since 1968 and, thankfully, in that order).

📖 Books by the Author 📖

A passion for writing has led to several books by the author, some of which are already available while others are scheduled for publication in the near future. His books have been published by three publishers. Below are brief summaries of each book, but for more detail and sample chapters, see our website (www.TheScriptureAlone.com/SS-Publications.htm).

From AMG Publishers

(www.AMGPublishers.com)

A Word for the Day: Key Words from the New Testament (2006)
and
A Hebrew Word for the Day: Key Words from the Old Testament
(2010)

Words matter! After all, we use words every day. They convey our thoughts, feelings, attitudes, ideas, purposes, goals, joys, sorrows—in short,

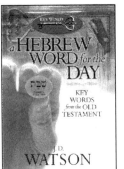

everything. While English is even more universal in our day than Greek or Hebrew were in Bible times, the wealth in studying these languages is inestimable.

The purpose of these books is to share with you the richness of some of the Greek words used in the New Testament and Hebrew words in the Old Testament and to help you make them practical in your Christian living. Since words matter, the words of Scripture matter most. And in a day when words don't seem to mean much, the need for precision in Christian doctrine and practice has never been more critical.

Each day of the year we examine a particular word by first presenting a brief word study and then a practical application to make that word real in your life. For reinforcement, each day also includes other related verses that you can study on your own.

It has been my desire for many years to write a daily devotional that would not only contain deep spiritual Truth but also be easy to read. In our day of Relativism, the absolutes of God's Word (and words) are desperately needed. I pray these book will bless your heart, enrich your mind, stir your soul, and empower your life. They should prove useful to pastors, teachers, and all Christian Believers who desire a deeper understanding and application of "God's Words." The writing of these books was one of the greatest joys of my life and one of the most profitable exercises of my ministry for our Lord. I pray it will likewise be a joy and profit to you.

Where to get them: Christian Book Distributors (CBD), Amazon.com, Christian book store, or the publisher.

From Wipf and Stock Publishers

(https://WipfAndStock.com)

The Doctrines of Grace from the Lips of Our Lord: A Study in the Gospel of John (2012)

The doctrine of salvation is the watershed doctrine of Scripture. Flowing from that doctrine will be not only all other doctrine but also personal practice and Christian ministry. The major controversy concerning salvation is whether it is a result of the sovereign grace of God alone or a mixture of "God's part" and "man's part." Addressing that issue is absolutely critical to the very foundations of Christianity itself.

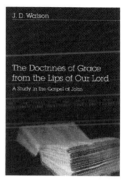

Whichever one of those premises is correct, we should expect to find it everywhere we look in Scripture, and that is precisely what we find. There is no truth that permeates the Bible more than the doctrines of God's sovereign grace. From Genesis to Revelation, in literally hundreds of verses, these doctrines call, capture, and command our attention.

Of the many books of the Bible we could choose, the Gospel of John is among the most compelling because of its foundational nature. It is there we find some of the most profound teaching on the Doctrines of Grace in all Scripture. Examining more than one hundred verses in John, this small volume presents these great biblical and historical doctrines directly from the lips of our Lord. (220 pages)

Where to get it: from the publisher, Christian bookstore, or use the enclosed order form:

1 or 2 copies $15.00   3 or more $14.00 ea.

From Sola Scriptura Publications

(www.TheScriptureAlone.com)

Truth on Tough Texts: Expositions of Challenging Scripture Passages (2012)

Was Matthias God's choice to replace Judas (Acts 1:15-26)? What is the identity of those "sons of God" referred to in Genesis 6? Are the "angels" of the seven churches real angels or pastors (Rev. 1:20)? Is there a so-called call to ministry (Eph. 4:11; 1 Tim. 3:1)? Is "deaconess" a valid church office (1 Tim. 3:11)? What is the "sealing" of the Holy Spirit (Eph. 1:13-14)? Is "regeneration" absent from the Old Testament, being a New Testament doctrine only (Isa. 57:15; Eph. 2:1)? What do other terms that appear in Scripture mean, such as: "fall away" (Heb. 6:4-6), "old man" (Rom. 6:6), and "new creature" (2 Cor. 5:17)?

Those are just a few of the "tough texts" we find in Scripture. While Scripture is infallible, never contradicting itself, and while it is literal and straightforward, not mysterious and ambiguous, there are some texts that raise questions and have therefore prompted varied "interpretations" throughout Church History. Again, such texts are certainly not "less inspired" than the rest of Scripture, rather simply more intricate and complex and thereby demand especially diligent investigation.

This 598-page book, therefore, addresses many texts of Scripture that have historically been debated, are particularly difficult to understand, or have generated questions among believers. The chapters that follow originally appeared in the monthly publication, *Truth on Tough Texts*, which was launched by the author in August 2005. They reappear here so that they might reach a wider audience, as well as provide a quick reference for longtime readers of the monthly offerings. This was the premier book of Sola Scriptura Publications, founded in 2012.

Where to get it: directly from the publisher using the enclosed order form:

Single Copy: $25.00   2–10 copies: $23.00 ea.
11–20 copies: $21.00   21 or more: $20.00 ea. (20%)

Also available on Amazon.com and for Kindle Reader

Upon This Rock: Studies in Church History and Their Application
(2012)

The sequel to *Truth on Tough Texts* above, this book is the collection of articles on historical issues from the first six years of the monthly publication, *Truth on Tough Texts*. The Reformation, for example, is misunderstood by many, ignored by some, and even attacked by others. It is, therefore, a major emphasis here in chapters 3 through 8. Even Church History itself, as is history in general nowadays, is viewed by many as unimportant, if not wholly irrelevant. "Why look backward?" it is argued. "We should only look forward and be about our Father's business in the here and now."

Such an attitude, however, is not only foolish but downright dangerous. As we will note in chapter 1, Spanish-born American philosopher and writer George Santayana (1863–1952) made the now famous statement, "Those who cannot remember the past are condemned to repeat it." Well, the Church as a whole has, indeed, forgotten much of the past, and the lessons we should learn from it, and is repeating many of the same errors.

This book, therefore, begins in Part I with "Our Foundation," in which we examine the value of studying Church History and then study the deep significance of the words of our Lord in Matthew 16:16–19, "Upon this rock." Part II, "The Five Solas of the Reformation," is the heart of our study in which we examine the core issues of the Reformation and are challenged with their importance for our day. Part III, "Other History Lessons," addresses other historical figures and events that are critical for our understanding in a day of growing indifference to these matters. There are also more than 60 illustrations, most of which were not in the original articles. (220 pages)

I pray these studies will be to God's glory and the reader's good. You can get your copy either by using the enclosed order form (published by Sola Scriptura Publications) or from Amazon.com (**will also be available for Kindle**).

Where to get it: directly from the publisher using the enclosed order form:

Single Copy: $12.00   2–3 copies: $11.00 ea.
4–5 copies: $10.00   6 or more: $9.00 ea. (25%)

(Also available on Amazon.com and for Kindle Reader)

We Preach Christ: The Bible Story (booklet, 2013)

This 28-page booklet reproduces a message first preached by the author on January 6, 2013. From Genesis to Revelation, from the beginning to the end, the Bible is all about Christ, and it is He who we preach. To underscore this central theme, the Bible story is briefly told in a seven act drama: the creation, the curse, the comfort, the calamity, the contract, the coming, and the consummation. The end purpose, then, is two-fold:

First, it is an encouragement to those who are already Christians to understand the central theme of the Bible, in contrast to the prevailing ideas in our day of what the Bible is about. While it is short, we pray it is comprehensive enough to challenge each of us with what our message really is.

Second, we also pray that God will use this little work in the lives of readers who are not yet Christian believers. Appendix B offers a clear, biblical presentation of the saving Gospel of Christ. We pray they will see what the Bible is truly about and how it addresses their real need.

Where to get it: directly from the publisher using the enclosed order form for $2.00 per copy ($1.00 each for 50 or more).

Also available in PDF or Kindle Reader FREE from the publisher via e-mail.

One FREE copy will also be included with every order using the enclosed order form.

A Light Unto My Path: An Exposition of Psalm 119 (2013)

Part of the incomprehensible miracle of inspiration is that God used the personality, experiences, and even words of each Scripture writer so that the result is not only what the *writer* wanted to say but also exactly what *God* wanted to say. There is no better example of this miracle than in the Psalms. We see the whole gamut of human experience—the positives and the negatives—but God is in it all and controlling it all. Sometimes we see a psalmist at the absolute lowest point of his life, and at other times at the highest, but God used it all to convey His truth with absolute precision.

Psalm 119 is such a psalm. We see the writer lofty and low, diligent and discouraged, fearless and frightened, victorious and vanquished. The more we read, however, we discover his secret. While many Christians today are looking for the newest trend for their excitement, or seeking the answers to problems by reading the latest self-help book, the psalmist *always* went to the Word of God. Why? Because it is there, and there alone, that he found everything: happiness (vv. 1–8), maturity (vv. 9–16), victory (vv. 17–24), therapy (vv. 25–32), consistency (vv. 33–40), confidence (vv. 41–48), and all else.

Simply put, *Psalm 119 is devoted to praising the virtues, merits, and sufficiency of the Word of God and demonstrates the author's total commitment to it.* While it cannot compare with a classic such as Charles Spurgeon's, this book is a complete, verse-by-verse, usually word-by-word, exposition of the Psalm. Because of the pivotal importance of the pulpit ministry, this book is based on a series of messages preached on consecutive Lord's Day mornings from July 2007 through January 2008. Rich in word studies, clearly outlined, and carefully applied, it is meant to be an encouragement, challenge, and source of growth to God's people. I pray that reading it will bless your heart as much as writing it blessed mine.

Where to get it: it will be available directly from the publisher and Amazon.com (including Kindle reader).

The Forgotten Tozer: A. W. Tozer's Challenge to Today's Church (2013)

Like many other Christians, the author became acquainted with A. W. Tozer through his classic book, *The Knowledge of the Holy*. Other than that classic work, however, he had read almost nothing else of Tozer until about 1999. It was then that someone handed him a copy of *God Tells the Man Who Cares*. He was astounded to learn that decades ago Tozer faced and addressed most of the same issues that are diluting Christianity and undermining the Church today. A year of research and writing resulted in the present book. While it contains some biographical material, it is not a biography. It is a review and analysis of Tozer's thought on contemporary Christianity. The method of presenting Tozer's thought is simple: state the problem, present the

Scripture, and permit Tozer to comment, making applications to our day as necessary.

Where to get it: it will be available directly from the publisher and Amazon.com (including Kindle reader).

Contending for the Faith: An Expository Commentary on Jude (2013)

How important could a book of the Bible possibly be when it is only twenty-five verses in length? The answer to this question is this: *The Epistle of Jude is one of the most vital books of God's Word in light of the 21ˢᵗ Century world in which we live.* In twenty-five verses Jude paints a picture of the present day so real that it could have been painted yesterday. The importance of Jude cannot be expressed enough.

Jude is progressive; that is, little by little Jude shows us the *reality* of apostasy and how to *recognize* the apostate. This is a book that every Christian needs to know. It is the only book of the Bible that is devoted *exclusively* to exposing false teachers and instructing us in how to defend the faith. As we progress in this exposition, we will see in a very practical way just how pervasive apostasy is in our society today. We will see how Jude, writing over 1900 years ago, exposes the cults and false religions of today. Jude's warning to true believers can be summed up this way: *be aware* of the apostasy *around* us and *beware* of apostasy lest it creep in *among* us

Where to get it: it will be available directly from the publisher and Amazon.com (including Kindle reader).

A Taste of Heaven on Earth: Marriage and Family in Ephesians 5:18—6:4 (2013)

Excerpted from Dr. Watson's 2-volume exposition of Ephesians (scheduled for 2014), this book covers just the section on the Christian home in 5:18—6:4. Its nine chapters include: Foundations of the Christian Home; The Meaning and Motives of Marriage; The Model for Marriage ("Solomon's Song"); The Responsibilities of the Wife; The Proverbs 31 Woman; The Responsibilities of the Husband; The Tragedy of Divorce; The Responsibilities of Children; and The Responsibilities of Parents.

Where to get it: it will be available directly from the publisher and Amazon.com (including Kindle reader).

The Christian's Wealth and Walk: An Expository Commentary on Ephesians (2 volumes, 2014)

This is what the author prays will be his greatest contribution to the Church, his three-and-one-half year exposition of the Epistle to the Ephesians. The aim of this work is to offer to the True Evangelical Church a comprehensive and readable exposition and application of the grandest, most awe-inspiring piece of writing known to man.

This work is an "expository commentary," offering not only the meaning of the text of this great Epistle, but also challenging each of us to what its truth demands from us. Based on a series of messages preached on consecutive Lord's Day mornings from February 2003 through August 2006, this work is the result of the author's passion *for* and immersion *in* this great Epistle for more than 20 years. In his own words, as he shares in the Preface:

"If I can leave anything behind when I go to be with our Lord, I wish it to be three things: a faithful life, a godly family, and this exposition of Ephesians. I pray that God will use it to His glory and perhaps even to spark someone else's passion for this Epistle as Martyn Lloyd-Jones' eight-volume work did for my own."

Where to get it: it will be available directly from the publisher and Amazon.com (including Kindle reader).

Salvation is of the Lord: An Exposition of the Doctrines of Grace by a Former Arminian (2014)

While *The Doctrines of Grace from the Lips of Our Lord: A Study in the Gospel of John* is a short and basic presentation of the Doctrines of Grace, this is Dr. Watson's full treatment of these biblical and historic doctrines. As a former Arminian and once very vocal critic of the Doctrines of Grace, he is uniquely qualified to write such a work. He knows the misunderstanding first hand that goes with this aberrant theological perspective; he knows the arguments, the mind set, and the attitudes all too well.

What are the Doctrines of Grace? Boiled down to their bare essence, the Doctrines of Grace say only one thing: *Salvation is of the Lord*. That's it. It's just that simple. It is this that provided the basis for the title of this book, for as the prophet Jonah declared: *Salvation is of the Lord* (Jon. 2:9).

This book is also unique is the way it presents the Doctrines of Grace. Instead of the usual *topical* approach, the approach here is *expository*. By expositing specific portions of Scripture that deal with the Doctrines of Grace, the danger of removing "proof texts" from their context is avoided.

Where to get it: it will be available directly from the publisher and Amazon.com (including Kindle reader).

Seek Him Early: Daily Devotional Studies on Knowing, Loving, and Serving Our Lord Jesus Christ (2014)

While Pastor Watson's third daily devotional book is, like the other two, thematic, word studies are not the foundation, although such studies appear often. Instead, the overarching emphasis is on knowing, loving, and serving our Lord and Savior Jesus Christ. In three distinct parts, each encompassing four months of devotional studies, the reader is first encouraged to know the Lord in a personal way, then to love Him like never before, and finally to be driven to more passionately serve Him. Like the other two devotional books, this one also includes additional Scriptures for extended study.

Where to get it: it will be available directly from the publisher and Amazon.com (including Kindle reader).

The Seven Churches of the 21st Century: An Exposition of Revelation 2 & 3 (2014)

Any study of the seven churches must not be entered lightly or hurriedly. Often a study of Revelation 2 and 3 is done quickly because people want to get to the "exciting parts" of Revelation. But the truth of these two chapters is truly some of the most important that a Christian can know. Admonitions and applications abound! Most of all, however, these letters show us how our Savior Himself views us, what He thinks of the condition of our lives and our churches. These letters are sobering indeed. I pray that God will use them in your life as He has used them in mine, and I pray that He will use these expositions to the glory and advancement of His Church here on earth.

Soli Deo Gloria!

Sola Scriptura Publications

P.O. Box 235 — Meeker, CO — 81641
970-878-3228 or 970-618-8375
sspmail1521@gmail.com

Order Form[1]

Name: _____

Address: _____

City: _____ State: _____ Zip: _____

Email (optional) _____

Qty.	Title	Price Each	Total Price
1	*We Preach Christ: The Bible Story*	FREE	FREE[2]
		Sub-Total	$
		Entirely Optional Shipping Donation	$
		TOTAL[3]	$

All proceeds go toward publishing other books to God's glory.

---

[1] PLEASE NOTE: We do not carry a supply of either *A Word for the Day* or *A Hebrew Word for the Day* (AMG Publishers). Best price is on Amazon.com.

[2] One FREE copy with any order. Additional copies may be purchased for $2.00 each or $1.00 each for 50 or more.

[3] We apologize, but to keep prices down, we do not accept credit cards at this time.

16640504R00116

Made in the USA
Charleston, SC
03 January 2013